Chinese Narrative Poetry

Chinese Narrative Poetry

The Late Han through T'ang Dynasties

Dore J. Levy

Duke University Press Durham and London   1988

© 1988 Duke University Press
All rights reserved
Printed in the United States of America
on acid-free paper ∞
Library of Congress Cataloging-in-Publication Data
Levy, Dore Jesse.
Chinese narrative poetry : the late Han
through T'ang dynasties / Dore J. Levy.
p. cm.
Bibliography: p.
ISBN 0-8223-0863-0
1. Narrative poetry, Chinese—History and criticism. 2. Chinese
poetry—221 B.C.–960 A.D.—History and criticism. I. Title.
PL2309.N47L48   1988 895.1'103'09—dc19   88-14712

For my parents

Contents

Preface

This study presents a critical model of Chinese narrative poetry from the perspective of comparative poetics. In formulating this model I have relied first on the Chinese critical tradition, then proposed correspondences and comparisons from European literary criticism. With these two sources in mind, I have tried to make this study of narrative poems in the *shih* form from the late Han through T'ang dynasties—roughly the second through ninth centuries—accessible to those with little or no experience of East Asian traditions, and at the same time of interest to specialists in East Asian studies. The result is not a historical account of the evolution of narrative *shih*, but an analysis of how narrative *works* in these poems. Specifically, what are the characteristics of narrative expression in a poetic tradition founded on lyric rather than epic poems? While Chinese poetic criticism and the poems themselves are definitely biased toward lyrical expression, there are principles of poetic form and composition, and distinctive features of Chinese poetic language which lend themselves to narrative expression. The challenge for poets using the *shih* form was as much in adapting the metrics and methods of lyrical expression to narrative composition as it was in telling a tale.

The distinctions between lyrical and narrative expression, and lyrical and narrative experience in Chinese poetry, form the main subject of the Introduction. The first chapter explores theories of Chinese poetic language and traditional literary criticism with an eye to defining those aspects of language and poetics which may allow for narrative. The chapters that follow suggest categories for analyzing the nature of narrative in *shih:* point of view, description, characterization, and sequential structure. These categories are intended to be suggestive rather than diagnostic, but all have roots in the Chinese critical tradition and are not dependent on European notions of narrative forms.

Any study of Chinese poetry or literary theory in a European language will inevitably garnish its material with European terms and cultural assumptions. These are foreign to the development of Chinese literature before the modern era, although they may not be irrelevant for comparative analyses. I have taken pains to emphasize this paradoxical aspect of the enterprise in the pages that follow. An awareness of this separation should be basic to comparative literary studies which deal with traditions without sustained intercultural relations. The reward may be a broader insight into the nature and function of art, transcending such cultural and linguistic barriers.

The field of narrative theory has enjoyed a bustling expansion in the last generation, and this is as true for Chinese as for European literature. In Chinese literary studies, however, narrative theory has focused on prose, particularly prose fiction. The relation of the Chinese novel to the Chinese poetic tradition is a matter for debate; however, traditional *poetics* certainly have their place in the study of prose fiction. Moreover, the essential and unselfconscious incorporation of verse narrative, with meters reflecting all the lyric forms of Chinese literary history in such masterworks as *The Journey to the West (Hsi-yu chi)* and *The Dream of the Red Chamber (Hung-lou meng)*, suggests that the narrative mode of expression in poetry made a direct contribution to the evolution of these texts. This study offers an introduction to the analysis of narrative in Chinese poetry: specifically, the literary as opposed to the folk tradition. Because of what I perceive as the characteristics of narrative composition, certain stylistic devices play a significant role in this analysis. Therefore, in quoting from the Chinese texts I have used my own translations, which reflect the importance of these devices. I have also attempted to preserve such features as word order, caesura, and parallelism wherever this was possible without sacrificing coherence. The four poems I discuss and quote most extensively—Ts'ai Yen's "Poem of Affliction" ("*Pei-fen shih*"), Po Chü-yi's "Song of Everlasting Sorrow" ("*Ch'ang-hen ko*") and "Ballad of the *p'i-p'a*" ("*P'i-p'a hsing*"), and Wei Chuang's "Song of the Lady of Ch'in" ("*Ch'in-fu yin*")—appear in their entirety in the Appendix. While I have sought to capture the distinctive formal features of these poems, I have also tried to convey the affecting power of their subject matter. Lapses in either aspect are due to my own shortcomings.

Acknowledgments

I would like to thank the many people who have helped me with care, knowledge, and dedication. In particular, Yu-kung Kao, Earl Miner, and Andrew H. Plaks of Princeton University constantly challenged me with their creative approaches to the study of literature, their critical insight, and their intellectual rigor. Stephen Owen first suggested a study of narrative poetry to me. Kang-i Sun Chang, Richard Davis, A. C. Graham, Charles Hartman, David Lattimore, Stephanie Merrim, Yang Hsien-ch'ing, and Anthony C. Yu have been unfailing in their encouragement, not the least because of the examples of excellence they have set.

I owe a great debt to the members of the East Coast Chinese Poetry Group, who over several years have provided constructive discussion and moral support on many aspects of this project. I am grateful to the staff of the Gest Oriental Library for their aid in gaining access to the great resources of that collection. My colleagues in comparative literature at Brown University have provided inspiration by treating East Asian literature as an integral part of their program, thus obliging me to present Chinese literature as a subject not of special, but of universal interest. Brown University granted me a semester's leave, allowing me to conduct new research and extensive revisions, and also granted funds toward publication. I am grateful to the editor of the *Harvard Journal of Asiatic Studies* for permission to reprint material published there, now part of my first chapter. Joanne Ferguson and the staff of the Duke University Press have been vigorous and imaginative in the handling of text and author. The calligraphy is by Hui-fen Lung, and Maggie Bickford delved deeply into the narrative tradition in Chinese painting to find a cover for the volume.

My friends F. W. Mote and Hsiao-lan Mote have inspired my interests in China and the humanities in general, and in all my endeavors I owe them my gratitude and affection. My husband, Jim, I thank for his wisdom, humor, and uncompromising criticism of my work at every stage. To my parents, my love. They saw this project at its beginning, and happily they now see the end—of this phase.

Introduction

A Model for the Study of Chinese Narrative Poetry

Chinese narrative poetry includes some of the most beloved and influential poems in the literary tradition. From the songs of the *Shih Ching* (*Book of Songs*) to the folk ballads of the Han dynasty, from the tours de force of Po Chü-yi's "Song of Everlasting Sorrow" and Wei Chuang's "Song of the Lady of Ch'in" to the verse passages of *The Journey to the West*, poetry's possibilities for narrative expression have made themselves felt in many genres over the entire history of Chinese literature. Their influence extends not only across generic lines, but also beyond the boundaries of China. Narrative poetry of the T'ang dynasty, for instance, had a crucial influence on the development of narrative in Japan. In chapter 25 of the *Tale of Genji* Prince Genji himself discusses the art of prose romances with his ward, Tamakazura, and his favorite consort, Murasaki. Throughout this work the author argues the merits and influence of Po Chü-yi's most famous poem: a double emphasis, since the *Tale of Genji* itself owes a debt of influence to the author of the "Song of Everlasting Sorrow."[1] In the Chinese tradition narrative poems provide many provocative historical and autobiographical documents, as well as vehicles for political criticism and social commentary. In addition, narrative techniques developed in poetry have influenced Chinese fiction, where the unique blending of prose and poetic narrative arguably brings the poetics of Chinese narrative to their full fruition. Poetic narrative helps to mediate between two fundamental concerns of artistic endeavor in Chinese culture; namely, personal expression and social commentary. Throughout the critical tradition the proper balance of expressive and didactic purpose in art is a source of debate, but seldom is one wholly forsaken in favor of the other. In a tradition founded on lyrical rather than narrative modes of expression, the blending of these two concerns in a given work of art tends to be implicit rather than explicit.[2] Narrative, however, allows the conflict of purpose to become explicit, both for the artist and the audience.

Seen in a comparative context, Chinese narrative poetry poses many questions, the most basic being: What is the nature of that quality we call "narrative"? Strange as it may seem, there is no comparable term in Chinese criticism, at least not in the traditional works of Chinese poetics. Such terms as *hsü-shih shih* (narrative poetry) and *ku-shih shih* (story poems) are neologisms coined in response to European critical terminology.[3] This is not to say that narrative characteristics or narrative as a distinct mode of expression went unrecognized in China before the advent of European influence. The apparent lack of a separate generic category for narrative poetry is not necessarily perceived as a lack in the Chinese tradition. China's narrative tradition, unlike that of Europe, has its literary foundations in historiography rather than in poetry, and accords to historiography the reverence which the West reserves for epic poetry as the founding model of narrative expression.[4] Not only does Chinese narrative poetry not derive from an "epic" model, it is not necessarily separated from other poetry on the basis of generic or formal considerations. Yet it exists as a recognizable category in both literary and folk traditions, and includes some of China's most popular and enduring works. The first problem for this study, therefore, is how to define, in generic terms, a body of literature whose own tradition does not recognize—or better, attaches little importance to—its generic consistency.[5] In view of this seeming contradiction it is essential that we understand as precisely as possible what "narrative" and the countervalent term "lyric" mean in traditional Chinese poetics before we consider the narrative poems themselves.

It should be clear from the start that broad distinctions between "lyric" and "narrative" refer only to *tendencies*. "Pure" lyric and "pure" narrative are theoretical categories, but for literary analysis they must be relative, not absolute. Indeed, in Chinese literature the distinctions between lyric and narrative genres as they are known in European traditions simply do not exist. Part of the richness of both the Chinese and Japanese traditions lies in the fact that lyric and narrative modes of expression interpenetrate to a far greater extent than they do in European literary traditions. Interpreting such works in terms of a critical tradition which assumes the primacy of narrative forms and narrative poetics is a complex and often frustrating business. In *The Interlingual Critic* James J. Y. Liu suggests that an awareness of the fundamental differences between East Asian and European aesthetics may be latent in the mind of the reader, and so the "response" to these differences, in literary criticism at least, is usually unconscious.[6] Unfortunately, even when conscious of the differences, critics tend to assume that the presence or absence of certain tendencies are criteria of artistic value. Perhaps the most striking example in this century is the enormously influential *Pai-hua wen-hsüeh shih*, by Hu Shih, which finds the Chinese tradition wanting by comparison with Western traditions precisely because of its bias toward lyrical expression rather than what Hu Shih regards as the more "dynamic" literary styles of the West.[7] But if the impulse to ascribe value on the basis of aesthetic criteria can be set aside, the fundamental contrast the Chinese tradition offers to European models allows new insights into the qualities of both.

Chinese poetic criticism focuses on lyric poetry and poetics, which make up the bulk of the classical tradition, and is founded on a profound belief in the possibility of "lyrical experience."[8] Lyrical experience on the part of the poet is regarded as the expression of a moment in time freed through the medium of poetry from the constraints of time. On the part of the reader or participant lyrical experience is regarded as somehow incorporating the creative process of composition, as well as internalizing the moment of inspiration. Western criticism takes for granted that creative experience is different from interpretative experience, which is in fact the experience of the reader. Chinese criticism sees them as parts of a single process because both are aspects of a universal possibility of aesthetic experience.

The sense of communion with the creative experience is an essential aspect of lyrical experience in any culture, not just Chinese. Technical considerations may be put aside because, ideally, a participant can follow through the entire experience which inspired the original composition by reading the poem. This is actually an *interpretative* process, but the nature of lyrical composition is such that the process of interpretation allows the participant to re-create, or at least feel affinity with the creative experience, even if he or she would not, in fact, be capable of composing such a piece. The participant may be convinced of actually capturing the author's experience, because interpretation has intuitive as well as analytical aspects. Based on evocation of personal experiences, a reader participates in the illusion of re-creating the poet's experience.

A lyric poem may be short because it relies on the evocation of what is presumed, rightly or wrongly, to be a shared body of human experience. A narrative poem, in contrast, usually provides at least some specific background knowledge which is intended to bear upon the central experience of the poem. It is the specificity of the experience described, not the experience in general terms, which stimulates the reader's most powerful response. The reader's sense of the nature of participation in the experience is therefore essentially vicarious; it is a substitute for actual participation in the experience. However vivid the presentation of events, the reader is inevitably separated from them. Unlike the shared body of knowledge and experience which the lyric poet presumes, the specific details the poet of narrative must provide reinforce this separation.

The intended response of the reader of narrative is quite different from the intended response to lyrical experience. Narrative poetry is conceived in terms of *empathy for* rather than *integration with* the experience described in the composition. No matter how sympathetic or enthralling the subject matter may seem, the reader cannot, finally, preserve the illusion of having participated in its events. Indeed, one of the major results of the choice of a narrative mode of expression is to stress the particularity of certain events, experiences, and emotions, and to preserve them in a particular context rather than free them from it.

In the European traditions the formal characteristics of a poem are fundamental to a critical decision as to whether the poem is narrative or lyric in mode. With rare exceptions there are formal, generic distinctions that accompany these distinctions between modes.[9] Such distinctions cannot be relied upon to distinguish between narrative and lyric in the Chinese tradition. Narrative poems do tend to be of greater length, though not extraordinary by European standards. The longest narrative *shih* I will discuss is a poem of 238 lines from the T'ang dynasty—almost monstrous by Chinese standards, but not to be compared with the epics of the West, which run to thousands of lines. While the length of narrative poems might give a clue to the reader, not all lengthy *shih* are narrative. Nor will the terms in the titles of longer *ku-shih* necessarily indicate the mode of expression—such terms as *shih* (poem), *ko* (song), and *hsing* (ballad) may appear in the titles of lyric or narrative poems.[10] If genres of narrative and lyric poetry are not to be distinguished by formal features—thus, not to be distinguished *generically* in the Western sense of the term—we must reconsider the criteria for the identification and analysis of narrative modes of expression.

At this point important questions arise regarding the relation between formal and generic considerations in narrative poetry. Are the qualities associated with narrative in fact only inherent in particular formal conventions, or can they be analyzed according to characteristics which transcend the divisions between those traditions that emphasize lyric and those that emphasize narrative? Of course, within a given cultural tradition certain poetic clichés dependent on formal features for their expression will inevitably develop. This is very much a function of increasing self-consciousness within a given poetic tradition, in particular of an awareness of that tradition vis-à-vis its own past. In some cases this awareness transcends immediate cultural boundaries. Vergil's *Aeneid* takes its character from the Latin hexameter, but not only from the possibilities and limitations of the meter itself. Vergil was fully aware that the Latin hexameter was created in emulation of the meter of Greek epic, and his perfecting of an essentially foreign form is an expression of the desire to place his poem and his nation on an equal footing with their Greek forebears.[11] Homer and Vergil, in turn, have heirs in every European language, and this common narrative heritage transcends linguistic and cultural differences. Narrative, specifically epic poetry, is the founding form of literary consciousness in the West. Just as the ancient interrelations of the diverse tongues of Europe can be studied from Indo-European or other roots, so can the aesthetics and development of their literary creation. Much theory of narrative in comparative literature reflects this assumption, which is concretely linguistic and cultural in its origins.[12] It is not surprising, therefore, that many points of narrative theory derive from the study of literatures which are fundamentally interdependent—which, in fact, manifest a single, broad tradition of literary aesthetics and cultural concerns. Preconceptions of appropriate formal and metrical qualities, even appropriate length, are good examples of such interdependence. Arguably, any comparative study of European literary materials or traditions must take into account not only a common heritage but repeated cultural contact and influence as well.

But what of traditions not stemming from these same roots? Can criteria fundamental to the analysis of narrative in traditions based on narrative forms be applied to traditions based upon lyrical forms? A major methodological aim of this study is to examine a tradition in which the characteristics of narrative cannot be explained in terms of intercultural influence, in order to reexamine the assumptions and principles of narrative theory. Narrative forms as they occur in Chinese literature offer a coherent model which stands in fundamental contrast to the material on which the bulk of current narrative theory is founded. The contrasts between the Chinese tradition and European poetic traditions are certainly recognized in the West, though their implications have perhaps been explored more by artists than by critics. Poets such as Ezra Pound have exploited their *impressions* of Chinese poetry and poetics for their own artistic ends, to lend an exotic legitimacy to individual attempts at innovation within their own tradition. While I do not intend to pursue a critical evaluation of such phenomena as Pound's chinoiserie in this study, it is interesting to note that such attempts to incorporate Chinese aesthetics have tended to reaffirm the primacy of narrative in the West, rather than to offer a functional alternative in lyric poetics.[13]

By discussing the conventions and aesthetics of Chinese narrative poetry in terms of its native critical tradition, and comparing Chinese models with models of narrative theory more current in the field of comparative literature, I hope to shed light on some of the cultural assumptions which have been incorporated as fundamentals of narrative theory and development. This should not only allow for an increased and more informed critical exchange, but may also offer a new perspective on the tendency to assume that genre, per se, in narrative is absolute. Another significant feature of such an analysis is the emphasis it places on the virtual tyranny of the founding poetics of any given tradition. The comparison of narrative-oriented traditions with a lyric-based tradition raises the issue of innovation within tradition, and thus has implications for artistic enterprise on the most general level. Histories of literary innovation deal as much with new ways to exploit existing conventions as with "new" creation; this is implicit in the fact that we are so acutely aware of artistic tradition. The creative process is like the critical process in that it involves adapting new material to a complex of inspiration *and* received notions of art. Recognition of the biases which underlie a tradition may lead to more flexible interpretations of traditional poetics, and hence to more universal models of literary theory.

This study focuses on narrative poetry in the *shih* form during the period of its first growth and development in the late Han and Six Dynasties periods, and the heyday of *shih* during the T'ang dynasty. Strictly speaking, the narrative poems discussed here are mostly *ku-shih* (old-style poetry), also known as *ku-t'i shih*.[14] The term *ku-shih*, used here to denote poems from as early as the second century A.D., was in fact not used until the T'ang dynasty, when it was coined to designate the contrast between these meters and the far more rigid and complex requirements of *chin-t'i shih* (new-style poetry) which began to develop in the seventh century. The syntactic requirements of *ku-shih* are much less rigid than those of the three main forms of *chin-t'i shih: chüeh-chü* ("broken-off lines," or quatrains), *lü-shih* ("regulated verse," or octets), and the long, parallel-structured *p'ai-lü* ("regulated couplets," a longer form which adheres absolutely to the syntactic structure of parallelism without recourse to discursive continuity and maintains a single rhyme throughout). There are also no requirements for tonal patterns in *ku-shih,* as there are for all the forms of *chin-t'i shih.* While the length of the lines was more or less fixed at five or seven characters, the comparative freedom of syntax and the variation of the rhymes in *ku-shih* allowed for a degree of liveliness which could enhance the presentation of certain kinds of subject matter. This feature of *ku-shih* suits the form more readily to narrative expression than the shorter, regulated forms or even the potentially infinitely long, but possibly tedious, sustained rhymes and parallelisms of *p'ai-lü.*[15] Another highly regulated form that became popular in the T'ang period, *p'ien-wen* or *p'ien-t'i wen* (parallel prose), features metrically identical couplets with parallel lines, usually of four or six characters, but this usually is not considered to be a "poetic" genre. *P'ien-wen* allows lengthy, expository compositions on topics of philosophical, critical, or political debate. While these compositions may contain anecdotes which employ narrative techniques of expression, *p'ien-wen* is not only formally distinct from *ku-shih,* but also distinct in purpose, being the premier form of artistic *critical* writing from the T'ang through the Ch'ing dynasties.[16]

A poetic form far more closely related to *ku-shih,* with even greater freedom of syntax and style, is *yüeh-fu* (originally, poems from the music bureau). The origin of this genre was said to be in 120 B.C., when Emperor Han Wu-ti (r. 149–85 B.C.) organized the Music Bureau (*yüeh-fu*) in the government; its purpose was to collect folk poetry in order to study the attitudes and opinions of the "common people" toward the state. The institution gave its name to the poems it collected and then to poems written in imitation of the folk models. During the reign of Han Wu-ti the Music Bureau was responsible for providing the court with a variety of poems and accompanying music for the enhancement of court ceremonies. To this end the bureau is supposed to have collected four types of composition: genuine, anonymous folk songs; ritual music with lyrics composed at the bureau itself; texts selected from works of known authors and set to music at the bureau; and poems written by men of letters in the style of the anonymous folk ballads. As with the poems of the *Shih Ching*, *yüeh-fu* have come down to us only in literary form, and the question of their ultimate origin in folk poetry or in the Music Bureau is much debated. Whether the official bureau took such an active role in the collection or composition of poems is difficult to document, but the four basic types of *yüeh-fu*-style poetry do appear in poems of the Han dynasty.[17] While line length in *yüeh-fu* may vary, there are many examples in which the line length is uniform and the style is virtually indistinguishable from that of *ku-shih*, except for perhaps a greater informality of language and minimal use of recondite allusions. Some of the poems termed *ku-shih* here might be classified by others as literary *yüeh-fu*. Metrically and in terms of subject matter the two genres are so closely related that it may be clearer to explain that while poems with more overt allusions to "folk" themes tend to be classified as *yüeh-fu*, as a *literary* genre the distinction between *yüeh-fu* and the form which came to be known as *ku-shih* in the T'ang dynasty is rather arbitrary.[18]

One feature to consider, however, is that even at their most literary, poems in the *yüeh-fu* style purport to be of a folk style and representative of a folk idiom in poetry.[19] This is not the case with the poems that are the main subject of this study. For the most part they are self-consciously literary compositions, written as much for the purpose of recording a particular experience or set of events in poetic terms as for pleasing a large popular audience. While the language and diction may be informal, they are never really of the folk idiom, and the poems may have highly complex tonal and syntactic structures, demonstrating a high degree of literary artistry.[20]

If narrative and lyric genres cannot be distinguished clearly according to formal considerations in the Chinese tradition, what criteria can be applied to analyze their contrasting modes of expression? Perhaps the first criterion to take into consideration is subject matter. Certain themes would seem especially appropriate to a narrative mode: journeys, for instance, might provide the kind of underlying structure which lends itself to narrative effects. In

Chinese poetry, however, the presence of narrative or lyric modes is not so much a question of the subject matter as the mode of presentation of that subject matter, which is dependent upon the artistic intent of the poet. Poems which treat similar or even identical themes bear out this distinction by representing different responses to their subject matter and therefore different expressive needs. In the following chapters I will compare poems which deal with similar subject matter—or poems by different authors on the same supposed event—which leave the reader with entirely different impressions, corresponding to the differences between lyrical and narrative experience outlined above. The mode of presentation is of crucial importance for the interpretation of a poem, reflecting as it does the poet's attitude toward the subject matter and thus his or her expressive intentions.

In order to clarify this method of interpretation, it might be useful to examine a pair of poems on a single theme, one written in lyric, the other in narrative mode. Not only do they deal with the same legendary event, but the second, narrative version seems to have been written in direct response to the first. The theme of "Peach Blossom Spring" originates in a composition by T'ao Ch'ien (365–427): a fisherman unwittingly stumbles upon a utopian community whose members claim descent from a group who fled the wars which preceded the founding of the Ch'in dynasty (221–206 B.C.).[21] Though charmed by the social harmony and innocence of the place, the fisherman longs for his own home. He therefore departs for the outside world, intending to return someday to this ideal world. When at some later time he does attempt to retrace his steps, he discovers that he is unable to find the path or the place again. T'ao Ch'ien's "Peach Blossom Spring" includes a substantial preface as well as a poem of thirty-two five-character lines. It has been suggested that T'ao Ch'ien based his composition on a contemporary account of the secluded community, and it is not difficult to imagine the appeal that such a story would have for a man like T'ao Ch'ien, with his preference for a life of retirement, founded, according to his own literary oeuvre, on complex political ideals and standards of conduct for the talented man in the proper service of the state. Given the poet's personal history the land of the Peach Blossom Spring would have presented a fantasy of an ideal environment for men of his own caliber.[22] In his version of the theme, the prose preface is a narrative of the fisherman's marvelous journey to the village beyond the blossoming peach trees, while the poem is a personal meditation on the meaning of this unrecoverable "discovery." The preface and poem are clearly meant to be read together, although the preface is so much admired for its style that it is often anthologized without the poem.[23]

There is a suggestion of the particular attraction that the story holds for the poet at the very end of the preface: "A high-minded gentleman of Nan-yang named Liu Tzu-chi heard the story and happily made preparations to go there, but before he could leave he fell sick and died. Since then there has been no one interested in trying to find such a place."[24] Liu Tzu-chi was said to be an eccentric recluse who refused all official appointments, spending his days wandering in the mountains in search of medicinal herbs.[25] T'ao Ch'ien himself left his modest official post in order to retire to the country and lead a simple life, perhaps as much to protest the modesty of the position given to a man of his talent as to escape the irritations of political office. The mention of another recluse of high principles and eccentric habits whose desire to find the land of the Peach Blossom Spring was unfulfilled suggests a strong sense of affinity between the poet and Liu Tzu-chi. T'ao Ch'ien laments that only one, "simple" person was able to find the place, and he was not able to appreciate fully his good fortune. After Liu Tzu-chi, literally, "there has been no one interested in 'asking for the ford,'" an allusion to the enlightened man's search for knowledge.[26] No one else was either sufficiently superior of mind or sufficiently unconscious of worldly things to seek or stumble upon this haven from the dusty world.

This gentle irony is the substance of the poem which accompanies the preface. The poet mentions the fisherman and his adventure only in passing (line 26), concentrating instead on imagining the place in all its peace and prosperity. When the refugees of the Ch'in fled, the workings of nature aided them by hiding the traces of their path of escape (lines 5–6). Then, "by agreement" (hsiang-ming), they proceeded to set up the ideal society of the mythical harmonious anarchy so dear to the Chinese philosophical tradition. Without ambition for further knowledge, the community endures without change until it is discovered (line 26). When the visitor leaves the place of his own free will, nature again obligingly covers his tracks behind him. The place is meant to exist beyond the actual experience of men. The poet, however, can imagine the place most clearly and longs in vain to find the land where his kind would be both appreciated and left to pursue the "simple life" in peace.

T'ao Ch'ien gives the "historical" account of the fisherman's journey in the preface. The poem is not a versification of the same story, but rather a reverie on the wonderful innocence he and those like him can never regain. The poem describes the place in loving detail, but the final impression is not of a place at all, but of a state of mind—the only place where people can live in harmony with nature and with themselves—and the poet, at once tantalized and frustrated by the fantasy, must be comforted by communicating his sense of loss.

The T'ang poet Wang Wei (699–761) was an ardent student of the poetry of T'ao Ch'ien.[27] Even as a young man Wang Wei admired T'ao Ch'ien's ideals of retirement and self-containment, but in his own "Poem of Peach Blossom Spring," written in 717, he shows a shrewd understanding of the earlier poet's relation to this special place. Wang Wei's version is both a reinterpretation of the original composition and a personal version of the journey, a journey he takes himself. Wang Wei combines the narrative content of T'ao Ch'ien's preface with his own response to the lyric poem in a single poetic composition:

Poem of Peach Blossom Spring

> My fishing boat follows the current, I rejoice in the mountain
>   spring;
> On both banks are peach blossoms, pressing my boat
>   upstream.
> I sit and admire the blushing trees, unmindful of the
>   distance,
> I come to the end of the blue stream without meeting any
>   people.
> The mountain has a mouth through which I pass that starts at
>   the bend of the hill,   5

The mountain opens on flat land extending as far as I can
  see—
I see in the distance a place where clouds and trees are
  gathered,
Near where I entered, a thousand houses, scattered among
  flowers and bamboo.
Some woodcutters first ask my name, using the speech of
  Han times;
The people who dwell here have not yet changed their
  clothes from the style of Ch'in!   10
The people who dwell here seem to live on the Wu-ling
  Stream,
And as if of a realm beyond this world tend their fields and
  gardens.
Under a bright moon and pines, their homes are at peace,
When the sun rises among the clouds, cocks crow and dogs
  bark.
Surprised to hear of a stranger, they jostle and gather
  together,   15
They squabble over inviting me home, they ask of my native
  place.
At dawn the village paths are swept clear of the petals of
  flowers,
At dusk the fishermen and woodcutters return with their nets
  and carts.
Originally they fled the world to leave the haunts of men;
I ask if they are immortals, enduring because they did not
  return.   20
In this enclave, who knows of the affairs of other folk?
And those in the outside world see only empty clouds and
  the mountain.
Unconscious of how hard it was to enter this spirit realm,
In my earthbound heart I unceasingly long for my home
  village.
I leave the cave without reason, cut myself off from the
  mountain and stream,   25
Though intending finally to leave my home and make the
  long journey again.

I rehearse with myself the paths I cross; so well known, I
    could not get lost—
How could I know that the cliffs and gullies would now seem
    changed?
Now I only remember that to enter the mountain's depths
A blue stream with many bends leads to a forest of clouds.   30
Spring comes, and everywhere there are peach blossom
    waters,
But I cannot find the fairy stream; where shall I look for it?[28]

Wang Wei uses the personal pronoun *tzu* (cf. line 27), which I
have translated as a first-person pronoun throughout to emphasize
the self-consciousness of his response to T'ao Ch'ien's composition.
When the master remarks, "Let me ask you, who are convention-
bound / Can you fathom those outside the dirt and noise?"(lines
29–30),[29] Wang Wei answers with a poem which questions T'ao
Ch'ien's reaction to the original legend and expresses his personal
longing to create within himself the contentment and equilibrium
imputed to the folk of the land of the Peach Blossom Spring.

    Wang Wei stresses his persona's *lack* of purpose (line 3) which
allows him to "find" the hidden land. While the inhabitants are
curious about the stranger, they have escaped the outside world
and have no desire to return to it (lines 19–20). However, the man
who originally had no thought of escaping soon wants to return to
his home (line 24). Once away, no matter how carefully he exam-
ines the route, he is foiled when he attempts to retrace his steps
purposefully. Nature is ever-changing, and as the seasons turn
he is bewildered: "Spring comes, and everywhere there are peach
blossom waters / But I cannot find the fairy stream; where shall I
look for it?" (lines 31–32). The answer, of course, is "everywhere"
(line 31)—if one has the imagination. And if the imagination is
there, what need is there for the place? Wang Wei gently chides
T'ao Ch'ien's "desire" (*yüan*, "Peach Blossom Spring," line 31), for
the man who *wants* to find such a place will be confused by the
patterns of nature and his own desire. A man truly content will see
that "*everywhere* there are peach blossom waters" (line 31, italics
mine), and he may make the journey to the "spirit realm" (line 23)
whenever he likes.

While the themes of these two poems are explicitly linked, the different techniques of expression reveal correspondingly different attitudes. T'ao Ch'ien tells the tale first in prose, and the following poem has the air of a personal commentary on the legendary experience. Wang Wei makes the story his own. Where T'ao Ch'ien reveals his emotion by explicit statements and by an admiring reference to Liu Tzu-chi, Wang Wei expresses his response through action, or more important, frustration in action, when trying to retrace his "actual" steps. As narrator, he makes for himself a character, that of the foolish and innocent traveler unconscious of his good fortune. Or was he simply not meant to turn his back on the world of men? T'ao Ch'ien, the genuine recluse, responds to the tale of another whom he regards as luckier than himself and leaves no doubt as to what his choice would be if he should ever find the elusive path.

The country of Peach Blossom Spring and its unaffected inhabitants became an archetypal, ideal state of being, individual and social, in later poetry. These two poems actually focus on the place itself, real or imaginary. They are both in the *shih* form—thirty-two lines—although T'ao Ch'ien's is in five-character lines and Wang Wei's is in seven-character lines. The main difference is in mode of expression. Unlike the earlier work, Wang Wei's "Poem of Peach Blossom Spring" has a narrative structure based on a sequence of actions, an explicit narrator's voice to tell the story, and even a "protagonist"—the unwitting fisherman. T'ao Ch'ien's poem is a glimpse of an ideal state of mind; Wang Wei follows him by taking the journey himself and recounting it *as* a journey.

This is, of course, a conscious choice: the poet may emphasize either an internal state or external events. This choice of emphasis governs both the mode of composition and the way the composition must be interpreted.[30] While our ability to distinguish between lyric and narrative in poems of the same genre may appear largely intuitive, such "intuitions" are most often responses to conscious literary artistry. The contrast between T'ao Ch'ien's and Wang Wei's versions of the story of Peach Blossom Spring provides a paradigm for the manipulation of *shih* poetics to suit widely varying expressive purposes.

In the chapters which follow I will focus on these aspects of *shih* composition as they are adapted for narrative expression. My principles of analysis are grounded in the founding aesthetics of Chinese poetry, which emphasize and elevate lyrical experience, yet provide for the development of narrative techniques. Some of these techniques are evident in the forms of poetic composition which precede the rise of *shih* at the end of the Han dynasty. The *Shih Ching* (*Book of Songs*) contains poems in several forms which suggest possible techniques for sustaining a longer composition than is usually thought characteristic of lyric poetry. Stanzaic form, for instance, is frequently associated with lyrics.[31] When stanzas are explicitly linked in an invariable order by such devices as refrains (which may themselves be varied to comment on the subject matter as it unfolds, but still anchor the structure and unify the poem as a whole), the units of subject matter they represent may take on a temporal coherence and specificity of the kind so important to narrative.[32] Another device used in the *Shih Ching* to link stanzas in a prescribed order is that of "catenation," the repetition of the final character or characters of one stanza as the first part of the first line of the following stanza. This device perhaps most explicitly suggests that the order in which the stanzas appear is logical and intended. Such a fixed formal sequence may also become the basis of a narrative sequence.

Other kinds of repetition may be used to reinforce the organization of a large body of material in a logical, sequential structure. Devices such as onomatopoeia, alliterative phrases, and "clichés" have been studied in terms of their possible origins in and relation to oral and formulaic language and composition.[33] Folk conventions of public performance certainly influenced the conventions of literary narrative poetry, along with the ancient tradition of literary composition intended for public display of political opinions.

Perhaps the most important and influential of the early poetic genres of public rhetoric is that of *fu* (rhyme prose or rhapsody). Poems in the *fu* genre reflect a concern with sequential structure and at the same time emphasize public expression of matters peculiar to a specific, designated context. The techniques of *fu* composition may well have inspired innovative treatments of similar subject matter in the genre of *shih*.

Early examples of narrative expression in poetry and poetic

criticism suggest three main criteria for distinguishing narrative in later works: point of view, characterization, and sequential structure. All three contribute to the sense of vicarious experience that is essential to narrative, as opposed to the sense of integration typical of lyric. Frequently they leave clear traces in the techniques of poetic composition: techniques developed for lyric require modification and innovation for the successful presentation of material in a narrative mode.

Point of view—the source of a set of perceptions on the subject matter of a given text—is the source of a reader's knowledge of the narrator's perspective in a poem. In *Art and Reality* the novelist Joyce Cary stresses the primacy of point of view in narrative: it is the controlling device through which the artist presents intuitions about the chosen subject matter to the audience, and it determines the reader's access to the author's own vision of events.[34] Further, the sense of a particular point of view, the poet's or the narrator's, not only controls the reader's perception of a poem's subject matter, but reinforces the specificity of the experience the poem conveys, and hence its separation from the reader's own experience. This is one of the areas in which poets most clearly manipulate the techniques of *shih* composition to produce narrative effects. A wealth of concrete detail can be called into service to enforce the distinctness of the narrator's point of view: definition of a particular voice or person, achieved through the use of pronouns, titles, or personal names; the use of framing devices to indicate particular speakers; the use of direct or indirect quotations; and details of time and place that help to anchor the source of these perceptions in a particular context. In each case the result is a heightened sense of sympathy, rather than integration, with the experience of the text.

Techniques of characterization enforce the awareness of a concrete point of view and a context of experience other than the reader's own. Chinese techniques of characterization stem from the historiographical tradition and differ fundamentally from those based on the Western, epic tradition. For example, heroic archetypes in the West derive ultimately from mythology and reveal their essential qualities through their actions. In a sense, what such a hero *does* is more important that what he *is*, because what he *does* reveals what he *is*. The heroes of early Chinese historiography tend to be conceived in terms of abstractions of aspects of ritual completeness. Their careers exemplify particular ideals of social conduct, which in turn define their characters. Following the Chinese propensity for emphasizing ritual rather than mythological patterns of culture, individual *quality* rather than action is the issue, and so quality reliably determines action.[35] The techniques of characterization which produce well-rounded, sympathetic characters in historiographical prose are also present in the poetic tradition. The most distinctive techniques involve direct and indirect discourse to express individual personality, and the use of symbolic associations to help define individual personality.

Another fundamental aspect of narrative expression is the role of sequential structures. As we shall see, the organization of events according to logical sequences led to the creation of explicit temporal contexts, a necessary feature of narrative. While not all poetic sequences are based on temporal patterns of organization, the sequential structures of narrative *ku-shih* usually purport to refer to specific contexts which reflect objective time, no matter how fictional the subject may be. (The fact that poem sequences show the tendency suggests yet another source of narrative in Chinese poetry.) Sometimes a sense of objective time is created by such mechanical means as the citation of a date in an attached preface or in the body of the composition. More sophisticated examples achieve balance between the requirements of *shih* poetics and the demands of narrative progression. In "Song of the Lady of Ch'in," the poet Wei Chuang successfully organizes his units of action, or narrative "tableaux," to correspond to such standard poetic units as quatrains and octets, creating a masterpiece of poetic technique and story-telling art which belies the assumption that *shih* is an essentially lyric form.

A study that attempts to cover some seven hundred years, even with reference to only one form of poetic composition, cannot claim to be comprehensive. The poems in the *shih* form contained in the *Complete T'ang Poetry* (*Ch'üan T'ang shih*) alone number many thousands, and it has not been possible to analyze even a fraction of that number. My purpose here is not to examine every example of narrative tendencies in *shih*, but to suggest a framework for the study of narrative, using other criteria than the formal or generic ones that Western criticism takes for granted. At the same time the consideration and application of Western critical terms may shed new light on the function of narrative in Chinese poetry and, by extension, in Chinese culture as a whole.

1

Narrative Elements in Traditional Chinese Poetics

Questions of the nature of narrative in the Chinese tradition—its techniques and forms of expression—are of increasing interest to scholars of Chinese literature and art, but are still defined only hazily by scholars of Chinese poetry. The three main criteria for the analysis of narrative expression as distinct from lyrical expression—point of view, characterization, and sequence—are familiar from European works of narrative theory.[1] The same criteria are present in traditional Chinese poetics, though they manifest themselves very differently from their Western counterparts.[2] Although Chinese narrative poetry may not be *formally* distinct from other modes of poetic expression as developed in various genres, the earliest extant texts of Chinese poetry and poetic criticism nevertheless show a clear awareness of the potential and utility of narrative expression. For an understanding of the functions of point of view, characterization, and sequence in traditional Chinese poetics we must consider the characteristics of Chinese poetic language as well as the documents of literary criticism in terms of the fundamental units of style which allow for narrative expression.

The earliest extant works of Chinese literature provide the basis for the formative statements of the nature of literary art and the general nature of the Chinese poetic language. The very term that we translate as "poetry," *shih,* serves as an example of some of the peculiar characteristics of Chinese critical discourse. The first documents of Chinese poetics, as they have come down to the present day, are based on the *Shih Ching* anthology, probably first compiled around 600 B.C., although many of its three hundred or so poems may date from centuries earlier. The word *shih* has its earliest usage in three of the poems in the *ya* (odes or elegantiae) section of this anthology. These usages of the term *shih* have been interpreted to indicate the existence of a conception of "poetry" as a *literary* art, definable by name and recognizable by nature in its application, as early as the sixth century B.C., and this definition of poetry is common in works of criticism.[3] The term is also used just as frequently to refer to that first anthology, the *Shih Ching,* and to the genre of poetry which is said to derive from the models of the *Shih Ching.* The interdependence of these uses of the term *shih* is readily apparent, and yet their precise relation and distinctions may seem baffling. Furthermore, Chinese criticism shows a tendency to define concepts either in terms of particular examples from the tradition or metaphorically, in terms of their effects. This makes the task of defining the abstractions which form the basis of Chinese critical terminology difficult in Western languages. Considering that the sources of the Chinese poetic tradition are lyrical, we can see that such terminology will also inevitably reflect the problems of describing the aesthetics of a lyric tradition and lyrical quality in art generally.[4]

Another important feature of the Chinese critical tradition which bears significantly on the development of a distinction between narrative and lyric modes of expression is the emphasis on the role of *intent* (*chih*) as crucial to the understanding of a work of art. The importance of authorial intention has already been implied in the introductory discussion of T'ao Ch'ien's and Wang Wei's versions of the legend of Peach Blossom Spring. Much of the significance of Wang Wei's poem derives from his shared interpretation of T'ao Ch'ien's *purpose* in composing his preface and poem. This is only a specific instance of the importance of the perception and understanding of authorial intention. In practical terms artistic emphasis on the perception and understanding of authorial intention is an integral aspect of Chinese literary criticism, a precept which was amply confirmed in Confucian doctrine, especially in interpretations of particular works of literature and statements on the nature of literary art.[5] The early Confucian impulse was to interpret *shih* in terms of their value for learning, if not precisely for their didactic content. What ultimately emerged was a bias toward political and social rhetoric, with literary language regarded as a means to various ends. The role of literature in such a system of social thought is as a medium through which one may acquire learning that may in turn stir and edify others; this is regarded as the proper end or use of learning.[6]

The Confucian emphasis on the ends of learning would seem to place as much importance on the act of reading as on the act of writing: what matters is the successful communication of the author's intent, and this requires a receptive audience. This purposive attitude toward literary criticism is evident from early statements on the nature of the arts in texts which express Confucian values. The *Classic of History* (*Shu Ching*), for example, attributes to Emperor Shun an admonition regarding the proper uses of poetic expression, as part of his charge to his new minister of music, the *T'ai-ssu yüeh*: "Poetry expresses intention (inclination, determination, or will) in words, songs prolong the sounds of words for chanting, and the pitch-pipes harmonize the notes. Make the eight kinds of musical sounds in accord and let them not interfere with each other, so that spirits and men may be brought into harmony."[7]

The "Great Preface" to the *Shih Ching* (*Shih ta hsü*), from the Mao edition of the anthology, dates from perhaps the first century A.D. and is attributed to Wei Hung.[8] This enigmatic text presents a complex statement on the nature of poetic expression which has proved to be perhaps the most tenacious and influential in Chinese criticism. This preface marks the foundation of Chinese literary criticism as a form of discourse in its own right. Incorporating the late Han revivals and reforms in Confucian doctrine, it attempts to formulate the process whereby poetry combines aesthetic quality and ethical substance. The preface reflects a background of Confucianism, grounded as it is in the pragmatic principle of the necessity of ethical purpose in literature, and this principle is in turn grounded in a conception of the nature of literature that makes the processes of writing and reading virtually inseparable. The relation of "intent" to "poetry" is part of a spontaneous creative process which proceeds from internal, individual response to the external world:

> Poetry is the fulfillment of intent; what dwells in the mind is intent, what comes forth in words is poetry. Emotions move in the core of one's being and take form in words. When speaking them does not suffice, then one sighs them or chants them; if sighing and chanting do not suffice, then one sings them; if singing them does not suffice, then unconsciously one taps them out with the hands, dances them, treads them and stamps them.
>
> Emotions come forth in sounds, and when the sounds fulfill patterns they are called musical tones. The musical tones of an age of peace are tranquil and incline to joy; their regulation is harmonious. The musical tones of an age of disorder are dissonant and incline to anger; their regulation is perverted. The musical tones of a kingdom in ruins are mournful and incline to nostalgia; their people are suffering. Therefore, to keep order in success or failure, to move Heaven and Earth, to touch the feelings of ghosts and spirits, nothing can approach poetry. The former kings used these means to guide the conduct of husband and wife, to inspire filial piety and generosity, to enrich social relations, to enhance education and culture, and to develop manners and customs.[9]

The significance of *chih*, or intent, in relation to poetry is to establish the purpose of expression; one intends, in response to the stimulation of inspiration, to express oneself in order to communicate this emotion (*ch'ing*).[10] With ethical purpose an underlying assumption of poetic expression, the critic here attempts to formulate a statement on the nature of artistic inspiration ("in the mind"), the process of expression ("if one does not suffice"), and the response of the audience. In order to achieve expression of inspiration the artist may call upon all his resources, verbal and physical. While expression in words must adjust to the limits of language, meaning lies under no such constraint; meaning may go beyond the literal level of the text—literally, "beyond words" (*yen-wai*)—and is limited only by the reader's imagination or capacity for understanding.

The concept of intent is central in the mainstream of Chinese literary criticism. This emphasis on the expressive quality of art is the basis of the Chinese lyric aesthetic.[11] In practical terms emphasis on the perception and understanding of authorial intent is integral to Chinese literary criticism. Again, it must be stressed that this statement from the "Great Preface" remained a crucial tenet of literary theory, and the primary statement of the significance of the relation of "intent" to artistic creation in the Chinese tradition, whatever the moral, philosophical, or political biases of the critic. Kao Yu-kung comments at length upon the formula:

> In its usual straightforward interpretation, this formula is close to a doctrine of didacticism: "to express through verbalization the poet's immediate message." Its purpose is clearly communication, its direction toward the external world. However, in early Chinese history the intrinsic distrust of discursive communication, and the absolute importance based on inner experience, prompted a subtler amplification of the same dictum, so here the word "to express" came to mean "total realization," embracing both semantic representation and formal presentation. Given this amplification in meaning, the word "intent" is no longer sufficient to encompass the object of poetic vision, and it is expanded to mean an integral part of the total experience, including all mental activities and attributes, of a particular person at a particular moment. Within this frame of reference, "intent" can be identified as the "meaning" of one moment in an individual's life, while "vision" becomes the realization of this meaning in its totality.[12]

According to the passage from the "Great Preface" quoted earlier, the poetic act implicitly has two parts: *perception* and *expression*. These two parts in turn determine the relationship between the acts of composition and reading. The act of reading implies the re-creation of the original act of perception, but the method employed by the artist to ensure this re-creation will to a large extent define the mode of expression and thus the experience of the reader. Lyrical experience fosters the illusion of reproducing the act of perception exactly as it was experienced by the artist. Narrative experience, on the other hand, invokes a vicarious perception, a sympathetic response tempered by awareness of the separation of the reader from the experience of perception. These two conventions of literary experience may also be seen as contrasting implicit and explicit expressions of meaning: implicit in fostering the illusion of precise reproduction of experience, explicit in the direct expression of particularized experience beyond the reader's immediate context.

In Chinese poetry these two kinds of literary experiences reflect not only fundamental differences in expressive intent, but also conventions and innovations in Chinese poetic language. On the most general level lyrical experience and narrative experience reflect the expressive tendencies of two basic conventions of syntax in Chinese poetry, as described by Kao Yu-kung and Mei Tsu-lin in "Syntax, Diction, and Imagery in T'ang Poetry."[13] The first convention is *imagistic* language, which requires no specific agent or context and exploits discontinuous syntax to produce arresting effects of rhythm and a vivid sense of perception. The second is *propositional* language, which implies the presence of an agent, perhaps indicated by a pronoun or other reference, and evokes action. In this case the syntax tends to a more continuous rhythm, and the presence of an agent determines the nature, intention, or result of action. The imagistic and propositional conventions of expression coexist in Chinese poetic language and can even occur in the same poem:

> Adopting a theory developed by Ernst Cassirer in his *Language and Myth*, we will propose a distinction of language into two poles, the *imagistic* pole and the *propositional* pole. . . .
>
> The two distinctions, imagistic/propositional and continuous/discontinuous, are based upon two different criteria. The first answers the question, what kind of "meaning" does a

verbal expression refer to and how is that meaning appre-
hended? That is, whether the "meaning" is primarily percep-
tual or conceptual. The second answers the question, what
kind of rhythm does the syntax of that verbal expression create? In practice, however, these two distinctions are frequently
related. If a line has minimal syntax, then its rhythm is likely
to be discontinuous and its imagistic function correspondingly
enhanced. If a proposition is to indicate the relations among its
component parts, it has to have a more complicated syntactic
apparatus, which at once weakens the image-making power
of the individual words and gives the sentence a fullness that
allows it to sustain a more continuous rhythm.[14]

The interrelation of these conventions provides a means of
understanding the interaction of the composition and reading of
poetry which is at the heart of poetic experience in Chinese literary
criticism. These same dynamics provide a key to the distinctions
between lyric and narrative in Chinese poetry. While Kao and Mei
focus on T'ang poetry in their study, the relation of imagistic and
propositional conventions of language is significant in all phases
of the tradition. Their tendencies affect the mode of expression
not only according to the subject matter, but also according to the
structure of an individual poem. The formal qualities of particular
meters and genres of *shih* may largely determine the proportion
of imagistic and propositional language. This in turn determines
the nature of the impact of the poetic act and reveals its underlying intent. Where imagistic language dominates, the lyric mode
will emerge; where propositional language dominates, the narrative mode prevails. The nature of the Chinese poetic language provides for the diversification of these modes according to authorial
intent. Because of its discontinuous and objective qualities, imagistic language promotes the reader's sense of integration with the
experience of the text. Propositional language, relying on the presence of an identifiable agent, and therefore more continuous in
syntax and subjective in reference, promotes the empathy characteristic of narrative experience. Kao and Mei suggest the association
of "objective" qualities with imagistic language and discontinuous
syntax (hence with lyrical tendencies), and "subjective" qualities

with propositional language and continuous syntax (hence, narrative tendencies). They explain these qualities in terms of "spatial" versus "temporal" axes. Imagistic language tends to objective expression because it is free from temporal reference, while propositional language asserts a context which implies temporal reference, and so provides a specificity which renders the expression subjective in quality. On first consideration it might seem as if lyrical expression should be subjective and narrative expression objective, because lyrical experience may vary according to the individual reader, while narrative experience seems far more set by the poet or speaker. From the perspective of the text and the functions of Chinese poetic language, however, the nontemporally referential, universalized expression of lyric is objective by virtue of its liberation from a specific context, while the grounding of narrative in a particular temporal context renders it subjective.[15]

The presence of an agent separates the reader from the context of the experience of the poem and so allows for the development of two important features of narrative: point of view and characterization. While the presence of these features may not require formal, generic distinctions between lyric and narrative poems, the interaction of the imagistic and propositional conventions of language suggests a sense of awareness of these distinctions on the part of the author and provides the reader with some keys to their analysis.

To go further, imagistic language emphasizes *quality*, while propositional language emphasizes *action*. Imagistic language thus relies upon the topic/comment structure in syntax, and makes extensive use of *stative* or *qualitative* verbs. Propositional language relies upon the presence of an agent and can accommodate the use of *performative* verbs. Qualitative verbs tend to describe states of being which are not dependent on specific temporal or spatial contexts for their significance. Performative verbs, on the other hand, tend to imply concrete temporal and spatial contexts, even if these contexts are not precisely defined.[16]

The relation between these two expressive conventions in Chinese poetic language is crucial to the understanding and appreciation of Chinese poetry. The problem of conveying their interaction is a difficult one for translators of Chinese poetry, especially lyric poetry. Given the predominance of lyrical expression, it is not surprising that Chinese literary aesthetics stress the imagistic rather than the active quality of language, and even in narrative literature it is the "lyrical" element which is elevated in criticism.[17] This element is virtually impossible to reproduce in inflected languages without nonsensical effects. The *sense* of a phrase or sentence may well be conveyed, but the expressive qualities of the syntax are quite another matter. Translators of poetry overwhelmingly substitute propositional structures for phrases that in Chinese are strictly imagistic. This tendency, of course, extends beyond the realm of translation and creates serious problems for those whom James J. Y. Liu has referred to as "non-native" readers of Chinese literature.[18]

By way of illustration, qualitative verbs provide an important component of imagistic conventions of expression in Chinese poetry. One of the most distinctive of the forms of qualitative verbs in early Chinese poetry is the disyllabic compound. According to George A. Kennedy, disyllabic compounds represent something of the essential character of Chinese language.[19] Some "strong" (explicitly referential) words, such as the pronoun *wo* (I), are monosyllabic and appear in poetry, but disyllabic compounds predominate and, in the *Shih Ching*, are essential to the quatrosyllabic (four-character) line which is the basis of the *Shih Ching* meters. Perhaps most typical of this type of compound in the *Shih Ching* are the "reduplicatives" (*lien-mien tzu*), which are difficult to translate into inflected languages but which are among the most distinctive Chinese conventions for establishing poetic intensity. The most familiar kinds of reduplicatives, "descriptives," function as qualitative verbs that either repeat a qualitative verb, in the case of "identical reduplicatives," or link two qualitative verbs with the same or similar initials or finals in a descriptive compound—the "unidentical reduplicative."[20] In "Reduplicatives in the Book of Odes," Chou Fa-kao cites and analyzes the first two stanzas of the first poem of the *Shih Ching* (Mao no. 1) "to exemplify the usage of identical and unidentical reduplicatives":

1 kuan kuan chü chiu
  Kuan kuan (cries) the 'chu chiu' bird,

tsai hê chih chou;
On the islet of the river;

yao t'iao shu nü,
the beautiful and good girl,

chun-tzǔ hao ch'iu.
she is a good mate for the lord.

2 ts'en tz'ǔ hsing ts'ai,
Of varying length is the *hsing* waterplant,

tso yu liu chih;
to the left and right we catch it;

yao t'iao shu nü,
the beautiful and good girl,

wu men chiu chih.
waking and sleeping he wished for her.[21]

These stanzas have been interpreted in nearly as many ways as there are translators and commentators, not least because of the reduplicative compounds they contain. James Legge leaves the first reduplicative in romanization, but suggests that it is an action, probably a cry, of the birds:

Kwan-kwan go the ospreys,
On the island in the river.
The modest, retiring, virtuous young lady:—
For our prince a good mate she.[22]

Bernhard Karlgren also leaves the "cry" of the birds in romanization: "*Kwan-kwan* (cries) the ts'u-kiu bird, on the islet of the river; the beautiful and good girl, she is a good mate for the lord.—"[23]

Arthur Waley anthropomorphizes the birds, putting the words of the people's approval into their beaks:

"Fair, fair," cry the ospreys
On the island in the river.
Lovely is the noble lady,
Fit bride for our lord.[24]

In *Grammata Serica Recensa* Karlgren defines this usage of the character *kuan* in the first line as a loan for a homophone indicating

a bird's cry.[25] Although Karlgren always suggests meanings for reduplicatives, in this case interpreting the reduplicative "*kuan kuan*"
as a sound rather than some other particular feature of the bird,
the basic function of a reduplicative in poetic usage is to intensify
the state of existence to which it refers—in this case the nature
of the birds. The figure of speech idealizes the state described: "The
ospreys are as *kuan* as *kuan* could be." In this case, while *kuan* may
refer to the sound made by the birds, it could refer to some other
feature, such as the tufts on their heads. (In the same entry Karlgren points out that *kuan* may refer to the little tufts tied into the
hair of small children, and indeed birds in this family of fishing
hawks have crested heads.) Another thing to consider in the interpretation of the stanza is the fact that this poem is an epithalamion,
and river islands are typical nesting sites for the species. In other
words, what is evoked by the original Chinese is more than just the
sound of the birds' cries; their whole environment of courtship and
mating is an image complementing the marriage and mating of the
young lady and lord. This kind of imagistic language is extraordinarily rich in evocative power and allows a very compact expression
to become the basis of a complex image and interpretation.

While the intensification of state described by a reduplicative
does *not* turn this verb into a performative or active verb in Chinese, this, paradoxically, is what all of the translators cited above
have done. Similarly, in Mao no. 3, "*Chuan-erh*," the first line, "*ts'ai-
ts'ai chuan erh*, " does not necessarily imply a repeated action, as
Legge would have it: "I was gathering and gathering the mouse-
ear."[26] It is far more likely that the word *ts'ai* is a loan character for
a word meant to describe some characteristic of this plant, as in
Waley's version, "Thick grows the cocklebur."[27]

When considering the specifically linguistic bases of narrative
expression in Chinese poetic language, it may be confusing to have
to deal with translations which convert imagistic into propositional
language. This difficulty is inherent in the task of translating from
Chinese into an inflected language. In this process it is frequently
necessary to substitute propositional for imagistic language, and
therefore to give the impression of active quality in language where
it did not exist in the original. Reduplicatives represent a small per-
centage of the qualitative verbs used in Chinese poetry but they

provide, as it were, intensified examples of both the expressive power and the interpretative ambiguity of the imagistic language which is the basis of lyrical expression in Chinese. While temporal particles, which indicate changes of status usually associated with tense or a fixed point in time, may provide a qualitative verb with a temporal reference, the first effect of such an expression in poetry will still be imagistic rather than propositional. According to Kao and Mei, this helps to explain Fenellosa's obsession with the expressive power of individual "pictographs":

> Fenellosa believed that Chinese written characters are eminently suitable as a medium of poetry, since one can see pictures in the characters. This is clearly nonsense; yet useful nonsense. What he noticed is that, unlike words in English poetry, the smallest unit in Chinese—namely, the individual character—is capable of image making. But Fenellosa assigned the wrong cause; isolative syntax, instead of pictographic writing, endows even the smallest units with the degree of autonomy they enjoy.[28]

The performative verbs typical of propositional language tend to be affiliated with temporal or spatial references, in the sense of indicating the relation of an agent to a definable context or physical space. The relation of the agent—usually but not always in the place of grammatical subject—to a predicate indicating the intention, performance, or result of action determines the nature of the statement. The agent may thus suggest the presence of a point of view other than that of the reader: either that of the agent itself, or of one who relates the agent's activity. Transitivity may also impart a structure to the statements, reflecting on the agent of the poem (I, or a third person). Considered as individual statements these cannot be said to establish a sequence; however, they may set up expectations for continuity which could allow for the establishment of a logical sequence. Suspense and the anticipation of resolution are important aspects of temporal sequence, again reflecting upon the mutual participation of poet and reader in the underlying intent of a particular composition.

In the case of verbs indicating intention of action, or *modal* verbs, the relationship to the agent is particularly well defined.[29]

The modal aspect of performative verbs is of great importance for narrative expression because it implies a specific agent; and the presence of such an agent is essential to point of view in narrative. This specific agent in turn provides the perspective which allows for the development of the second necessary criterion, characterization. Modal verbs anticipate the agent's intention to change the state of an object (which may be the agent), through the performance of some action, to a different state of existence. The poem "*Chuan-erh*" mentioned above provides a typical example. The first couplet is descriptive, setting the context for the introduction of the speaker-agent, represented in the second couplet by the demonstrative pronoun *wo* (I). The speaker longingly awaits the appearance of a friend or lover after a lengthy separation, and the natural setting reflects the speaker's state of mind. The speaker hopes for a change in his or her emotional state, but the surrounding scenery remains stubbornly constant, suggesting that no gratification is imminent.

A third category of statements, one that often mediates between imagistic and propositional language in poetry, should be mentioned here. This is the set of statements depending on *relational* verbs, which are nontemporal and nonspatial in connotation and yet depend on the presence of an agent for meaning or interpretation. These verbs in Chinese include *yu* (literally, "to have," but often in the sense of "there is," or "there exists") and *ju* (to be like, to resemble). In relational statements the state of the agent and the state of the object to which the agent is compared are semantically equivalent. The crucial distinction between relational and propositional verbs is the intention of the agent—"I" or a third person—which usually has the effect of specifying a context in time and space.[30]

These general statements regarding the conventions of reading may be said to apply to all aspects of Chinese language, but for the purposes of this study it is most important to consider how these conventions affect the development of poetry. Most obvious is their effect on lyric and narrative tendencies. Imagistic language makes possible a total lack of temporal and spatial references for lyrical expression, allowing for the fullest integration and appreciation of lyrical experience. Propositional language, on the other hand, with its explicit agents and performative statements, exploits the potential for narrative by specifying the agent's experience and enforcing the vicarious nature of the reader's experience. Neither imagistic nor propositional language is used to the total exclusion of the other; what is in question is the relative proportion of use, the pattern of their distribution, and the intent governing the composition.

Understanding the relation of these conventions is only part of the interpretation of a complex composition. An awareness of the historical evolution of language may also add depth to the meaning of particular words or phrases, as their many connotations may be brought to bear on their context in a poem, thus enriching the structure of the poem's meaning.[31] This evocative quality allows for extraordinarily dense effects, establishing texts which reveal their full meaning only after substantial interpretation by a reader. The latitude granted a word or phrase to partake of various syntactic, semantic, and allusive functions not only allows for a variety of uses and meanings for a word in multiple contexts, but these multiple connotations may also be brought to bear simultaneously upon a word or phrase in a single context. Although these multiple levels of meaning can be experienced emotionally, their complex totality may be impossible to articulate, even though its components can be articulated and analyzed in interpretation, translation, or commentary.[32]

For the purposes of interpretation we can study the function of words according to their context in a given work of art. On the syntactic level, especially in poetry, usage can be very free, and our evaluation is interpretative as well as strictly grammatical. Contextual, syntactic, and semantic analyses all play a part in determining meaning, and the conventions of a poetic form or style may affect all three levels of analysis.

The evolution of poetic expression through the T'ang dynasty tends toward a more self-consciously lyrical convention. Pronouns and other specifiers increasingly drop out, and the ratio of imagistic to propositional usage increases and is formally underscored by the perfection of the conventions of parallelism, the lyrical trope par excellence. Since parallelism tends to equivalence and discontinuity rather than to the sense of progression vital to narrative, the dominance of parallel over continuous sentence structures in *shih* reflects a preference for imagistic over propositional expression and, by extension, for lyrical over narrative, or integrative over vicarious experience.

From the Han through T'ang dynasties the adaptation of lyrical conventions to the requirements of narrative was an increasingly complex process, offering the most severe challenges to the poets of narrative. The structure of such compositions had to conform to the formal requirements of the poetic genre represented, and manipulate the technical features of that genre to establish the logical sequence essential to the vicarious experience of events in narrative. With this in mind we may recognize that the most easily perceived and important aspect of narrative poetry in a tradition based on narrative, namely, *temporal* sequence, is simply not of primary concern in the Chinese tradition. Nevertheless, Chinese poets did construct sequences of various kinds, and some of these poetic sequences produce effects very similar to what European literary criticism calls "narrative." The ambivalence of Chinese poetic criticism toward drawing generic distinctions based on the *kind* of poetic sequence may suggest that traditional Chinese poetics are not simply inimical to narrative expression, as is often assumed. Rather, this tendency in the critical tradition underlines a fundamental distinction in attitude between traditions of narrative-based and lyric-based poetics as regards what constitutes proper material for poetic sequence. In order to explore the concept of sequencing in Chinese poetry, we may again turn to some of the earliest surviving texts of poetics, and the sources of some of the basic concepts in Chinese critical theory.

Here the focus will be on the critical principle of *fu*, known from its inclusion among the "six principles" (*liu-yi*) of the "Great Preface" of the *Shih Ching*. There has been a tendency in poetic criticism, in China and in the West, to isolate one or another of Wei Hung's six principles as the basis of poetic expression and to study it in isolation. Chen Shih-hsiang follows just such a procedure, focusing upon the principle of *hsing* (motif), and describing it as "the essence of the *Songs'* generic character."[33] Although I will concentrate here on the principle of *fu*, it should be kept in mind that studying any one of these principles in isolation from the others "doth murder to dissect." My own conclusions regarding the nature of the principle *fu* are the result of returning to this group of concepts and trying to achieve some understanding of why these six terms are regularly mentioned together, their interrelation apparently taken for granted.

Critics have tended to focus on the relation of the principle *fu* with the genre of the same name with an eye to explaining the development of the genre alone. What seems not to have been recognized is that an examination of the poetic principle *fu* in terms of its relation to the genre *fu*, and to other poetic genres as suggested by the relevant criticism, may shed light on Chinese attitudes toward poetic sequence, especially methods of sequencing which are not necessarily dependent upon temporal progression. The inquiry may be extended to the construction of temporal sequences as well, for temporal sequence does occur in Chinese poetry and is an important aspect of poetic structure even if it is not regarded as the universal basis of narrative.

While most critics approaching the problem of *fu* would cite its inclusion among the six principles found in Wei Hung's "Great Preface," there seems to be no consensus as to what *fu* is. The authority most frequently quoted is Pan Ku, from his preface to his "Two Capitals *Fu*" ("*Liang tu fu*"): "Someone has said, '*Fu* have their origin in the ancient *Songs*.'"[34] This statement, however, refers to the poetic genre of *fu* rather than to the poetic principle. While the idea that the genre evolved from the principle is generally accepted, the tradition provides no systematic explanation of how this occurred.[35] Starting with the commentary of Mao Heng (second century B.C.), critics applied the six principles to categorize and analyze the poems of the *Shih Ching*; and they applied the term *fu* to poems which bear no generic resemblance to poems of the *fu* genre. This apparent but persistent anomaly provides a starting point for a new examination of the meaning of *fu* and its role in the evolution of Chinese literary genres.[36]

While there might seem to be no relation between the shorter, often stanzaic poems of the *Shih Ching* and the highly complex, sustained compositions of the *fu* genre, in Chinese critical terminology both may be linked by the principle of *fu*, which I suggest should be translated as "enumeration." This term was first suggested in

David Hawkes's study, "The Quest of the Goddess," although in that context it is used to describe characteristics of the genre and has no reference to the principle: "In the first place, the *fu* [genre] is not truly descriptive any more than it is truly narrative. The genre would never have been exposed to the attacks of moralists if it were merely descriptive. The ancient, no doubt highly dubious derivation of '*fu*' from a word meaning 'spread,' 'unfold' comes quite close to our word 'enumerate' and is still serviceable to the extent that it can warn us away from definitions like 'narrative' and 'descriptive.' "[37]

There are many nonliterary meanings of the word *fu* based on "counting" or "allotting": for example, "to give," "to bestow," "to pay out," or "to pay or levy taxes."[38] The etymology suggested here is in response to the need for a satisfactory translation of the term *fu* as a poetic principle: one that would be general enough to apply to the many uses of the term, and to evoke both what the term seems to represent in Chinese critical theory and the technical implications of *fu* as a principle of poetic composition.

Most definitions and translations of the term reflect the confusion between the principle and the genre. However, it is interesting to note that attempts to define the principle *fu* as distinct from the genre *fu* lead almost immediately to the term *narrative* in Western languages, although that term is not necessarily or obviously applicable to the material being discussed. In fact, this translation tends to be used when the term for the principle appears in isolation, and so the problem of its application to specific works does not really arise. The definition/translation offered by Georges Margouliès in *Evolution de la prose artistique chinoise* reflects the confusion of the two terms: "La traduction la plus exacte du terme fou serait: exposé, narration ou description poétique."[39] James Legge, who includes translations of the commentaries of Chu Hsi with his translations of the poems of the *Shih Ching*, uses the term "narrative" for the principle *fu*.[40] When David R. Knechtges comments upon Pan Ku's famous line in his notes on the "Two Capitals Rhapsody," he accepts the same term:

> According to the *Rites of Zhou*, a work that purports to be a description of the Zhou Dynasty administrative system (com-

piled no earlier than the Warring States period) *fu* as [*sic*] one of the *liu shih* ("six song techniques") taught by the Grand Music Master to blind singers (*Zhou li* 6.13a). The "Mao Preface" to the *Classic of Songs* (see *Wen Hsüan* 45.21a) also refers to *fu* as one of the *liu yi* ("six principles") of the *Songs*. Ban Gu was probably basing himself on one or both of these sources in associating the literary genre *fu* with the *Songs* tradition. Strictly speaking, the *Rites of Zhou* and "Mao Preface" notion of *fu* is not generic. It is rather a term for a rhetorical mode or a recitation technique that involves direct narration.[41]

The term "narrations" is suggested by Chen Shih-hsiang.[42] Chen applies it to pieces of expository statement, whether descriptive or narrative. His intention is to affirm K'ung Ying-ta's observation that, of the six principles, *fu* is a term of "poetic technique" (*shih chih suo yung*), or perhaps more appropriately, "application," as opposed to a term of "poetic form" (*shih chih ch'eng hsing*) or "substance."[43] In his commentary on the *Shih Ching* K'ung Ying-ta analyzes the six principles and concludes that *feng, ya,* and *sung* are terms distinguishing types of subject matter, while *fu, pi,* and *hsing* are methods of presentation or composition—"modes of expression" according to James J. Y. Liu.[44] C. H. Wang follows Chen Shih-hsiang, but uses the term "narrative display."[45] In "Metaphor and Chinese Poetry," Pauline Yu avoids the temptation to link *fu* with narrative, mentioning the term as "description" or "exposition," and later as "direct description." She remarks that "even though the *Great Preface* lists it first, *fu* ('description' or 'exposition') generally proved to be of lesser interest than *bi* ('comparison' or 'simile') and *xing* ('association' or 'motif')," and her interest is likewise in the last two principles.[46] It should be kept in mind that while there are important formal differences corresponding to the differences in subject matter of *feng, ya,* and *sung*, it is theoretically possible for all three technical principles to be present in a single composition, and commentators do occasionally ascribe all three principles to a single poem.[47]

To my mind the rendering "enumeration" better evokes the meaning of *fu*, and allows us to consider its implications for narrative poetics without committing it to the concept of "narrative," with its Europocentric connotations. It also better allows us to cross over generic boundaries in its application, a need clearly indicated in the applications of the term in Chinese criticism, and to reconsider its precise relation to its sibling terms, *pi* and *hsing*. For usage in criticism, these three principles, which suggest techniques or processes of composition, should not be confused with the poetic structures or conventions that are the results of these techniques. Nor, obviously, should these terms be considered to connote any qualitative judgment in themselves.

The principle of *fu*, or enumeration, denotes the techniques whereby certain structures, in this case poetic sequences, may be achieved. A simple, necessary condition for establishing a sequence is that three or more elements must be present. Furthermore, the order of these elements is not arbitrary, but set in the text to produce a certain effect, whether of meter, rhyme, or sense. This second necessary condition distinguishes a poetic *sequence* from a *series*, for in a series the elements may be reordered without detriment to the integrity of the text. It should be noted that the nature or content of the elements may vary from one sequence to another, and with them the nature of the sequence itself. The principle is thus able to encompass such apparently diverse structures as a list of animals or plants, an expository statement as to the elements of a given situation, a parade of historical figures and their actions or attributes, and a chronology of events leading to an individual crisis. This point is vital to the application of the principle of enumeration in narrative sequence and will be discussed more fully below.

The principles of *pi* and *hsing* may be related to the principle of enumeration by considering the kind of poetic conventions with which they are associated. According to Karlgren, the basic meaning of *pi* is "to compare," with the connotation of a comparison of two elements of similar, if not precisely equal, ontological status.[48] This helps to explain why *pi* has been translated as "simile." In practical terms *pi* is applied when there are two elements to be compared with one another within a given poetic unit, such as a couplet or stanza, and both elements for comparison are explicitly juxtaposed in the text itself.[49] In the *Shih Ching*, *pi* usually occurs when a stanza presents a two-part image. One element is often taken from nature to be compared with another element, usually describing the emotional state of the poet or speaker. In Mao no. 63, "*Yu hu*," the state of a solitary fox is juxtaposed to the state of a solitary speaker (probably female) musing upon the pitiful figure of a poorly clad man. This has been interpreted as comparing the solitary state of a fox cautiously seeking a mate to the situation of a young woman who for some reason must choose her own husband without help.[50] In Mao no. 124, "*Ko sheng*," the first two stanzas juxtapose a dreary landscape rampant with weeds to the lament of a new widow.[51]

The principle of *hsing* has been treated as the most exalted, perhaps because it seems to be the most difficult to define or generalize. In his preface to the *Shih p'in* Chung Jung (fl. 502–19) lists *hsing* ahead of *pi* and *fu*, and describes it as conveying meaning beyond the literal level of the text: "When the text is finished, but the meaning resonates [literally, has more to it], that is *hsing*."[52] Karlgren lists "lift, raise; rise; prosper" among the meanings of the graph, and suggests that originally it depicted a sail held by four hands.[53] Chen Shih-hsiang states that the central part of the graph is a tray rather than a sail or boat, and suggests that this configuration—hands all around lifting a tray of ritual offerings—is meant to evoke the kind of spontaneous response that the application of *hsing* in poetry should elicit from an audience.[54] In poetry *hsing* is certainly evocative, and this is reflected by translations such as "allusive" (Legge), "association" (Yu), or "motif" (Chen).[55] I would suggest that the unifying characteristic of *hsing* as it is used in literary criticism is that it is an element of a poem which evokes associations beyond the immediate context of the poem and invites the reader to bring these associations to bear upon the matter of the text. As such, it may occur only once, or it may be repeated, as in a refrain. *Hsing* may occur as an ejaculation or hortatory locution ("Look at those recesses in the banks of the K'e / With their green bamboos, so fresh and luxuriant!" [Mao no. 55, "*Ch'i ao*," lines 1–2]), a vivid image meant to focus the imagination to be receptive to the "comments" which follow ("There are the branches of the sparrowgourd," [Mao no. 60, "*Wan lan*," line 1]), or a refrain meant to unify the preceding material of the text ("How is it, how is it / That he forgets me so very much?" [Mao no. 132, "*Ch'en feng*," lines

5–6, 11–12, 17–18]).[56] Whatever its precise form or function, *hsing* as it occurs in poetry consists of a unified, apparently self-referential figure of speech that draws upon material beyond the literal level of the text for appreciation of its full significance.

Following the order of these three technical principles from the "Great Preface," *fu* organizes and integrates three or more units, *pi* coordinates two units, and *hsing* manipulates a single, self-referential unit to evoke certain responses and produce certain poetic effects. The utility of this analysis is that it allows us to apply these canonical terms as broadly as they in fact are applied in the Chinese tradition of literary criticism and textual exegesis. It also allows us to appreciate, from a foreign tradition, the assumption of the vital interrelation of these three principles in Chinese poetics.

We may now turn with more assurance to the principle of *fu* as enumeration and its relevance to the development of narrative poetry. Enumeration includes the idea of counting or organizing units in order, and its usage in literary criticism relates it to the organization of such units as stanzas (in the case of the *Shih Ching*), descriptive catalogues (as in *fu*), or even units of action suggestive of temporal sequence. The term may be applied to compositions in which units of imagery or action are organized in a logical progression—one of the foundations of narrative expression. The principle *fu* does not define a poetic genre, "narrative," but a technique of composition which involves the enumeration of units of subject matter. The mode of expression in a given composition is determined by the nature or content of these units. In poems attempting narrative modes of expression, these units of subject matter may contain actions, and the enumeration of these units forms the kind of logical, sequential structure of events which is associated with narrative.

It is probably this characteristic of "enumeration" which led to the assumption that the critical principle of *fu* was the origin of the poetic genre *fu*, although by the time the critical principle was isolated and being debated the genre had reached its height of achievement as the sanctioned form of public poetic display at the Han court.[57] The *fu* genre, however, displays only some of the possible kinds of enumeration; many other kinds may be found in the *Shih Ching*. It has been asserted that the use of refrains, special descriptive phrases and grammatical constructions, and alliterative phrases reflects the influence of oral composition.[58] Whether this is indeed the case, what should be noted here is that all these devices are treated as units to be enumerated. The genre *fu* may be said to comprise the techniques of organizing subject matter in a poetic composition through enumeration.

Thus, the formal features of the genre *fu* are not the only manifestations of the principle, although they are arguably the means whereby the *principle* achieved its greatest expressive success. One aspect of the works of the genre shared by works categorized by the principle is an assertive rhetoric intended for public display. This intention of public expression is vital to the development of narrative in *shih* and other genres. Furthermore, the passion for detail and description—concrete or general—characteristic of the genre *fu* is at least as important as temporal sequence in Chinese narrative, and may also be a component of the poetic principle in the eyes of Chinese critics.

Let us consider how enumeration is applied in K'ung Ying-ta's, and later in Chu Hsi's commentaries to the *Shih Ching*. According to K'ung Ying-ta, the principle as it appears in the *Shih Ching* seems to be reinforced strongly by stanzaic composition. The stanzas in a given poem may function as units in their own right, to be placed in sequence by enumeration. In this K'ung follows the suggestions of Cheng Hsüan, who justifies the order of stanzas as set by Mao but does not always identify his ordering principle with *fu*. The poems designated *fu* by K'ung are usually three or more stanzas in length. Of those poems so designated which contain fewer than three stanzas, he occasionally comments that they may be sequels of the poems which precede them in the anthology, as in the case of Mao no. 67, "*Chün-tzu yang yang*," which is described as the sequel of Mao no. 66, "*Chün-tzu yu yi*."[59] Chu Hsi follows K'ung Ying-ta precisely, but while K'ung sets his categories according to the technical observations of Cheng Hsüan, Chu Hsi's justifications for the assignment of the principle *fu* suggest that he may have confused the principle of enumeration with one of its frequent results; namely, a more particularized composition tending to specific rather than general expressions of emotion.[60] This characteristic is also suggestive of narrative and, considering the enormous influence of Chu Hsi's edition of the *Shih Ching*, perhaps accounts for the persistent confusion of the principle of enumeration with narrative in the minds of (particularly European) critics.

Among the most consistent examples of the principle *fu* are poems written in stanzas about legendary or historical topics which either relate some story vital to the explanation of social conventions or codes of behavior, or glorify heroic figures from the past. Poems such as Mao no. 243, "*Hsia Wu*," and Mao no. 244, "*Wen wang yu sheng*," use repetition of lines to carry the subject matter forward. "*Hsia Wu*" links six four-line stanzas by the process of catenation, represented here by repeating the last line of one stanza as the first line of the next. The lines are sometimes identical (stanza 1, line 4, and stanza 2, line 1: "The King was their worthy successor in his capital"; stanza 5, line 4, and stanza 6, line 1: "They will receive the blessing of Heaven"); and sometimes only one character is repeated (stanza 4, line 4, and stanza 5, line 1: "He brilliantly continued the doings [of his fathers] / Brilliantly! and his posterity . . .").[61] The effect is still to enforce the relationship of the stanzas in the logical sequential order of the subject matter. The fact that the middle stanzas are not absolutely consistent does not really undermine the pattern established in the first two stanzas. It is clear that the subject matter as presented was intended to follow this order, setting the exemplary King Wu in his proper context as the heir of legitimate rulers and the father of other legitimate rulers. The sequence does not focus explicitly on the actions of the ruler, but rather on the results of actions which have become facts of the accepted social order: in stanza 1 the king comes to power; in stanza 2 he tries to win over the population; in stanza 3 he wins over the population; in stanza 4 he consolidates his power with his increased popularity; in stanza 5 the people are reconciled to the new order; in stanza 6 the people contemplate the secure future of the now established order. The concern of the poem is not with the actions of King Wu himself, but with the process of transfer from martial to civil authority in a new political order. This is a logical sequence whose causal links are historically dependent upon temporal sequence for their significance, but whose ultimate significance transcends the historical context of the foundation of the Chou kingdom.

"*Wen wang yu sheng*" also uses a repeated line to link its eight five-line stanzas but, rather than using catenated lines, these stanzas are linked by a refrain "*Wen wang cheng tsai*" ("A sovereign true was King Wen!").[62] The refrain itself is identified by Chu Hsi as *hsing*, though not until the last stanza. In this poem the refrain functions to define the stanzas and enforce their sequence. It is not simply repeated: the last two characters, *cheng tsai*, are consistent, but the first two characters change according to the subject matter of the stanza. The first four stanzas focus on King Wen, who is either referred to by name (stanzas 1 and 2), or styled "royal prince" (*wang hou*, stanzas 3 and 4). Stanza 5 switches back to the deeds of King Wen's predecessor, King Wu, who is referred to as the "Great King" (*huang wang*, stanza 5) or by name (stanzas 6 and 7). The compositional sequence, whose movement is chronologically backward, culminates with the establishment of a sequence in fact, a structure for the orderly transfer of power from father to son which will ensure the security of the people. There are more elaborate examples of *fu* as an applied principle in the *Shih Ching* but, whatever the kind of enumeration involved, all seem intended to build a sequence which will culminate in a particular interpretative conclusion.

The applications of the principle of enumeration thus vary according to form and subject matter in the poems from the *Shih Ching*, but how do these uses bear upon the workings of the principle *fu* in the genre of that name? The earliest examples, by anyone's reckoning, occur in the *Ch'u Tz'u*, an anthology which in its present form dates from the second century A.D., but whose contents may date from as early as the eleventh century B.C. These poems, from the catechism of "*T'ien wen*" to the *itineraria* on which the genre is supposed to be based, employ a variety of sequencing techniques.[63] David Hawkes, in "The Quest of the Goddess," has termed poems such as the "*Li sao*" and the "*Chiu ko*" ("Nine Songs") *itineraria* because of their subject matter. It is said that these poems are based on the magical flight of the spirit of a shaman to a union with a corresponding deity.[64] Hawkes observes that the influence of Ch'u *itineraria* was crucial to the development of *fu*, but he does not consider the type of sequence underlying the structure of the poems to be narrative: "If we apply the term 'narrative' to the *itineraria*, its absurd inappropriateness is at once apparent. . . . The reason why the term 'narrative' is so immediately unacceptable is that the development in these poems is conceived of as a spatial sequence. In the ritual circuit whose object is the accumulation of magic power, the actual passage between one power-nucleus and the next, though indispensible, is not of intrinsic interest."[65]

The poet's reflection of this process is the enumeration of significant places or visions, not the experience of seeking or achieving them. *Itineraria*, then, are not primarily concerned with temporal patterns of organization. While the structure of poems such as the "*Li sao*" may not be strictly temporal, there is still a distinct sense of progression as the poet-shaman describes his exploration of the cosmos. Nor is this progress unsystematic. In most *itineraria* it can be argued that the ritual sequence overwhelms any other kind, but it may also be argued that the primacy of the ritual is supported by techniques which render the ritual sequence more understandable to the layman, and these techniques may include temporal and descriptive elements which influence the poetics of the composition.

This variety is acknowledged by Chinese critics in their categorization of *fu* according to subject matter, starting with the *Wen Hsüan* of the early sixth century and continuing at least to the *Yü-ting li-tai fu-hui* (published in 1706).[66] In the preface to the *Wen Hsüan*, Hsiao T'ung (501–531) draws distinctions on the basis of subject matter between the descriptive *fu* of Ssu-ma Hsiang-ju (179–117 B.C.), Yang Hsiung (43 B.C.–A.D. 18), and Chang Heng (79–138), and the lament, termed "*sao*," of Ch'ü Yüan, who inspired so many later poets to emulate him in poetry, if not biography. The first nineteen *chüan* of the *Wen Hsüan* are poems in the *fu* genre, containing fifty-six examples, but *sao* make up only two *chüan* (32–33), containing seventeen examples, all of them perhaps more familiar from their inclusion in the *Ch'u Tz'u*. The designation *fu* is further divided into fifteen categories, which Knechtges calls "sub-genres," based on subject matter rather than formal features.[67] These categories were accepted with only minor changes by later compilers, for instance by Ou-yang Hsün in the *Yi wen lei–chü*, and so on to the *Yü-ting li-tai fu-hui*.

The critical material on the genre *fu* and theories of its evolution reflect the tenacity of these categories. But in spite of the tremendous range of topics, *fu* seem to fall into two main categories, which for convenience I will call "descriptive" and "personal." Although the Chinese terms for these categories vary, there is a clear awareness of difference in kind and even in origin. The most common pair of terms is *ta fu* and *hsiao fu; ta* (major) referring to the long, cataloguelike, descriptive type, and *hsiao* (minor) referring to the expressive, "personal" type.[68] *Ta fu* are in fact usually longer, but some sort of qualitative judgment also seems to be implied by the term. *Hsiao fu*, because they are fewer and shorter, tend to be regarded as somehow outside the mainstream of *fu* composition. Other pairs of terms which describe the same division are *shih-lei fu* (*fu* on specific things) and *yen-ch'ing fu* (*fu* that express the emotions); and *ching-fu* (*fu* on capital cities) as opposed to *hsiao-fu* (minor *fu*, or *fu* on lesser matters). Again, "*fu* on specific things" or "*fu* on capital cities" tend to include descriptive *fu*, while "*fu* that express the emotions" or "*fu* on lesser matters" tend to deal with personal themes.[69]

When we consider specific examples of the genre *fu*, the application of the principle *fu* as enumeration should become clear. It is evident not only in those *fu* whose purpose seems to be descriptive, but also in *fu* which seem to attempt a more personal, individualized expression. In the first type, "descriptive" *fu*, the emphasis is on a place or object; the description will reveal the object's qualities as an exemplar. The *fu* of Ssu-ma Hsiang-ju are of this type. The second type, "personal" *fu*, attempt to make explicit a poet's internal feelings of conflict, often through description, sometimes with a strong sense of temporal context or even progression. Chia Yi's (c. 200–168 B.C.) "Owl *fu*" ("*Fu-niao fu*") is an example of this type and is often cited as the first example of the type after the "*Li sao*."[70] Whether metaphorically or actually, the poet attempts to recapture or articulate the elements of an experience in a highly personalized fashion, still using the technique of enumeration as the basis for structuring the sequence. There are several possible levels of enumeration in the "Owl *fu*." The first is the standard, three-part structure of the poem as a whole, which consists of the owl's introduction (lines 1–11), the main body of philosophical discourse (lines 12–49), and the conclusion (lines 50–54). The main body of the poem is further subdivided into three sections which reveal a logical sequence of persuasion as the poet attempts to comfort himself by putting his plight—in his eyes, he has fallen victim to slander and has been exiled unjustly—into some kind of perspective. The first section deals with the greatest level of generality, stating the nature of the cosmos and the relation of men to it (lines 12–21). The second asserts that these tides of fortune are part of an organic and impersonal process (lines 22–29); and the third perspective uses examples of the vanity of striving to exploit causality (lines 30–49). Within each subsection are further instances of enumeration, such as the list of historical figures who preceded Chia Yi in misfortune (lines 18–21) or the pageant of the foibles of human nature (lines 34–45).

The presence of these divergent strains of expression—descriptive and personal—is not surprising when we consider the two main theories of the origin and development of *fu* as a genre. The first theory is based on the origin of *fu* from the lyric sources of the *Shih Ching*, following the leads of Pan Ku and Hsiao T'ung. The Ch'ing critic Ch'eng T'ing-tso gives a history of the genre based on this assumption in his essay "*Sao fu lun*." Ch'eng T'ing-tso posits that *sao* and *fu* developed with the inspiration of the poems of the *Shih Ching*, which allowed the poet Ch'ü Yüan to apply the six principles to his own source of inspiration. He regards *sao* and *fu* as subdivisions of a single genre, called *sao-fu*, or simply *fu*, after the poetic principle of enumeration which distinguishes the poetic form. This theory of development, first advanced in the "Bibliographical Treatise" ("*Yi wen chih*") in the *Han Shu*, attempts to explain the shift from a *sao* type of personal expression of emotion (corresponding to the concerns of "personal" *fu*) to a *fu* type of self-conscious, public poetry ("descriptive" *fu*). Ch'eng writes:

> The act of composing the "*Li sao*" was truly a product of the life and time of Ch'ü Yüan. In the compositions of later times which were written in the style of *sao*, could even Sung Yü, who, carrying on the style of enterprise he received from Ch'ü Yüan, composed the *Chiu P'ien* . . . be compared to him? How could others compare to him? They did not have the experience of his life and time; they could not possibly achieve his

heights merely through force of effort. In examining *fu*, we find that its foundation is entirely different from that of *sao*. . . . They are as clearly delineated as household ranking and social class. The Commentary (by Mao, *Shih Ching* no. 50, cited in the *Han Shu*, 30.1755–56) says, "If you wish to ascend to great heights and are able to compose *fu*, you will be able to become a great minister." Cheng K'ang-ch'eng (Cheng Hsüan) says, "*Fu* are a form of display which lay in order matters of government and education, beauty and evil of the present time." The subject matter used by the masters of *fu* ranged from the royal court to ancestral temples in outlying districts, from mountains and rivers to the grasses and trees; there was nothing they did not set forth in writing. Therefore the authors, certainly such a one as Ch'ang-ch'ing (Ssu-ma Hsiang-ju) embraced all of the universe and considered all men and phenomena. There are some who have the inspiration from the mountains and rivers within themselves, but who do not realize or express it, and so the degree of difficulty of *fu* is as great as of *shih* or *sao*.[71]

In contrast to the theory of the lyrical origins of the genre, Knechtges traces the development of *fu* as epideictic rhetoric from the tradition of "persuasions" (*shui*).[72] This is a very ancient form of prose in China; in fact, much extant early artistic prose is some form of persuasion, suggesting a thematic as much as a generic distinction. These works, composed with a view to public presentation, placed great emphasis on persuasive rhetoric. Perhaps the most famous example is Mei Sheng's "Seven Stimuli" ("*Ch'i fa*"), said to have been composed for the admonition of the prince of Wu. It is a masterwork of the use of rhetoric as a vehicle for conveying personal opinion into the public domain. On the surface the purpose of the poem is to entertain Mei Sheng's ailing and apathetic prince. When the piece is examined rhetorically, however, it becomes apparent that the seductive emphasis on the pursuit of sensual pleasures is an important part of the theme of persuasion. The illness of the prince cannot be cured with physic alone; it must be "persuaded to depart" ("*shui ch'ü*"). This recalls the techniques of summoning spirits in "*Chao Hun*" of the *Ch'u Tz'u*, except here the process is reversed. Instead of calling back the prince's wandering spirit, Mei Sheng banishes the evil influences which are weighing on the spirit in its proper home. Again, the technique of enumeration produces a sequence which proceeds cumulatively rather than strictly temporally, and yet the given order of the subject matter cannot be revised without a radical change in the effect of the persuasion.[73]

Mei Sheng's prosody and techniques of persuasion influenced many later writers of *fu*, especially those associated with the central court. Ssu-ma Hsiang-ju, in his "Tzu-hsü *fu*" and "*Fu* on the Shang-lin Park," described magnificent hunts in sumptuous surroundings in order to criticize unnecessary extravagance. The concerned statesman could use *fu* to describe an object, a place, or a person in such a way as to evoke the desired response from his prince, fulfilling both his political responsibilities and his artistic aspirations in the best Confucian tradition.

Whatever the ultimate origin of *fu* as a poetic genre, these two theories of the source of *fu* poetics seem to reflect not so much on the evolution of the form itself as on the distinction drawn between what came to be its two main categories of subject matter. The "expressive" or "personal" tendencies exemplified by Ch'ü Yüan and his heirs would seem to ally themselves with "personal" *fu*, while the tradition of persuasions would seem closer to "descriptive" *fu*, the manifestation of "word magic" at its best. Neither type, of course, turns away from the intention of public display. Personal *fu*, such as Chia Yi's "Owl *fu*," were usually written as first-person monologues and were probably intended as self-justification, to be "overheard" or given into sympathetic hands when public channels of appeal were closed. Descriptive *fu*, on the other hand, were ostensibly written for the moral and political edification of their audience, but were conceived in terms of the public context and lack the self-referential element of personal *fu*.

During the Six Dynasties period a sense of the appropriateness of *fu* to public display seems more than ever to have directed the construction of sequences in long works of the genre. Indeed, among works of this period the distinctions between descriptive and personal *fu* are as dependent on the treatment of subject matter as they are on differences of form or in the nature of the subject matter itself. While structurally there may seem no great difference between Yü Hsin's (513–581) "Lament for the South" ("*Ai Chiang-nan fu*") and many other *fu* about the same region of China that are classified under "geography" (*ti-li*) in anthologies, in the minds of editors their treatment of subject matter makes them absolutely discrete. It is not just the technical aspects of meter, rhyme, and so forth that determine the distinctions between descriptive and personal *fu*, but also the perceived intentions of the author of a given composition. While the basic technique of enumeration in *fu* may remain fairly consistent, the content of the units to be enumerated and the underlying purpose of the organization of sequences is crucial for an understanding of the piece in relation to the tradition of its subject matter and to the genre itself.[74]

In the case of "The Lament for the South," not only does Ch'en Yüan-lung place it in his anthology's *wai-chi* (outer collection) with the other personal *fu*, he goes so far as to place it in his first category, *yen-chih* (to speak of one's true self).[75] This is partly because Yü Hsin makes extensive use of *sao* meters and frequently alludes to the "*Li sao*," thus allying himself with the very beginning of the tradition of personal expression in *fu*. But by placing the poem in this most significant category, first in the *wai-chi*, Ch'en indicates that in his mind the expressive purpose and force of the poem goes beyond the particular events of Yü Hsin's life to be linked with the very essence of poetic expression, *yen-chih*, according to the tradition of *Shih Ching* criticism.[76] Again, it is necessary to make some distinctions between the techniques of poetic expression and their effects on the reader. "The Lament for the South" is explicitly autobiographical. While its graphic account of the destruction of the Liang dynasty (502–556) from within and without could be analyzed as merely descriptive of a most unhappy chain of events, the sure knowledge of the author's historical context, enforced by details of his own experience related in his own voice determines the interpretative stance of the reader. The intricacy of the poem's structure of meaning on every level—metrical references, poetic and historical allusions, figures of speech peculiar to the *fu* tradition in general and the sixth century in particular—is staggering, and allows us to appreciate and apply the complexity of enumeration to the larger tradition.[77]

For the purposes of this study the poem's underlying sequential structure is most important. Yü Hsin gives three accounts of his plight in "The Lament for the South," comprising three different perspectives on his temporal context and the sequence of events. The preface gives a condensed version of the material of the poem proper without suspense, from the point of view of one who knows the results of the actions involved. Yü Hsin provides specific literary and historical contexts for his work and compares himself to other statesmen who fell into evil times and transcended their personal failures with works of art—Ch'ü Yüan and Ssu-ma Ch'ien.[78]

In the second "account" Yü Hsin provides his genealogy (lines 1–40), and by its intricacy suggests his intention to record his own experiences in great detail. There are compelling reasons for the length of this genealogy, which is forty times as long as its model from the "Li sao."[79] The sequence of his ancestry is enforced by chronology on the literal level of the text and by rhyme and meter on the poetic level, but there is a new level of significance. While a genealogy is bound to culminate in a particular generation or individual, Yü Hsin adds the irony that, in his family's seventh generation of service to the imperial court, he will in fact end this sequence with his death. The chronological sequence of the rest of the poem is thus overlaid with two layers of foreboding, which influence the remainder of the poem even in the first reading. Yü Hsin deliberately manipulates temporal references and sequence to enhance his poem's tapestry of meaning, to bind events to his unique experience, and to give that experience significance in the stream of history.

The third account, the bulk of the poem (lines 41–520), attempts to reproduce the whole of Yü Hsin's world in words. He begins with his early career, taking his place in the Yü family genealogy and making the transition between his background and his own life and times (lines 41–84). He then shifts to the state's unpreparedness for rebellion (lines 85–110) and the omens of disaster for the Liang's founder, Emperor Wu (Liang Wu-ti, r. 502–549). The omen of "Seeing a man with streaming hair at Yi-ch'uan / One knew that within the century there would be barbarians there" (lines 109–10),[80] provides the transition to the menace of the barbarian Hou Ching (d. 552), the first of the serious external threats to the state (lines 111–40). Lines 141–230 describe the siege of the Liang capital Chien-k'ang (Nan-ching), Hou Ching's triumph, and the miserable death of Emperor Wu. Yü Hsin makes it clear that, in his eyes, the victory of Hou Ching was due as much to the internecine struggles of Emperor Wu's potential successors as to any alien force:

> Chin and Cheng refused to help;
> Lu and Wei were not in harmony.
> They struggled to move the gate of heaven,
> Fought to turn the axis of the earth.[81]

In line 231 the poet suddenly reappears in his own person, fleeing to the court of the emperor's seventh son, Hsiao Yi, later Emperor Yüan (Liang Yüan-ti, r. 552–554). This flight up the Yangtze to Chiang-ling makes Yü Hsin's experience seem like a nightmare version of the story of the Peach Blossom Spring, speeding away from one fallen ideal to another, each doomed in its turn, and driving his boat up a stream hedged by rebels and fire instead of beckoning peach trees (lines 231–52). Lines 253–86 describe his new post under Hsiao Yi, but the death of his father (lines 275–82) erases his hopes for success in his lifetime, and he determines to avoid holding office to honor his father's memory (lines 283–86).

The poem then turns again to the war, detailing the Liang campaign against Hou Ching and the recapture of Chien-k'ang (lines 287–312), and then setting the triumph against the dreadful losses of the rebellion (lines 313–48). The final fall of the Liang comes swiftly afterward (lines 349–460). Line 349 speaks of "the Restoring Emperor," but hopes that the restoration will last under Emperor Yüan are immediately dashed:

> Though he restored the ancient institutions of the Governor
>   of the Capital
> And brought back the customs of the Cheng-shih period,
> Sunk in suspicion, he followed only his own desires;
> Concealing his faults, he prided himself on his
>   accomplishments.[82]

Emperor Yüan's actions result in the ruin of his people, and the Liang dynasty is finally destroyed at its secondary capital of

Chiang-ling (lines 415–24). Yü Hsin surfaces in the midst of the turmoil, sent by the emperor as an ambassador to the court of the Western Wei (lines 409–10). His mission of pacification is of course unsuccessful, and he helplessly watches the ruin of his people as they are led into captivity in the north (lines 435–60). The last section, lines 461–520, focuses again on the author alone, lamenting his exile and his shame in surviving to tell his tale.

Yü Hsin thus uses his own career as a frame for the larger tale of the fortunes of the Liang. The interweaving of individual voice with more general historical description is a technique also used extensively in narrative *shih,* and it suggests that authors of autobiographical poems found this doubled sequencing an effective means of grounding personal experience in an unmistakable temporal context. Certainly there is a strong awareness of the efficacy of temporal sequence in creating a powerful context "to speak of one's true self."

In terms of general application in Chinese poetics the principle of enumeration is extremely pervasive. It can be seen as comprising the basis of all poetic structures which involve a logical and considered ordering of elements; in short, the sequences which underlie the textual integrity of any self-conscious work of literary art. Enumeration allows for sequences made up of units of any kind: from phrases and compounds ordered according to set patterns of tonal values and rhyme, to the ordering of elements in a catalogue, to the poems in a unified poetic sequence or events in a narrative poem. In the Chinese tradition the principle of enumeration ignores generic distinctions and spans a wide range of expressive purposes, including, but by no means confined to, the desire for narrative modes of expression.

In terms of the development of poetic narrative, this discussion of *fu* suggests two important features. First is the poet's use of his own voice to describe a specific experience or object which in some way reflects on or reveals an important personal or individual experience. This seems to be a definitive characteristic of personal *fu.* The second feature is a more general manifestation of the critical principle of *fu* as enumeration, namely, poetic sequence. The sequences presented in *fu* are *not* necessarily temporal ones; there are sequences of objects, of perceptions or observations, of results of a single action or condition, and finally even of actions themselves. While these sequences may not build up a sense of narrative suspense dependent on a causal relation of events, they do build tension and anticipate some resolution, either in a publicly oriented moral pronouncement or in a sudden focus on an individual poet striving for recognition. This is especially pertinent to the development of narrative, which deals with particular rather than general experience. The individual experience may of course be relevant to a general context, but the emphasis in the work of art is on an experience which is, for the reader, essentially vicarious. While the poetic principle *fu* provides a basis for the construction of sequences, the genre provides a reconciliation of two aspects of poetic expression vital to the narrative poet: the impulse to reveal the private self and the desire to captivate an audience.

2

Setting Specific Contexts
Point of View and Description

In narrative poetry, as in fiction, point of view determines the reader's access to the artist's intuition and interpretation of events.[1] Just as physical description particularizes the context of experience, point of view particularizes the experience itself. Together, point of view and description allow the poet to control the reader's response to the circumstances recounted in the text. The point of view of the narrator or primary speaker in a poem reflects the expressive intent of the poet, who may or may not be identified with that speaker. In addition to the narrator, other speakers may introduce "their" individual points of view, which in turn complicate and enhance the reader's interpretation of events. The greater the reader's awareness of differing points of view, the greater the chance of realizing a coherent interpretation of events through their various perspectives.[2]

The apparent merging of poetic voice and identity with the

reader's voice and identity is an important aspect of lyrical experience in Chinese poetry.[3] In a lyric poem the point of view of the poet is the same as that of the speaker, which in turn, if the illusion of integration with lyrical experience is achieved, is assumed by the reader. This point of view is *inclusive* and *objective;* that is to say, it allows the reader to assume the full experience of the poem as his or her own, and communicates emotion in a potentially universal mode, rather than emphasizing the specific context of the poet's experience. Northrop Frye speaks of the lyrical "radical of presentation," which allows for transcendence of specific context[4]—a feature of the objectivity of lyric conveyed so well by the dominance of imagistic language in Chinese poetry.

Narrative poetry may present many points of view, none of which is meant to merge with that of the reader. The narrative point of view is *exclusive* and *subjective.* Insofar as specificity of point of view does not encourage integration of reader and speaker, the reader remains separated from the point of view of the narrator. The separation of the speaker from the reader in a lyric poem is inherently ambiguous, while in a narrative poem point of view deliberately reveals perspectives beyond the context of the reader. The reader may be affected primarily by the point of view of the narrator, or by those of other participants in the events of the poem. In contrast to lyric poetry, each speaker and/or participant in a work of narrative poetry may assert an *individual* identity. The ultimate aim of these complex patterns of narrative presentation is to enable the reader to synthesize material presented by multiple points of view from the unique perspective of a particular reader outside of the text itself.

This is not to say that lyrical expression does not convey a sense of the individual personality of the author. One of the clichés of Chinese literature and criticism is that the character of an author may be understood from his writing; in fact, this evocative quality is the natural outgrowth of the author's intent (*chih*). The informed reader may therefore experience something of the personality of the author, as well as something of the experience which inspired the poem, through the act of reading.[5] This interpretative tendency permeates both artistic creation and scholarly or critical analysis in Chinese literature. The expression of intent (*chih*) gives plausible authenticity to the experiential interpretation of a poem and forms the core of experience for the informed reader. In artistic creation awareness of this purposive undercurrent affects the author's presentation, because appreciation of intent is a consummately *critical* experience, a mutual exchange between poet and reader relying upon the vitality of this interpretative convention for fulfillment. If a poet's original intent in composing is to reveal the self as well as to convey a particular experience, it requires a sophisticated reader to extract both the experience as presented in the poem and the intent underlying the expression. In lyrical experience the reader may achieve the illusion of integration with the intent of the poet through the act of reading, and takes this on, if only momentarily, as if it were part of his or her own personality and consciousness. In the case of an informed reader this provokes a realization that this response—the illusion of integration with the experience of the poem—is in fact inspired by the impression of the poet's own personality and consciousness, thus promoting a sense of insight into the actual experience of the poet as an individual.[6]

While this convention of reading is taken for granted in the study of Chinese lyrics, it applies to other modes as well. We will find, however, that in poems which introduce particular points of view, the task of fully realizing the author's intent is not left to the resources of the reader alone. It is not difficult to see this qualification of the convention in the study of the *fu* genre, especially personal *fu*. As we have seen, by particularizing experience with details of specific context—temporal and otherwise—the poet of personal *fu* eschews reliance on the conventions of lyrical reading in favor of a blunter but perhaps more forceful instrument. Poets such as Chia Yi might well doubt that an informed reader of the "Owl *fu*" would exercise such critical acumen as actually to come to the aid of the poet in distress, without particulars of the poet's immediate plight.

Narrative poetry goes even further, explicitly invoking these critical conventions by emphasizing subjective experience. Let us consider, by way of example, a poem by Han Yü (768–824), written on his way into exile after the political fiasco engendered by his memorial on the bone of the Buddha. "The Officer at Lung River" ("*Lung shih*") is in the form of a dialogue between the disgraced poet-statesman and an articulate security officer at the Lung River in Kuang-tung.[7] Because of the exigencies of his situation (in T'ang times, exile to pestilential Ch'ao-chou was tantamount to a death sentence), it is literally a matter of life and death for Han Yü to convey his intent to a sympathetic audience, preferably to the emperor himself. While he might have relied upon the critical convention of extrapolating a poet's underlying intent from a lyric poem to convince his audience, Han Yü has used a more explicit mode of expression to ensure communication of his urgent message. With understandable consciousness of his relation to such poets as Chia Yi, he balances particularizing details of his predicament and more conventional landscape description to convey his inner state. While the poet and the officer are firmly located in space and time, the physical context at first seems subordinate to the increasing emotional wildness of the environment. Far as it may be from Ch'ang-an to the head of the Lung River, it is just the beginning of the end of the earth for Han Yü, who is on his way to the southern edge of the empire. The officer obliges Han Yü's inquiries with a fearsome description of the place, but this is a generalized, terrifying landscape, a fitting image of the harshness of exile for the devoted Confucian statesman. The officer's intimations as to why Han Yü has been exiled fill the poet with shame, and as a result he is enlightened not to the misery and waste of his exile, but to the great bounty of the emperor, whom Han Yü in his intransigence has so inadequately appreciated. "The Officer at Lung River" is not so much a narrative of the poet's experiences and emotions in exile as it is a "memorial" to the emperor, acknowledging the poet's shortcomings and expressing his undying (and by virtue of the circumstances, intensified) respect and loyalty.[8]

The poet's intent, then, is unambiguously political, which allies this poem strongly with the tradition of personal *fu*. The poetry of Tu Fu also contains outstanding examples of this use of a more particularized mode of expression to convey political intent; such monumental poems as "From the Capital to Feng-hsien: Five Hundred Words Chanting My Feelings" ("*Tzu ching fu Feng hsien hsien yung-huai wu-pai tzu*") and "Journey North" ("*Pei cheng*") both tell of travel through the empire that details the progress of the An Lu-shan Rebellion, with its devastating effects on the land and people, and the despairing attempts of the disillusioned poet to progress—physically, professionally, emotionally, and morally—in this environment. The sense of spatial progression and the strong personal voice recall the expressivism of personal *fu* in the more densely evocative form of five-character *ku-shih*.[9] Similarly, because of his specificity, Han Yü's "Officer at Lung River" moves away from "pure" lyricism: the experience is not integrative. Han Yü shapes his journey into exile as a journey into self-knowledge, but maintains the distance between himself and his audience. We can see that as soon as the motive for expression becomes more important than the expression itself, lyrical experience will be compromised. Although specificity in and of itself does not transform "lyric" into "narrative," it may well work against the integrative tendencies of lyric. The choice of a narrative mode suggests that when it is urgent to convey *particular* intent to a broad enough audience, or the right audience, the poet may not be prepared to rely upon the critical convention of realizing an artist's personal experience through the act of reading.

According to the Chinese critical conventions discussed above, the illusion of integration with poetic experience does not imply that lyric lacks point of view, or that the voice of the poet actually merges with that of the reader. Personal voice is conveyed to the reader by an implicit point of view, one that is meant to be identified, ultimately, with the poet. In the case of narrative poetry the point or points of view are made explicit. It is a feature of lyric that the point of view of the poet and the point of view of the speaker of the poem are meant to be the same; in narrative there can be no such assumption.[10] Indeed, the multiple points of view which narrative brings to bear may produce a sense of dislocation. Events treated in narrative poetry are to some degree separated in time and space from the narrator, from the poet, and certainly from the reader. The reader is aware of these separations or distances; however, on the level of interpretation all points of view—poet's, narrator's, reader's—may be brought to bear simultaneously upon the events in a narrative. These points of view may be contemporaneous with the events of the text, or they may be quite distant in time and space. While the resulting complexity requires an adjustment on the part of both poet and reader, it is a crucial factor in the interpretative richness of narrative.[11]

Although the explicitness of point of view in Chinese narrative poetry is a function of Chinese poetic language generally, the techniques whereby point of view is made explicit involve two basic methods: the explicit identification of speakers and the use of description to set *subjective* rather than *objective* contexts.[12] The most obvious indicators of the presence of particular speakers are personal pronouns, personal names, or epithets, which I will call "personal references." Such particularizing terms are far less evident in lyric poetry. When these more blatant identifying features are absent, description may serve to indicate particular points of view.

The use of specific detail helps to shape a reader's perception of subject matter through points of view other than the poet's. The success of the narrative mode of expression depends on stimulating audience response to a world outside its immediate context. Chinese narrative poetry may contain a substantial proportion of passages which seem to be purely descriptive in content, but clearly set particular rather than general contexts when they are considered in terms of their position in the poem as a whole. Depending upon the structure of the poem, the *context* of a descriptive passage will allow the interlude to refer to and reflect upon a specific rather than a general situation, thus converting the essentially "objective" mode of description to the needs of narrative. This is vital to narrative expression in the Chinese tradition because it allows the technique of description, which exploits the properties of imagistic language to the fullest, to be turned to the subjective purposes of narrative.

Let us first consider the matter of the explicit identification of speakers, or personal references. While some pronouns, such as *wu* (I), *yü* (I), or *fu* (he), may indicate precise personal references, pronouns frequently are discarded in favor of proper names, epithets, or "titles"—the "king" (*wang*), the "bride" (*chia-nu*), the "old wife" (*lao-fu*), and so on, terms which may substitute for proper names and have the force of pronouns. Pronouns may themselves be ambiguous in identifying the speaker or subject of a narrative; for instance, as mentioned in the note to my translation of Wang Wei's "Poem of Peach Blossom Spring," it is unclear whether the narrator is using the first person or third person. The word *tzu* in line 27 ("I rehearse with myself the paths I cross") may also be read *"he* rehearses with *him*self," as in Pauline Yu's translation.[13] *Tzu* is reflexive but does not in itself indicate the person involved. For the purposes of identifying point of view, however, the use of *tzu* as either "I" or "he" indicates the explicit presence of a narrator and/ or actor who enforces the reader's separation from the events in the poem. Whether that narrator may be identified with the protagonist of the poem is not essential to the narrative, although for the reader a precise identification might suggest variations in the style of the experience. The impact of the use of the pronoun *tzu* is to single out a particular actor whose experience is intended to be evocative rather than integrative.

The presence of straightforward personal references is a distinctive feature of the poems of the *Shih Ching*, and of *yüeh-fu* as well. They convey an impression of specificity, even if upon careful examination the more discursive diction of such poems still rests upon a very generalized context. In the "Ballad of the Orphan" ("*Ku-er hsing*," A.D. 100–200?), a *yüeh-fu* poem with lines of uneven length and no refrain, repetition of the speaker's or protagonist's "title," *ku-er* (orphan), emphasizes the particularity of the speaker and prepares the reader for a lament: "Whether born an orphan / Or to become an orphan / This fate is one of lonely suffering!"[14] The orphan's misfortunes seem to come in pairs, and the rhythm of the couplets shows his tasks and miseries taking him back and forth, back and forth, from hard labor to hard words. While the process of his demoralization is detailed by a specific personal voice, the context of his expression is still very generalized. Again, it is possible to interpret this poem as either a first- or third-person statement. The ballad "Southeast Fly the Peacocks" ("*K'ung-ch'üeh tung-nan fei*"), a *yüeh-fu* with consistent pentasyllabic lines, is much more explicit. A complex, third-person narrative, it contains a good deal of dialogue between identified speakers within a frame controlled by an omniscient narrator.[15]

We have also seen that poets of personal *fu* often use first-person pronouns to identify a speaker. Their literary progenitor, Ch'ü Yüan, set the example in the "*Li sao*," which most insistently identifies the poet with the speaker of the poem. The entire "*Li sao*" is written in the first person, not casually, as an assumed persona, but constantly enforced by the use of personal pronouns:

> *I* will no longer care that no one understands me,
> As long as I can keep the sweet fragrance of *my* mind . . .
> Enough! There are no true men in the state: no one to
>   understand *me*.
> Why should I cleave to the city of my birth?
> Since none is worthy to work with in making good
>   government
> *I* will go and join P'eng Hsien in the place where he abides.[16]

Ch'ü Yüan created an archetype of the rejected courtier for countless generations of poets and statesmen, and would-be poets and statesmen, to emulate in their poetry if not in their lives. Chia Yi's "Owl *fu*" and Yü Hsin's "Lament for the South" both show the overt influence of Ch'ü Yüan's model. Such personal references are characteristic of the tradition of personal *fu* and suggest a strong influence on the development of techniques for presenting point of view in narrative *shih*.

Description, the second major technique for indicating specific contexts in Chinese narrative poetry, is often used in conjunction with narrative *frames*. In Chinese poetry description relies on conventions of poetic language that are generally associated more with lyrical than with narrative expression. The narrative frame provides a concrete location in time and space for the experience in a poem. This invokes the reader's sense of separation from the context of the experience, while adapting description to the needs of narrative expression by virtue of its context within the frame. Framing devices present particular points of view which set the contexts of telling, separating what follows from what has gone before, yet maintaining explicitly delineated relations of structure and subject matter among the parts. As we will see in the analysis of specific poems, particularly the "Ballad of the *p'i-p'a*," frames are an overt manifestation of the methods developed by narrative poets to adapt the objective mode of description to the subjective needs of narrative.

There are many styles of literary frames, with a broad range of functions. Some, like prose prefaces, appear in all prosaic and poetic genres throughout Chinese literary history. Others may be particular to a certain genre. Framing is a structural rather than syntactic feature and, in the case of narrative *shih*, owes much to both *yüeh-fu* and personal *fu*. The framing devices in *shih* of the Han through T'ang dynasties take many forms. They may be poetic and integrated into the main body of the text, as in "Poem of Affliction" ("*Pei-fen shih*"), by Ts'ai Yen (discussed in chapter 3). In this poem Ts'ai Yen sketches the precise historical context of the beginning of her adventures in a few terse lines, focusing the larger context of the fall of the Han upon her personal tragedy. Framing devices may be prosaic and separated from the poetic text, as with Po Chü-yi's prose preface to the "Ballad of the *p'i-p'a*." Frames may also form an integral part of the poem, giving the narrator a first-person voice to introduce his own tale. The T'ang poet Shen Ch'üan-ch'i (c. 650–713) couches his wistful reminiscence of his fall from political favor in the form of a letter to his family in "Response to a Troll: A Letter to My Family" ("*Ta chih-mei tai-shu chi chia-jen*"). The frame sets the context of the narrator's speech by describing how, in his exile, he met a troll who inquired just how he came to be in that wild, forsaken place; while the main body of the poem consists of the poet's frank recital of his travails.[17] Framing devices may be expository, with an omniscient narrator using the third person. Shih Ch'ung (249–300) uses this approach in his prose preface, then changes to first person in the body of his poem, "Song of Wang Ming-chün" ("*Wang Ming-chün tz'u*"), in which the unlucky consort of a Han emperor relates the misfortunes attendant on her refusal to bribe the court painter to enhance her portrait. Believing the evidence of the homely portrait, the emperor gives Wang Ming-chün to a Tatar chieftain as part of a treaty settlement, and the lady dies in exile. A frame may present a speaker claiming direct participation in the events to be narrated, as Po Chü-yi does in "Ballad of the *p'i-p'a*," or relating events of distant times and places, as he does in "Song of Everlasting Sorrow." Framing devices at once set the context of the experience of the poem and free the poet to explore that experience from any point of view, in any role. However they are used, framing devices serve to maneuver the reader into a position of direct observation of the experience of the poem as determined by the point of view of the narrator. The advantage of the frame is that by incorporating description into a framed passage with a specific temporal context, a poet may adapt the expressive potential of imagistic language to the subjective mode of narrative without lessening the intrinsic, objective force of the description. This enforces the sense of vicarious experience typical of narrative and fosters a sense of participation, not so much in the events themselves as in the creation of their memory.

The device of the frame integrated directly into the text is familiar to us from the tradition of personal *fu*, which includes prosaic and poetic frames integrated into the tripartite structure frequently seen in Han *fu*: introduction (*hsü*), main body, and summation (*luan*). The centrality of an individual point of view typical of these *fu* is reinforced by the use of a frame to set a specific context for a personal statement. Chia Yi's "Owl *fu*" combines the functions of frame and introduction in a completely integrated verse composition. The frame provides the context for the poet's "dialogue" with the foreboding owl by precise date and even time of day (lines 1–11). The main body of the poem, presented as indirect quotation of what the owl would have said if it could speak, is the poet's self-justifying lament. The summation reveals the true purpose of the frame, for the owl has disappeared and the poet directly presents his own thoughts.

Ts'ao Chih's (192–232) "*Lo-shen fu*" has a double frame. The first frame consists of a prose preface that sets the context of the poem's composition, rather than the experience described in the poem. The poetic introduction, with its prose excursion into the driver's speech imploring his master to describe the goddess (lines 1–28), also functions as a frame for the experience described in the main body of the poem; namely, the noble poet's fantasy of personal delight and spiritual attainment. Ts'ao Chih closes his frame with an image of his reaction to his own powers of imagination: mounted on horseback, yet hesitating on the riverbank, he seems unable to accept the dissolution of his fantasy.[18]

Yü Hsin's "Lament for the South," discussed in chapter 1, provides another example of this kind of double, self-referential frame. Yü Hsin's prose preface gives a condensed version of the destruction of the Liang dynasty from a historical perspective, while his poetic introduction (lines 1–40) functions as a frame personalizing the subject matter of the text. The prose frame thus injects a note of foreboding which pervades the poetry. The frame is again closed in the summation, focusing on the poet alone, speaking in his own voice.

The nature of the narrative frame makes it extremely flexible and adaptable as a structuring technique. Some writers may employ several frames in one composition or combine several functions in a single frame. One of the most striking examples of complex frame technique in *shih* is also, perhaps, the most famous "private" musical entertainment in Chinese poetry. I am referring, of course, to Po Chü-yi's "Ballad of the *p'i-p'a*," written in 816 while the poet was in exile in Hsün-yang.[19] This poem has two main frames in the first-person voice of the poet-narrator, the first a prose preface attached to the poem, the second integrated into the body of the poem. Furthermore, within the body proper there is a digression meant to be from the point of view of the musician. In spite of the intricacy of the frame structure, these multiple points of view are explicitly refracted through the mind of the narrator. Even the musician's tale is given as indirect discourse rather than quoting her own speech. In this Po Chü-yi follows the models of personal *fu* like Chia Yi's "Owl *fu*" and Ts'ao Chih's "*Lo-shen fu*"—and, incidentally, perhaps, introduces the same note of fantasy to the experience.[20] In the prose preface the poet provides a synopsis of the events, set in their precise temporal and spatial context. The preface explains the reason for the poet's susceptibility to the experience: "I became a provincial official and was sent out two years ago. I had been tranquil and at peace with myself, but, affected by the words of this person (the musician), this evening I finally began to feel what it meant to be degraded and banished."[21] While the catalyst of the event is a dear though anonymous friend, from whom Po Chü-yi is taking a sorrowful leave, the central experience of the poem lies in the profound and unexpected sympathy between the disgraced politician and the forlorn singing-girl. The strong attraction of their two natures lies in the fact that both are artists, lonely and unappreciated in the backwaters below the Yangtze River. Their disappointments are narrated in simple terms; and, indeed, their situations are actually by no means unusual. Whatever the musician's degree of talent, what makes her unique is the chance meeting between herself and Po Chü-yi. In the context of his poem her talent is appreciated as truly exceptional. Po Chü-yi sets her beyond the stock types of aging courtesans, and under her hands even familiar music is magic with fresh emotion.

The narrator, who in this case is explicitly identified with the poet, assumes the controlling point of view from the first line to the last. Po Chü-yi manipulates the imagery of landscape and music to reflect his own emotional state. Moreover, the other possible points of view in the poem, those of the departing guest and of the musician, support the centrality of the poet. The prose preface sets out the particularity of the experience, down to precise location, date, and time of day. The first six lines of the poem provide an atmospheric setting, describing a melancholy autumn landscape with friends parting on a riverbank. "Suddenly" (line 7) another presence makes itself felt, through the sensuous artifact which is the musician's identity. The introduction of the musician completely changes the nature of the experience and the original purpose of the poem. Instead of composing a farewell poem to honor his departing friend, Po Chü-yi composes the poem which we in fact read, and which in turn describes the circumstances of its own composition. Rather than concentrating on the emotions of friendship, the focus turns to the affinity between the two artists in the practice of their art.

The introduction of the music which had been so conspicuously lacking to the occasion changes the gentlemen's plans: "I forgot all about going home, and my friend did not set out"(line 8). The "Ballad of the *p'i-p'a*" is in three parts, with each part comprising a tableau of the poet's consciousness of the significance of the encounter, and each part entailing a shift in point of view. The first part (lines 1–38) is the frame for the musician's tale, in which the poet describes the night, the musician's appearance, and her first performance for the company. The astounding personality of the music and the nature of the performance seems to obviate the need for any physical description of the lady herself:

> She turned the pegs and plucked the strings for several
>   notes,
> Even before they became a song, they began to reveal her
>   emotion.

With every string she pressed or released, each note was full
    of memories,
As if to complain that throughout her life she had never
    fulfilled her desires . . .
The large strings drummed with a noise like the rush of rain,
The small strings whispered as if they told a secret,
Drumming and whispering mingled in her playing
Like big pearls and small pearls pouring into a dish of jade.
There was the call of a hidden oriole, rolling out from under
    the flowers,
And the muffled sob of a flowing spring as its water poured
    down the bank.
The water of the spring seemed cold, as if the strings were
    freezing,
Their freezing kept the spring from flowing; the sound
    gradually choked to a halt.
The music ceased in deep melancholy, then hidden griefs
    came forth,
Those moments of silence were more powerful than those
    with sounds of music.
A silver pitcher suddenly broke, the liquid burst out,
Armored cavalry rushed forth with the ringing of blades and
    spears,
At the end of the piece she paused with her plectrum, then
    struck right across the heart;
All four strings gave one sound like the tearing of silk.

                                   (lines 15–18, 23–36)

There is no indication of specific person or particular context
in these passages. Taken out of the context of the "Ballad of the
p'i-p'a," we have an extraordinary musical event as evocative and
timeless as the themes of farewell, banishment, and personal fail-
ure themselves. It is the placement of these descriptive passages in
the particularizing context of the narrative poem that makes them
appear to function as sources of detail unique to a unique occasion.
Read in this manner the passages serve as individuating description of the unnamed musician and, furthermore, also illuminate
the emotional state of the poet at this particular time.

In the second part (lines 39–62) the lady sets down her instrument, lifts her (undescribed) face to the audience, and tells her life story. It is significant that, while the poet clearly introduces another point of view here, he does not do so by direct discourse. Instead, he narrates her story without the use of quotation, which directs attention as much to his strong response to the tale as to the woman as an individual. The musician's history is not unusual in itself, although Po Chü-yi infuses it with odd, small details:

> As she grew older, she made a match, to be a merchant's
> wife.
> The merchant valued his profits, and made light of being
> separated from her—
> Last month he went out to Fu-liang to buy tea.
>
> (lines 56–58)

While the figure of the preoccupied husband ignoring the languishing wife is conventional, the homely detail of his errand is not and lends verisimilitude to the recital. In a sense the tale as "told" contains no personal detail which had not already been revealed in the musical passage quoted above. Since the poet so carefully retains control over the point of view of presentation, however, the fact that the music so perfectly mirrors *his* state of mind comes as no surprise. The narrator explicitly reveals this in the third tableau in his own voice, by direct quotation, and the revelation of the musician's complementary experience serves to enhance the narrator's remarks on his sorrows.

In the final tableau (lines 63–88) the poet frankly centers on his own emotions. Instead of detailing his feelings, he "quotes" his own speech to the lady, his own tale of banishment and disillusionment. The poet implies that the lady's skill has uncovered a hidden self-knowledge; the music has finally brought the reality of his exile home to his consciousness. The delight of having such entertainment at hand awakens him to his deprivations, not just of the intellectual delights of the capital, but of emotional communication as well:

> "In spring on the river are flowery mornings, in autumn are
> moonlit nights,

But any time I go to fetch wine, I must always drink alone.
Oh, I'm not without 'mountain songs' and 'village pipes,'
But they do sound uncouth and shrill, and grate on my ears.
This evening, when I heard the voice of your *p'i-p'a*,
It was like hearing immortals' music, and my ears became
    clear again.
Don't refuse me! Sit down for a while and play another song,
And I will in return compose a 'Ballad of the *p'i-p'a*' for
    you."

(lines 75–80)

Hearing her *p'i-p'a*, the poet has joined the tradition of those who instinctively appreciate the personal worth of another, *chih-chi*, *chih-jen*, or most appropriately here, "*chih-yin*"—"one who understands the nature of the music"; that is, one who recognizes and acknowledges a deep affinity with another through artistic, particularly musical expression.[22] The poet acknowledges this bond by speaking of the similarity of their plights: "We are both lost wanderers at the ends of the earth; Meeting here, what need have we to have known each other before?" (lines 65–66). In order to make the bond complete the poet must respond in kind, with his own art of poetry. He writes for the lady a song to commemorate the occasion, one that will set her apart forever from other singing-girls.

Although Po Chü-yi's stated intention is to record an extraordinary personal experience, there are several possible interpretations of just what this record is meant to represent. On one level "Ballad of the *p'i-p'a*" is an artifact—a song written by a famous poet for an obscure entertainer. On another level it represents the life of the poet in exile. The story of the lady's past life leads to her meeting and spiritual communion with the poet, both in terms of their actual meeting and the description of this revelation in the poem. The poet's realization of their affinity and its significance points to the emotional center of the poem. Finally, "Ballad of the *p'i-p'a*" is a narrative of the creation of the poem itself. The interest of the narrative depends less on action than on the characterization of the musician achieved by the description of her music, her "speech," which with the emotional interplay between the two artists leads us to an understanding of the poet's intent. These levels of experience are controlled by the relation of particularizing frames. The ultimate effect of the narrator's point of view is to reveal that communion with the musician—or the departing guest—is secondary to the poet's revelation of "what it meant to be degraded and banished." The guest, the landscape, and the musician's exquisite performance and sad story are manipulated by the narrator to reveal his insight about his own state. The first narrative frame sets the context of a conventional parting poem, but the body of the poem shifts the emotional focus from the one who is free to leave Hsün-yang to the ones who must stay on there. The poet implies that the intensity of the musical experience makes them forget their original purpose. By the end of the poem the departing guest who started it all has simply dropped out of the text. The poet finds a fellow in exile who brings home its meaning to him; but this insight brings him a feeling of utter forlornness:

> Of those among the company, who wept most of all?
> I, sub-prefect of Chiang-chou; I soaked my blue sleeve
>   through.
>
> (lines 87–88)

Po Chü-yi's autobiographical poem uses framing devices to assert the poet's authority as narrator, and description to emphasize his perception of the situation and how the audience should receive it.[23] All the poems discussed above present points of view in the first person. However, this kind of explicit, individual point of view is not just a property of first-person, autobiographical poems like the "Ballad of the *p'i-p'a*." Third-person narratives may also employ framing devices in order to incorporate description into a larger narrative, and even to manipulate various points of view in a style which evokes the tradition of the storyteller's performance. Such a presentation combines the sense of vicarious experience of events with a perspective mediated by the explicit point of view of an omniscient narrator.

The framing devices of omniscient narrators are perhaps most familiar from *yüeh-fu* and the literary works inspired by them. *Yüeh-fu* often have a performative, or perhaps more accurately, mock-performative context. The most obvious manifestations of this type of *yüeh-fu* are the omniscient narrators who use the third person, as in "Southeast Fly the Peacocks."[24] Here the narrator sets up the frame with an emblem of the plight of the unhappy lovers, a peacock hesitating in its flight because it misses its mate. The burden of the tale is then left to dialogue, with the narrator occasionally stepping in to describe a flood of tears or other external manifestations of turbulent inner states. After the suicide of Lan-chih and her husband the narrative provides a reconciliation of sorts: the lovers are buried in the same grave, the trees around them entwine their branches, and faithfully mated pairs of birds make their nests there. In the last couplet the narrator steps out of the frame, directly addresses the reader, and enjoins all to heed the moral of the tale, suggesting, at least here, that the considerations of the romance outweigh the couple's "unfilial" defiance of their families' wishes.

One explanation for this frame structure is the assumption of performative context; that is, that *yüeh-fu* were originally intended for oral performance.[25] The "singer" would have the double task of narrating and of impersonating a cast of characters, which would vary the performance and encourage the audience's sense of involvement. Whether "Southeast Fly the Peacocks" and poems like it were in fact composed in performance, the technique is definitely suited to creating a varied narrative. The narrator must fill in details of nonverbal actions, but the fact that the different characters speak for themselves gives a sense of several individual personalities and several points of view. These are all ultimately unified by the omniscient voice of the narrator, who closes the frame with an appropriate moral, bringing down the curtain, as it were, on his performance.

These framing techniques were emulated by writers of *shih* in their third-person narratives. The effects of this kind of narrator's point of view are perhaps nowhere better demonstrated than in Po Chü-yi's most famous poem, the "Song of Everlasting Sorrow" ("*Ch'ang-hen ko*," 808).[26] The framing techniques used in this third-person narrative *shih* evoke the performative context of *yüeh-fu*, but with a difference. A performative context may have the effect of suggesting to the reader a participation in the experience of hearing a recitation. However, the experience of "hearing" the recitation is deemphasized in a poem like "Song of Everlasting Sorrow." Here, the function of the frame is similar to the function of a frame in personal *fu:* even the context of establishing the frame is separated from the reader's experience. The poet in the role of narrator assumes overt control over all aspects of the reader's experience, even of "hearing," and can dislodge the reader from the role of integration into a more active, if more removed role in the experience of the text.

Writing in a time of peace fifty years after the An Lu-shan Rebellion, Po Chü-yi created a world which centers on the doomed love of Emperor Hsüan-tsung (684–762, r. 715–55) for his "paramount" concubine, the notorious Yang Kuei-fei (718–756).[27] The story is drawn from the T'ang's most urgent political crisis; however, though a lesson may certainly be taken from the downfall of the emperor who brought the T'ang to its zenith of cultural achievement and prosperity, the poem definitely subordinates the consequences of his folly for the empire at large to the sorrow and ruin he brings upon himself. The narrator elevates the theme of passionate, even eternal love to the position of chief importance. To enforce this point of view Po Chü-yi brings all his descriptive gifts to bear on those aspects of the affair which emphasize the personal tragedy of the actors: the luscious beauty of Yang Kuei-fei, as a woman and later as an immortal; the impotence of the aging emperor in the face of his mutinous troops; his terrible loneliness after the death of his love. While poets living under the reign of the Emperor Hsüan-tsung, notably Tu Fu (712–770), lamented and indirectly reproached the emperor for the ravages brought by the rebellion to the general population, Po Chü-yi draws from the same events a legend of transcendent romance.[28] "Song of Everlasting Sorrow" transforms the story of the emperor and his favorite concubine from the most foolhardy intrigue of the century to one of the greatest love stories of China, in spite of the fact that the emperor was sixty years old when he first beheld the languid and fascinating Yang Kuei-fei. Po Chü-yi is able to create a compelling sense of the pathos of the fall of a great ruler into old age, despair, and, above all, loneliness.

The descriptive passages and their placement in the poem, however, do intimate the consequences of the actions of the lovers for the empire at large, even while providing a sympathetic perspective on their romance. In this sense the descriptive passages enhance the suspense which makes the tale so compelling. For instance, the narrator invokes in lavish detail the renewal of the old emperor in this romance, creating an "ideal" world waiting to be shattered:

> Her clouds of hair, her lovely face, her swaying, gold-shod
> steps,
> Within hibiscus canopies they passed their spring nights in
> warmth.
> The spring nights seemed very short, the sun would rise
> high;
> But from that time His Majesty would not attend the early
> court.
> They took their pleasure at feasts and entertainments without
> pause,
> The spring came, and passed on as night followed night.
> There were three thousand other beauties in the women's
> palace;
> For him, all their three thousand charms were combined in
> one body.
> In the golden room, her toilette complete, she seductively
> attended him all night,
> In the jade tower, the feasting finished, she harmonized with
> spring delights.
> Her sisters and brothers were all given rank and titles;
> To the dismay of many, her glory reflected on her family,
> And so throughout the empire the hearts of mothers and
> fathers
> Did not value the birth of a boy, but valued that of a girl.
> In the upper stories of Li Palace, piercing the blue sky,
> Fairy music wafted on the wind, to be heard everywhere,
> Slow-paced songs and languorous dances were played by
> strings and flutes:
> Though he gaze all day, His Majesty could not gaze on her
> enough.
> Then the war-drums from Yü-yang came, shaking the earth,

Abruptly breaking off the songs of the "Rainbow Skirt" and
the "Robe of Feathers."

(lines 13–32)

The court and empire of the T'ang are bathed in the rosy glow
of the emperor's delight in one woman. But this ambiance of sensual delight hints that all is not well. The proper order of the empire is inverted by the centrality of Yang Kuei-fei: with the inner
court now his entire realm, the emperor no longer meets his early
court or tends to the affairs of state. Night is turned into day, spring
never ends, titles and political power are bestowed against the
meritocratic principles so sacred to the empire. Even the common
people invert their perspective, wishing for lucky girls to make a
man in his autumn years feel springtime come again, rather than
for boys to carry on their family lines. Then, in only two lines (31–
32), the illusion dissolves: the sound of war drums stops the gentler
music of the emperor's fantasy world.

After the death of the concubine and the emperor's return from
exile, the sense of the passage of time returns with a vengeance:

In the spring wind the peaches and plums blossomed with
the days,
In the autumn rains the *wu-t'ung* trees shed their leaves in
season.
The West Palace and the Southern Enclosure were full of
autumn grasses,
Falling leaves covered the stairs with red, and were not swept
away.
The attendants of the Pear Garden, had newly whitened hair,
The Pepper House eunuchs' young eyebrows began to show
their age.
Fireflies flew in the evening halls; he thought quietly of her,
The wick in his lonely lamp burnt out, and yet he would not
sleep.
Slowly, slowly, the bells and drums began each long night,
Brighter, brighter the Milky Way, urging the sky to dawn.
The roof-tile mandarin ducks were cold, the frost was bright
and thick,

His kingfisher-feather covers were cold, for who was to be
    with him?
His thoughts were on the distance between life and death,
    year after year without end,
But her spirit would not return, or come to enter his dreams.

(lines 61–74)

Every aspect of the emperor's surroundings reflects his own sense of loss and his awakened awareness of his helpless old age. The dream of love dissolved, he is appalled by the realities of aging, ruin, and decay, and finds that no sleep can return him to the precious dream. His inverted world of pleasure has been reinverted, and the pain and passage of time is excruciating as his environment reminds him of the past and reproaches him with it.

The two descriptive passages quoted above are absorbing in themselves, but in terms of the narrative as a whole they provide more than images of unconditional enjoyment and cold and lonely old age. Each reflects on the context of its presentation in the narrative. The description of the world of pleasure is not concrete; with a pleasing progression of conventional hyperboles, the poet lures the reader into the fantasy of the romance. At the same time, however, the passage creates tension, and the expectation of the end of the idyll grows as each pleasure is detailed. The chilled world of the bereaved emperor similarly anticipates some kind of resolution, in this case the tenuous communication between the spirit of the lady and her lover through the medium of a Taoist adept.

In both cases the narrator manipulates the sympathies of the reader through the use of description. The passages provide an intimate perspective which enhances the story of the lovers and absolves them from the consequences of their actions except as they affect their own lives. For the narrator this is tragedy enough, as he speaks in his own voice for the final comment: "Heaven endures, earth's span is long, but sometime both will end / This sorrow everlasting will go on forever" (lines 119–20). While the emperor's actions cannot be condoned, the poet carefully refrains from actually condemning him, even if the empire is turned upside down by his inverted sense of priorities. The narrator's point of view causes the events to be seen from the perspective of the doomed lovers rather than in the larger context of historical events. Po Chü-yi creates in the context of the poem a world in which the lovers ironically bring about their own ruin, and this world effectively substitutes for the empire in a dark and unsentimental period of Chinese history. Po Chü-yi's participation as narrator in this text evokes the style of *yüeh-fu* narrators but, again, he does not relinquish the control of his point of view to any other speaker in the context of the poem. The third-person narrator plunges straight into the romance and only emerges explicitly in the final couplet, to lament the sad fate of the emperor and his lady and point to the artifact he has created to ensure that his interpretation of their story will bring them immortality.

I have concentrated my analysis on Po Chü-yi's two classic narratives to show that a single poet can easily adopt more than one approach to the manipulation of description for narrative expression. These poems are praised at least as much for passages such as the ones quoted above as for any plot or story. Yet the essentially vicarious nature of the experience for the reader stands, and is reexperienced with each reading.

Set in a temporally or spatially specific context, description invokes the particularity so important to narrative experience and reveals the areas of emphasis in the mind of the poet. Framing and description strengthen the effectiveness of a controlling point of view, either by reflecting directly on its source or by presenting details of subject matter that enhance the narrator's interpretation of events. In short, framing and description as manipulated by the narrator help to maneuver the reader into a position to see and understand what the narrator sees and understands, without the illusion of integration.

These features, however, do not in themselves define narrative as compared to lyric modes. Potentially ambiguous techniques, including point of view, are sometimes used deliberately to encourage a sense of personal participation in events, while at the same time indicating the reader's separation from the events of the text in the contemporary context. In poems of this type explicit points of view may seem to set specific contexts, but if a temporal or a detailed physical setting is not firmly established, the poetic expression may detach from an apparently specific context and impart instead a universal one.

This is frequently the case with poetry that conveys political criticism. The technique of universalizing point of view combines with the tradition of allusion in *shih* to create extremely forceful documents of protest. By invoking through allusion a vision of the past which is based on the poet's present, the universalizing point of view conveys the impact of the specific context while at the same time preserving, however tenuously, the poet's margin of safety from charges of subversion and lèse-majesté.[29] Tu Fu, for instance, was inspired by the devastation caused by the An Lu-shan Rebellion to compose many critical poems and protest ballads. In "Lament at the Riverside" ("*Ai Chiang-t'ou*"), written in 757 (soon after Yang Kuei-fei met her death), Tu Fu meditates on the utter desolation of the imperial city in the grip of rebellion. Although the poet is standing in the ruins of the T'ang imperial park, he deliberately sets the carefree scenes of former times in the reign of Han Ch'eng-ti (r. 32–7 B.C.) and compares the life and death of "the first lady of the Chao-yang Palace" (line 7) to the former splendor of Ch'ang-an and its present ruin. While the poet seems to relate the separation of the lovers ("The one who has gone and the one who remains cannot exchange their tidings," line 16), he may also be referring to his own separation from the court he wishes to serve and to that court's exile from its proper place in the capital. The poem creates a chilling impression of a land disrupted by war without ever explicitly stating the poem's reference to the An Lu-shan Rebellion. Tu Fu provides a speaker with a controlling point of view, yet the ambiguity of the context of the experience makes the mode of expression finally more objective than subjective, transcending the particular context in favor of a universalized vision of the disaster of civil war.[30]

Even when a point of view is specified, the context of its identification can defy particularity and so make the mode of expression ambiguous. Tu Fu's series of six poems, "Three Conscripting Officers" ("*San li*") and "Three Partings" ("*San pieh*"), written in 759, presents six different points of view on the themes of the horrors of war and the sorrows of parting, which combine to describe poignantly a time when all partings seem to foreshadow useless deaths. The poems are not linked by a temporal sequence, or even a specified context; however, as a group the poems implicitly represent all members of society affected by the An Lu-shan Rebellion. In "The Conscripting Officer at Shih-hao" (*"Shih-hao li"*) the poet actually participates as an eyewitness observer of events and presents the actors explicitly, even to the point of quoting their speech:

> I heard the old woman go forward and speak to him,
> "My three sons were in the garrison at Yeh.
> One son sent a letter which arrived here:
> Two sons have just been killed in the fighting,
> The survivor still for the time being hangs on to his own life,
> But the dead ones are already gone for good . . ."
>
> (lines 7–12)[31]

While the poet does not identify himself by the use of a personal pronoun, he presents the confrontation between the officer and the old woman, whom he refers to as "the wife" (*fu*) and who refers to herself as "the old woman" (*lao fu*), from his point of view as witness to the incident. What he overhears is an eloquent protest from the old woman, who confronts the conscripting officer directly to protect her husband. The bitterness of her losses pours out—two sons gone, no hope for the third, a grandson at the breast not likely to survive if the mother is taken to serve the troops. She ironically offers her services to the men of the garrison, and it seems that this offer is accepted, for when the traveler resumes his journey in the morning only the old man is left in the house, "alone" (*tu*, line 24).

The "Three Partings" consist of monologues spoken by three victims of the war around them: a new bride, an old man, and an orphan, who has returned from military service to find his family gone and his village destroyed. The poet is not present as an implied observer or questioner. In "The Parting of the New Bride" (*"Hsin-hun pieh"*), the bride's situation is full of contradictions based on the systematic disappointment of all her expectations of marriage:

> For a maiden to marry a soldier
> Is worse than being cast away by the roadside!

I put up my hair and became a "wife,"
But the marriage bed has not been warmed . . .
I sigh to be the daughter of a poor family;
A long time I spent making these silk clothes,
Silk clothes which I will never wear again,
And for your sake I must wash off my cosmetics.
I look up and see birds by the hundred flying,
Large ones and small, yet they always fly in pairs.
Human affairs are mostly at cross-purposes;
With you I share our eternal longing for each other.

(lines 3–6, 25–32)[32]

The paradoxes of the young woman's position seem bound to
have tragic consequences. Married and abandoned, but not repu-
diated, the bride cannot return to her own family, but with the
marriage unconsummated she cannot yet present herself to her
husband's household. The poignancy of her isolation is emphasized as she addresses her absent husband directly (lines 9, 17, 19,
32). Her only concrete experience of marriage is her longing for
her departed husband, and all the trappings of joyful domesticity
must be set aside in favor of an untimely widowhood. In the final
quatrain she laments that the human world is out of joint with the
natural world, which seems to mock her isolation.

There is a great temptation to interpret "Three Conscripting
Officers" and "Three Partings" together, although they are not
linked by the kinds of temporal and syntactic elements that usually
define poem sequences (see chapter 4). These poems are linked by
a universalized context of adversity, joining the people portrayed
in them in a universal human family in a world at war. Though the
poems might seem to be linked by complementary family relationships, the "implied" relationships are in fact the reader's intuitive
impression of the connections between these laments. All of these
people are affected by the same forces, which overwhelm their personal individuality. Tu Fu underlines the pathos of the perversion
of social values in times of war, especially when the victims, such
as the old woman and the young bride, speak out, deploring and
yet accepting their fates. The presentation of the depredations of
war from the six points of view in the series ultimately has the
effect of emphasizing their sameness rather than their diversity.

In terms of the role of point of view, "Lament at the River-side," "Three Conscripting Officers," and "Three Partings" seem to partake of both lyrical and narrative tendencies as discussed in this chapter. Tu Fu exercises his controlling point of view to create a sense of disjunction between the reader and the events, encouraging the reader to sympathize with the situations described in the poems. At the same time the precise context of the events is deliberately ambiguous. There is no detailed description or precise historical reference to anchor the events in a context clearly removed from the contemporary one. The reader is drawn into a sense of indirect participation, rather like the observer in "The Conscripting Officer at Shih-hao."

While the points of view invoking this ambiguity may be quite explicit, a sense of particular contexts and individual personalities of the speakers or participants is conspicuously lacking. For this the complementary techniques of framing and description must provide particularizing detail that illuminates the individuality of these contexts and personalities; namely, details of character. These poems by Tu Fu demonstrate how the universalization of point of view reduces the sense of specific context conveyed by the poem, causing the devices of framing and description to inspire integration with the experience of the text, rather than separation from it. The intent of the poet is to inspire horror of a particular war, but the restrictions and conventions governing political protest in literature obliged him to express this intent in objective rather than subjective terms. Description in the subjective mode is the basis of characterization, and in the chapter that follows we will see how this feature is relevant not just to the evocation and creation of personalities, but to the creation of narrative contexts in their own right.

3

Character Types and Character Roles

Characterization in Chinese narrative poetry depends on the techniques that make points of view explicit in a text and that give these points of view individual identity. Furthermore, once the vicarious nature of the experience is established, the interpretative convention of understanding a poet's personality through a poem may be applied to the development of a sense of the individuality of the various speakers and/or actors in a text. In other words, when a narrator explicitly exercises a controlling point of view, the reader quite naturally relates the experiences described in the text to that narrator, speaker, or actor, rather than directly to the personality of the poet. This mode of characterization, relying primarily on direct discourse and description, is a logical outgrowth of the particularizing tendencies of point of view discussed in chapter 2. Indeed, it may be considered an extension of these tendencies to their logical culmination.

    This is perfectly consistent with the general emphasis in Chinese narrative on revealing the essential quality of a hero or heroine rather than portraying such figures in a process of growth.[1] Chinese techniques of characterization also reflect the differences in approach to the representation of human reality in narrative from the expectations of European traditions. The basic distinctions in approach have been described in terms of "types" and "individuals" as characters. "Types" are seen as formed more in the mold of exemplar, while "individuals" are more mimetic.[2] Chinese principles of characterization have been described as emphasizing type over individuality, thus denigrating the Chinese tradition. Andrew H. Plaks points out that, at least in the case of prose fiction, "the whole question of individuals and types, of course, is generally raised with the purpose of leveling at the Chinese narrative texts the accusation of failing to present fully rounded individuals."[3] In his discussion of characterization Plaks develops the notion that the concepts of "unique individual" and "stereotype" are not mutually exclusive; indeed, it is the interplay between individuality and recognizable type in a given role that creates a character in narrative.[4]

While prose fiction may present more complex characters, if only because of the far greater length of the narratives involved, the techniques of characterization in narrative poetry reflect these same principles, even in the more compressed form of *shih*. The concomitant abridgment of character development in the text, however, does not emphasize type to the exclusion of individuality, or vice versa. Rather, techniques of characterization in narrative poetry exploit the tension between these two aspects of the perception and presentation of character to compensate for the relative brevity of the narrative. The properties of Chinese poetic language that form the idioms of narrative *shih* determine the nature of characterization and character development both in terms of the conventions of reading and the conception of character in narrative. The shift from a lyrical persona, with ultimate reference to the poet, to a narrator not necessarily identified with the poet is an essential feature of characterization here. Recognition of the nature and importance of *archetypes* in narrative poetry allows us to appreciate how the techniques employed affect our perceptions of character, and even to apply these principles to the more complex characters of extended prose narrative.[5]

A narrative archetype in poetry may be considered in terms of two complementary parts: an individual with distinctive traits who comes to represent a particular character "type" (often, in fact, identified as the original individual, by the same name), and the events and experiences with which that figure is associated—the character "role."[6] A germinal archetype combines both type and role, but these need not occur together in later uses. In the case of the adaptation of a particular character type, like Ch'ü Yüan or the courageous warrior maiden Mu-lan, who disguised herself as a man in order to save her father from military service,[7] the composition usually undertakes to retell the original story with the original character, though there may be some topical modifications, as in a T'ang adaptation of the type of the Han poet Ts'ai Yen. In the case of character roles, individuals are defined in terms of their experience, as the unnamed fisherman who remonstrated with the despondent Ch'ü Yüan on the banks of the Mi-lo River,[8] or the fisherman who blundered into the land of Peach Blossom Spring. These roles may be adapted to new individuals in order to enhance their topical significance, while still alluding to the original archetype. In the autobiographical "Ballad of the *p'i-p'a*," for instance, Po Chü-yi styles for himself, or at least for his narrator, the role of the insightful Chung Tzu-ch'i, while the *p'i-p'a* musician stands in the role of the lutenist Po Ya. Po Chü-yi revitalizes the generalized role of *chih-chi* by reassociating it with thoroughly up-to-date music and applying the role to his position as artist and government official in exile.[9]

The life of an archetypal character in the evolution of narrative *shih* can be demonstrated by a selection of poems based on the story of the late Han poet, Ts'ai Yen (late second–early third century), also known as Ts'ai Wen-chi. The historical Ts'ai Yen was the daughter of the eminent poet and statesman Ts'ai Yung (133–192), who died in prison after his associate, the frontier general Tung Cho (d. 192), rebelled against the central government. After the deaths of her father and her first husband, Ts'ai Yen was caught in the upheavals of the Tung Cho Rebellion; in 192 she was captured by a raiding party of barbarian mercenaries, who carried her off to become the wife of a chieftain of the Southern Hsiung-nu. When this chieftain died she was married again, to his son by a previous marriage. Ts'ai Yen bore her husbands-in-exile two sons and lived among the Hsiung-nu until about 206, when she was ransomed by Ts'ao Ts'ao (155–220), who had finally succeeded in establishing control over the floundering Han court. Ts'ai Yen was escorted back to China, but was forced to leave her children behind with the nomads. When she returned to the court Ts'ao Ts'ao gave her a fourth husband, the statesman Tung Ssu. Although her clan, of which Ts'ai Yen found herself to be the sole survivor, had been restored to its official status by Ts'ao Ts'ao, the lady was ostracized at court because of her family connections and her multiple marriages, considered shameful by the Chinese aristocracy.

This was not the end of her troubles, as recorded in her biography in the *Hou Han Shu*, "Biography of the Wife of Tung Ssu" (*"Tung Ssu chi chuan"*).[10] Eventually Tung Ssu offended Ts'ao Ts'ao and was condemned to death. His wife, fully aware of her notoriety, challenged Ts'ao Ts'ao's decree before the court and asked him if he would provide her with yet a fifth husband. Tung Ssu was spared. Ts'ai Yen's identification as "the wife of Tung Ssu" in her official biography would seem to suggest that this incident defined the historical figure for later generations, but in fact the power of the lady's plea for her husband rested on the known facts of her long exile and political victimization. The biography, compiled between 424 and 445, includes the poem in five-character-line *shih* meter on which the narrative archetype was based, "Poem of Affliction" (*"Pei-fen shih"*). A second poem, of the same title and subject matter but written in *sao* meter is also included, but it never enjoyed the popularity of the poem in *shih* meter.

There is much debate over the authenticity of Ts'ai Yen's authorship, but there is no doubt that this poem is the first presentation of one of the most powerful archetypes of exile, political upheaval, and personal alienation in Chinese narrative poetry.[11] Moreover, the techniques of characterization employed by the author of "Poem of Affliction" are typical of narrative *shih* from the time of its composition until at least the end of the T'ang dynasty. For the purposes of this discussion of characterization, the final identity of the author of the poem is not crucial. The author certainly intended the work to function as an "autobiographical" narrative, identifying a particular context and set of experiences which became inextricably identified with the historical figure of Ts'ai Yen. "Poem of Affliction" is all in the first-person voice of the lady narrating her experiences as she was captured by barbarians, lived in exile among the nomads of the northwest, and finally returned to her home. The narrator represents Ts'ai Yen herself, and the lament is one of the longest five-character *shih* in which the narrative is sustained throughout by a single voice. The style of narration follows a typical pattern for characters in narrative *shih*; namely, the narrator focuses on the unique qualities of a particular experience more than on her own participation in that experience.[12] The events are related in chronological order and, like Po Chü-yi's "Ballad of the *p'i-p'a*," from the point of view of the poet looking back on an experience of which she is the center, if not precisely the catalyst. The narrator's point of view is therefore affected by her hindsight on the significance of this experience as a whole, and, given the persuasive power of the narrator's voice, the hindsight in turn shapes and reinforces the reader's sense of the veracity of the experience.[13]

Like the personal *fu* evoked by comparable experiences of exile and alienation, "Poem of Affliction" may be divided into three main sections, each corresponding physically and emotionally to a distinct stage in Ts'ai Yen's experience. The first part (lines 1–40) gives the background of the mercenary raid in which the lady is captured, first presenting the matter of central political importance, the fact that a trusted general raised his hand against his emperor:

> In the later phases of the Han, when it lost hold of its power,
> Tung Cho rebelled against the abiding principles of Heaven:
> He had a perverted ambition to usurp his ruler's place,
> But first he murdered all the worthy men and the wise and
>   noble lords.
> He forced a migration to the old imperial capital,
> He got control of his lord and exploited him to make himself
>   strong.
>
> (lines 1–6)[14]

Tung Cho upsets the equilibrium of the empire by seizing the emperor, and the resulting demoralization and terror make it impossible for the Chinese troops loyal to the Han to resist the mercenaries of the Hu and Chiang tribes employed by the rebels (line

12), who take this opportunity to pillage the countryside. Ts'ai Yen is captured during such a raid:

> They surrounded the cities as if they were hunters in the
>   fields,
> And where they struck, there wasn't a thing left alive.
> They killed people wherever they turned until no one was
>   left,
> Corpses and dry bones propped each other up.
> On their horses' sides they suspended the heads of the men,
> Behind them on their horses' backs they carried off the
>   women.
>
> (lines 13–18)

If all were well in the empire these "hunters in the fields" would be the kind celebrated in the great hunt *fu*, which embody the court image of the Han. As it is, all of the known and supposedly invincible patterns of order have been disrupted. The description of the prisoners' march out of China (lines 19–40) reflects the lady's sense of total deracination, terror, and exhaustion. Her past life is violently obscured: "I gazed back into the dark and blurry distance" (line 21). The mass confusion of the captives mirrors the narrator's inner hysteria in such an alien context. The Hsiung-nu warriors are portrayed as brutal and easily moved to violence, embodying the worst fears of an aristocratic Chinese in a foreign and uncouth environment:

> Although those they had captured numbered tens of
>   thousands,
> We were not allowed to camp or meet together.
> There were times when we might be near our next of kin,
> But though we wished to speak, we dared not say a word.
> If they felt displeased at the least little thing
> They'd bark out, "Kill the captives!
> Anyone who holds back his blade
> Will not be left alive."
> How could we even wish to go on living?
> We could not endure their cursing;
> Sometimes they would just pick up and start beating us

So bitterness and pain were mixed as the blows came down.
By day we wailed and cried as we trudged along,
By night we grieved and groaned as we sat down.
If we wished to die, we were unable to manage it;
If we wished to live, we were hardly able to do that, either.

(lines 23–38)

In the second section (lines 41–80) Ts'ai Yen shifts the imagery of her mental state from the mass of suffering captives to the cold and threatening landscape of her new home. She is literally devastated when confronted by the "frontier wastes":

The frontier wastes are not at all like China,
The customs have little righteousness or order.
Everywhere there is plenty of frost and snow
And the nomads' wind begins to blow in spring and summer.
Whipping up, the wind whistled through my clothes,
Wailing, it entered my ears . . .

(lines 41–46)

Once settled in the nomadic way of life, Ts'ai Yen's emotional life focuses on longing for home and hoping for news from China. Her perspective on the world has become inverted because of her location in exile: "When a traveler came from the *outside world* / I always felt happy to hear of it" (lines 49–50, italics mine). The use of the word "outside" (*wai*) is ironic because in her own terms it is *she* who is "outside" among the barbarians, while the travelers she so eagerly awaits have come from "inside," from China.

It is not until Ts'ai Yen finally is ransomed that she offers any details of her personal life among the nomads. Though she longed for home, the lady in exile did establish strong domestic ties within her strange environment, and these ties change the happiness of her release to a tragedy of separation:

Unexpectedly, my wishes for help were finally granted,
An envoy from my family came to take me home.
But though I was able to have myself released,
When I returned, I still had to abandon my sons.
There were natural ties which bound our hearts together,

I brooded that I would be parted from them, without hope of
    meeting again.
In life or death we would always be separated,
And I could not bear to take my leave of them.
My children came forward and hung around my neck,
Crying, "Mother, where are you going?
They say you have to go away,
But how will we ever be reunited?
Mother, you have always been so loving, so indulgent,
How can you now be so unkind to us?
We have not yet grown to manhood,
How could you not look back and long for us?"
To see them this way crushed my very vitals,
Distressed as I was, I became as one demented.
Wailing and crying, hands clutching, caressing,
As I was about to go, I turned back yet again.

                                         (lines 53–72)

The pathos of the scene and the lady's anguish are strength-
ened by the direct quotation—the only passage that can be so interpreted in the poem—of her sons' entreaties (lines 62–68). The
children reveal new facets of Ts'ai Yen's character. She is represented by them as a tender and loving mother, with a genuine
attachment for her nomad family which clearly transcends any cultural barrier. This scene destroys any sense of relief at Ts'ai Yen's
redemption. She is a woman without any free or happy choices,
with no prospects for fulfillment. As she departs, her surroundings
now reflect this new awareness: everyone weeps and wails, and
even the horses hesitate to leave the nomad camp behind (lines
73–80).

In the third section (lines 81–108) Ts'ai Yen's thoughts on her
return are filled with her children, paralleling her brooding on her
own parents while adjusting to life in the lands of the nomads (lines
47–48):

Go, Go! My lingering ties were cut.
Marching fast, as days rolled by we were farther and farther
    away;

> With the vastness of three thousand *li* between us,
> When would I again meet with those I loved?
>
> (lines 81–84)

When she returns to her old home she discovers a wilderness of desolation even more chilling than the frontier. Here the barren landscape again reflects the narrator's emotional state, facing the cruelest blow she has yet endured:

> When I arrived, my family was all gone;
> Again I was without even a distant relative.
> The city walls had become a mountain forest,
> The courtyards and pavilions sprouted brambles,
> There were white bones of who knows whom
> In all directions with no one to cover them up;
> I went outside the gates, but not a human sound—
> Just the wolves howling and yelping;
> Desolate, I faced my orphan shadow;
> Grief and anger swelled in my entrails.
>
> (lines 87–96)

While she continues to live, she regards her life as a burden, only maintained out of her sense of consideration for those who have acted kindly toward her (lines 99–100) and her new husband (lines 103–4). The extirpation of her clan and home village, however, suggests that at least in her own eyes she is a woman without a future precisely because her past has been destroyed. Her life seems all bitter paradox, all actions and consequences leading to shame and grief, but not death:

> My homeless life completes my suffering;
> My constant fear is to be cast off again.
> How long can one person's life endure?
> I shall harbor my grief to the very end of my days!
>
> (lines 105–8)

In historical terms Ts'ai Yen was an unfortunate victim of war and politics. From the point of view of the narrator of "Poem of Affliction" she is a person whose life is full of dilemmas whose outcome inevitably is determined by outside forces over which she has no control. Her role in all the choices concerning her fate is passive. This is reflected by the emphasis on the consequences of the "choices" made for the lady rather than the choices themselves, and by her emphasis on her inner state rather than her actions. Because Ts'ai Yen's role is passive, the interest in her character is in her responses to her situation and emotional conflicts. Moments of indecision or inability to act are due to her inability to reconcile herself to the inevitable, or perhaps more correctly, to her utter helplessness. One of the strongest emotions conveyed is her frustration with the impersonality of the forces, however violent, which cause her displacement, alienation, and grief.

While the narrator's many explicit statements of her misery may seem melodramatic, in the light of her complete frustration and emotional isolation they find some justification. Her fear when she falls into the hands of the barbarian rebels, her psychological and physical estrangement in a foreign land, and her love for her children and frantic despair over their enforced separation all evoke a sympathetic response, not only to her plight but to her as an individual. Ts'ai Yen's final return to China, to be faced with a scene even grimmer than the northwestern wastelands, is especially pathetic because the confrontation with the desolation of her home is a final blow to her spirit. From this supposedly autobiographical narrative emerges a powerful character who commands personal respect. Although Ts'ai Yen's endurance of the events detailed in the poem is passive, it finds active expression in the personal narrative itself. The fact that her individuality survives all her suffering reveals a gritty dignity and even defiance which effectively establishes a new archetype for a situation which at the time of writing was itself new—the fall of a great dynasty.

The narrative archetype of Ts'ai Yen has endured in several forms and through many transformations. Some of these have taken on lives of their own which may seem at first glance quite removed from the late Han original. The poem sequence attributed to Ts'ai Yen herself, "Eighteen Songs of a Nomad Flute" ("*Hu-chia shih-pa p'ai*"), is at least as influential in the transmission of Ts'ai Yen's archetype as "Poem of Affliction."[15] The transmission of the Ts'ai Yen type—that is, the individual identified as Ts'ai Yen herself, as distinct from the set of experiences and responses originally associated with her—was profoundly affected in the T'ang dynasty by a new version of the "Eighteen Songs of a Nomad Flute," by Liu Shang (fl. 770–73).[16] On the other hand, Ts'ai Yen's character *role*—the experiences originally associated with her life that could be adapted without direct reference to the historical figure of Ts'ai Yen—was preserved in narrative poems about other exiles, notably the Han noblewoman Wang Chao-chün (first century B.C.) and the unnamed lady from the capital city in Wei Chuang's "Song of the Lady of Ch'in."

Let us first turn to the transformation of the character type, that is the figure of Ts'ai Yen herself, that took place in the hands of Liu Shang. Liu Shang was active in a period known to literary historians as the mid-T'ang, roughly 766–835, a period which also includes the work of some of the most popular and influential writers in Chinese literature, such as Po Chü-yi and Han Yü.[17] The pervasive influence of the mid-T'ang on later artistic creation has rather obscured the fact that poems such as Liu Shang's are anomalies in the T'ang as a whole. The distinctive themes of mid-T'ang narrative poetry seem to be in part responses to the shock of the An Lu-shan Rebellion and its aftermath, and perhaps to a lesser degree to the weight of the brilliance of the poetry and culture of the High T'ang, particularly under the reign of Emperor Hsüan-tsung (r. 715–55). The trends most apparent in Liu Shang's work are the rise in emphasis on explicit didactic purpose in poetry and poetic criticism and, more important for our understanding of the evolution of the narrative archetype of Ts'ai Yen, the focus in didactic purpose on revising history, a tendency conspicuously lacking in the Chinese tradition in general. Liu Shang's "Eighteen Songs of a Nomad Flute" is perhaps the most influential of the mid-T'ang's sudden flurry of "new" versions of old topics, now reworked to soften the impact of their grim subject matter. Liu Shang followed this sentimental aesthetic in his version of Ts'ai Yen's story, and in doing so erased the central moral and historical issues of his model. Liu Shang's sequence follows the events as presented in "Poem of Affliction" and the original sequence quite faithfully until the final poem:

When I returned to my old home, I met with my kinfolk;
The fields and gardens were gone half wild, but the spring
    grass was bright green.
Bright candles again were burning from among the rubble
    and ashes,
In the cold spring I washed again, a jade piece sunk in mud;
As I put on my headcloth and comb, I felt how good our
    rituals are—
Once I plucked my silk-stringed, *t'ung*-wood lute, I could
    have died content.
Since I went out through the passes, it has been twelve years:
My sorrows are all set down in these "Songs of a Nomad
    Flute."

(poem 18)

Compare this bland finale with the earlier description of Ts'ai Yen's return to her home village. In "Poem of Affliction" any joy of returning from exile is undercut by the fact that the lady's children were left in the steppe and her home, upon her return, has literally been transformed into a howling desert. Liu Shang's treatment of the story indicates a willingness not only to avoid painful subject matter in art but even to subvert events and personalities to "inspirational" ends. The emotional endurance and essential identity of the narrator of "Poem of Affliction" and the original "Eighteen Songs" has been sacrificed. In those poems Ts'ai Yen embodied the sensitive individual denied control over her own fate through violence, the crisis of the Chinese in exile with cultural superiority no longer taken for granted, and the emotional trauma of witnessing a hitherto "invincible" political system come down like a house of cards. Liu Shang's Lady Wen-chi has become merely a helpless female whose terror and hardship are soothed by an apparent restoration of everything deprived her while she was in exile. Liu Shang's smug affirmation of the power of Chinese culture transformed the late Han type of Ts'ai Yen, and at this point in its literary evolution the figure of Ts'ai Yen as an individual (the character *type*) was decisively separated from the issues and events which inspired the original poems.

Liu Shang's version, with its happy ending, was the inspiration for many later poets, and also became the subject and even the text for a number of paintings, particularly narrative handscrolls.[18] The Sung poet and statesman Wang An-shih (1021–86) wrote a poem sequence entitled "Eighteen Songs of a Nomad Flute" in which the figure of Ts'ai Yen corresponds to the type as presented by Liu Shang rather than to the tougher-minded original.[19] The happy ending of the story and the refurbished type of the protagonist gained new significance under the first emperor of the Southern Sung, Kao-tsung (r. 1127–61). Before his consolidation of the Southern Sung, Kao-tsung himself had been a hostage of the Chin Tatars, along with his wives, his father (the emperor Hui-tsung [r. 1101–26]), and his brother, Ch'in-tsung (r. 1126). Kao-tsung was the only one of these to return to China. When Kao-tsung's mother was finally returned to China in 1142, the endurance of the happy ending was ensured in the tradition, in painting and poetry.[20]

The grimmer archetype of Ts'ai Yen established in "Poem of Affliction" survived in the character role, which was adapted to the cases of other women either to give depth to historical figures such as the Han noblewoman Wang Chao-chün, or to address contemporary issues, particularly the impact of political instability and war on innocent civilians—or at least innocent aristocratic civilians. While the background of the historical Wang Chao-chün is quite different from Ts'ai Yen's, two crucial similarities encouraged poets to borrow from Ts'ai Yen's imagery and characterization to achieve the desired effects. Like Ts'ai Yen, Wang Chao-chün was forced to marry a barbarian chieftain and live among the nomads far from her homeland; and Wang Chao-chün was also a helpless and circumstantial victim of a diplomatic crisis, though not a victim of war and the kind of violence associated with Ts'ai Yen. Within these broad correspondences the details of Wang Chao-chün's background and experience make her a distinctive character. Wang Chao-chün (also known as Wang Ming-chün) was an obscure concubine of the emperor Han Yüan-ti (r. 48–32 B.C.). The legend states that the ladies of his household were so numerous that the emperor commissioned a painter to make portraits of all of them so that he might better allocate his attentions among them. The painter deliberately painted an unflattering portrait of Wang Chao-chün because she refused to bribe him to improve on her beauty. When the chief of the Hsiung-nu requested a royal bride from China as part of a pacification treaty, the emperor selected her because of the homely portrait. The lady was then discovered to be, of course, the loveliest of the concubines, but while the emperor regretted his choice he was obliged to stick by his bargain.

Like Ts'ai Yen, whose reputation as a literary archetype rests on two crises in her life—her experiences in exile and her challenge to Ts'ao Ts'ao's condemnation of Tung Ssu—which tend to be treated as independent of one another, the reputation of Wang Chao-chün rests on either the lady's defiance of the portrait painter and the emperor's poignant realization of lost romance or on the tragedy of the Chinese lady languishing, however luxuriously, in barbarian captivity.[21] The Chin courtier and wealthy racketeer Shih Ch'ung (249–300) concentrated on the theme of exile—the sense of isolation, estrangement, and despair of the Chinese aristocrat—in his narrative poem "Song of Wang Ming-chün."[22] Shih Ch'ung ignored the romantic possibilities of the circumstances under which the lady was chosen, and even the incident of the painter, in favor of the calamity of her fate, her helplessness, and her total alienation from her new environment. In his prose preface he also outlines the circumstances under which such a narrative would have been written, and in describing them explains his own source of inspiration:

> When the Hsiung-nu were flourishing, they asked the Chinese emperor Han Yüan-ti for a bride. In the Inner Palace there was a girl of good family called Ming-chün, and she was given to them in marriage in order to cement the treaty. On a previous occasion, when a woman had been given to the Wu-sun tribe, a *p'i-p'a* musician accompanied her on horseback, playing music in order to alleviate her feelings of homesickness. When they sent Ming-chün into exile, this must [also] have been the case, for she composed a song full of sounds of sadness. I have subsequently composed one like it.[23]

Shih Ch'ung's Wang Ming-chün evokes the role of Ts'ai Yen in events and emotions, with some modifications because she is an unwilling bride given by treaty rather than snatched by force during a rebellion. Wang Ming-chün's fright, alienation, and frustration about the value of her life of shame remind us of Ts'ai Yen's emotions in exile:

> My misery wounded me to the very vitals,
> My tears soaked my vermilion tassels . . .
> I could never feel at home with folk of such different kind,
> No matter how much honor I had, for me there was no glory
>   in it
>
> (lines 7–8, 13–14)

Several images in this poem echo those associated with Ts'ai Yen. The drawn-out farewells, down to the horses' apparent sympathy with Wang Chao-chün's reluctance to leave China (lines 3–6) remind us of Ts'ai Yen's departure from the steppe, when she was taking leave of her children ("Poem of Affliction," lines 73–80). Overwhelmed by terror and strangeness, neither lady can decide whether death is preferable to life among the nomads ("Song of Wang Ming-chün," lines 17–20; "Poem of Affliction," lines 37–38; "Eighteen Songs," poem 2). Wang Chao-chün watches the flight of the wild geese in order to tell the passing of the seasons and imagines communication with home, as Ts'ai Yen does in poem 9 of "Eighteen Songs of a Nomad Flute." In contrast to Ts'ai Yen, the story of Wang Chao-chün ends, geographically, in exile—she is said to have committed suicide when she was told after her husband's death that she would be married to her husband's son, an ordeal which Ts'ai Yen survived. Wang Chao-chün's lament ends with her longing for death and her desire to leave her special tale for later readers:

> It is hardly worth the time to rejoice for the morning flower,
> It would be sweeter to be among the autumn grasses.
> I tell this tale for people of later generations:
> Married in an alien land, my feelings are bitter indeed!
>
> (lines 27–30)

The main interest of Shih Ch'ung's poem is the reaction of a refined Chinese to the strange, harsh, and hostile land and society of the nomads. As first-person narrator, the lady bewails her displacement and sense of apathy in a position of great honor among the Hsiung-nu: "They received me in a vast tent / And granted me the title of 'Yen-chih'" (lines 11–12). The role resembles Ts'ai Yen's because of the geography and the place of the lady in nomad society, but the type is different because of the circumstances from which they came into exile. While Ts'ai Yen certainly felt a deep sense of personal shame over her experience, her emotions are more afflicted by the violence she has witnessed and endured. Wang Chao-chün is a victim not of violence but of calculated and impersonal politics. While her new home is dreadfully crude by her standards, she is not physically threatened, and while she is separated from her home and family, they are not destroyed. Ts'ai Yen's endurance of grief transcends her personal resentment in a lament for the destruction of the whole Han order. In contrast, Wang Chao-chün as an exile is an isolated case, and so seems ultimately self-centered. The imagery of exile and the expressions of loneliness and alienation are very similar in "Poem of Affliction," "Eighteen Songs of a Nomad Flute," and "Song of Wang Ming-chün," but the narrative presentation makes it clear that their characters are not similar at all. The configuration of events and the women's verbal responses to them are closely related, but because of the context from which they have come to these circumstances, the underlying motivation of the characters is revealed as different and distinctive. Seen in their entirety, the particularity of the circumstances helps to generate a sense of the individuality of these two figures in exile.

The comparison of the character of Ts'ai Yen as she appears in "Poem of Affliction" and Liu Shang's "Eighteen Songs of a Nomad Flute," and Shih Ch'ung's Wang Ming-chün illustrates the essential features of characterization in Chinese narrative poetry. Considering the relative brevity of the poems, these characters and the distinctions among them stand out with surprising clarity. Chinese techniques of characterization rely heavily on symbolic attributes which become attached to certain types (Ts'ai Yen's grief upon leaving behind her nomad children, for instance), imagery which is associated with some crucial aspect of a character's role (adjusting to a barbarian "husband," telling the passage of time by watching the migrations of the wild geese on the steppe), and direct discourse. These devices are well known from historiography, where all characters' actions have predetermined outcomes or consequences.[24] Narrative archetypes in poetry are also subject to this kind of determinism, and while narrative poetry may be less discursive than historiography, it displays the same techniques in its own idiom.

Because the narrative is so compressed in *shih*, the characterization must be more evocative—it must do as much, if not more, with less. The character is tersely but vividly sketched, relying on the reader's sense of empathy and knowledge of literary convention for understanding. But because of the concentrated significance of the elements which define a type, a role, or both in the process of evolution of an archetype, these components may be used in a hackneyed fashion and the character may become stilted. It is up to the poet to breathe new life into the basic configuration of character "traits" by reaffirming that character as a temporally grounded and significant figure, in other words, to preserve the recognizable features but also to make them new. We have seen how Liu Shang and others adapted the type of Ts'ai Yen to suit a more sentimental aesthetic and audience. Liu Shang co-opts the symbolic impact of the late Han heroine to the needs of mid-T'ang literary culture for reconciliation with the political order, but in doing so the essential character is subtly yet certainly changed. In general, adapting a character *role* to a new set of circumstances allows for a great deal more flexibility and topical significance because the character which emerges is not just compared with better-known ones. Instead, a new character arises combining the potency of the original archetype with the power of its own experiences and qualities. The poet may use allusive imagery and follow the basic configuration of events from the career of a character like Ts'ai Yen, but set the character and events in a new, topical context to demonstrate the continued vitality of the archetype.

Perhaps Ts'ai Yen's most effective literary descendant is Wei Chuang's "lady of Ch'in"—a poetic term for a female citizen of the capital, Ch'ang-an. A comparison of the "Song of the Lady of Ch'in" with "Poem of Affliction" reveals the continued life of the archetype of Ts'ai Yen, its broader significance in the light of the more cosmopolitan world of the late T'ang dynasty, and, perhaps most important, a sense of a tradition of poems in this style which reaffirms the truth of Ts'ai Yen's experience as an archetype in Chinese culture. Her role is preserved, along with the themes of rebellion, impersonal violence, sexual exploitation, loss of self in a strange environment, loss of self in a familiar environment which has been changed by violence, and the comprehensive inversion of known society as a great dynasty falls.

Wei Chuang revives the archetype, evoking the Tung Cho Rebellion by relating contemporary events in the context of the Huang Ch'ao Rebellion (874–884), which presaged the final fall of the T'ang dynasty in 905.[25] "Song of the Lady of Ch'in" was written in Loyang perhaps in the spring of 884, after Wei Chuang had fled Ch'ang-an and escaped the fury of Huang Ch'ao's occupation. The poem was said to have been based on his own experience (Wei Chuang was in Ch'ang-an waiting to sit the *chin-shih* examinations when Huang Ch'ao's troops descended), and is unusual both as autobiography and history. While narrative poems containing political criticism were by no means unknown, they were usually couched either in allegorical or symbolic terms, or at least written from a safe distance in time. Tu Fu's "Lament by the Riverside," for instance, sets the romance which caused the fall of the emperor Hsüan-tsung in the context of the Han emperor Ch'eng-ti's fatal passion for his consort Chao Fei-yen; while Po Chü-yi's "Song of Everlasting Sorrow" was written in 808—half a century after the An Lu-shan Rebellion—and still refrains from overt criticism of the main characters. "Song of the Lady of Ch'in" was composed directly after Huang Ch'ao's sack of the capital in 880–81, and Wei Chuang makes no attempt to disguise the event in any way.[26] And where Ts'ai Yen lays the blame for the downfall of the Han emperor's righteous rule on the rebel Tung Cho, Wei Chuang describes a court panicked, its members unhesitatingly sacrificing the populace to save their own skins. Wei Chuang's only concession to the convention of removing himself from the context of topical political criticism is the use of a narrative frame in which the poet as narrator encounters a victim of the rebellion—the lady of Ch'in—in a peaceful landscape a good distance from the fallen capital. The narrator assumes the role of questioner, leaving the bulk of the narration to be presented from the point of view of the lady:

In the third year of the Chung-ho reign, the third month of
the spring,
Outside Loyang's city walls the blossoms massed like snow;
East, west, south, north the people on the road had
vanished,
The green willows were quiet and still, the fragrant dust had
settled.
At the roadside I suddenly came upon a lady like a flower—
Alone she had gone to the green willows, and sat down to
rest in the shade.
Her phoenix clasp was tilted, bell-bird hairpins askew,
lock-ends falling every which way,
Her rouge smeared off, her brow paint beaded, the line of her
eyebrows broken.
"Young lady, where have you come from?" I asked.
She composed her features and started to speak, but her
voice first broke into a sob,
So she turned her head to adjust her sleeves, then
courteously answered me.
"Swept along by the waves of rebellion, how can I bear to
speak of it?"

("Song of the Lady of Ch'in," lines 1–12)[27]

The frame of this initial encounter of the primary narrator (the
poet) and the lady establishes a context in which the tale of Huang
Ch'ao's sack of Ch'ang-an may be told from the point of view of
an anonymous eyewitness. The lady's disheveled appearance prepares the reader for a tale of violence; it is obvious from her natural
distinction that this is not her proper state. After the preliminary
courtesies are exchanged, the lady plunges into the tale in earnest,
and the presence of the poet is forgotten until the last couplet. Even
then he himself does not speak, but is directly addressed by the
lady:

"I pray you, Sir, to raise your oars and go farther and farther
east
And chant this long song as an offering to His Excellency of
Chin-ling."

(lines 237–38)

Within this frame the lady also uses framing devices and description to introduce other points of view, with the intention of revealing the universal destruction brought on the Chinese people by their careless rulers. The violence and alienation of exile which tormented Ts'ai Yen are even more sinister here because the inversion of the known world of the lady of Ch'in takes place suddenly and violently *in* her known world: the city which has been her home and the center of the empire is transformed overnight into a frightening wilderness. Most important, the Chinese themselves, as rebels against the government, are mercilessly revealed to be no better than the barbarians they despise.

The lady briefly describes the calm before the storm, then the complete helplessness of the undefended city as the rebels approach (lines 17–32). Deserted by the emperor and his entourage (line 31), the city is sacked and much of the populace slaughtered (lines 33–84). The lady is captured, laments her loss, and details her life with the rebels—which includes, of course, a new "husband":

> From that time on I could never again return to my old ward,
> From that time on there was no place I might look to find my
> kinfolk;
> It has been three years since I first fell into the rebels'
> hands,
> Each day I have trembled and grieved, with my heart and
> courage broken.
> At night when I rested a thousand ranks of swords and
> spears surrounded;
> At the morning meal, each taste seemed like slivered human
> livers.
> Although I "entered the curtains of marriage," how could I
> enjoy "marital bliss?"
> Although I had plenty of precious goods, they were not
> things I could enjoy.
> His hair unkempt, his face filthy, his eyebrows bright red!
> If I gave the man even a sidelong glance, I still could not bear
> the sight.
> His clothing was put on inside out, the language he spoke
> was uncouth,

On his face there were boasts of his deeds—the words being
   tattooed there!

(lines 89–100)

The details of the lady's captivity and sexual exploitation are
far more complete than Ts'ai Yen's descriptions, with even a bris-
tling description of her husband, not as a person but as a caricature
of the physical and moral repulsiveness of the rebels. Nor is the
lady disconcerted merely by strange customs: in their attempts to
administer the imperial government in the capital city itself, the
rebels desecrate Chinese society with their parodic rituals (lines
101–8). After the rebels repel an imperial relief force, the lady con-
templates the wasteland that was her home, combining Ts'ai Yen's
emotional desolation as reflected in the landscape of the steppe and
the landscape of her razed village:

Ch'ang-an lies so still, so still; what is left there now?
Ruined markets, desolate streets where shoots of wheat are
   sprouting,
For firewood they chopped down the last of the trees that
   bloomed in the Apricot Gardens,
For building their fortress they doomed the willows along the
   Imperial Canal.
Splendid coaches with paint-patterned wheels were all
   smashed and scattered,
Of the mansions with their vermilion gates, not even half
   survive.
On the floor of the Han-yüan Audience Hall foxes and rabbits
   roam,
The approach to the Hua O Tower is filled up with brambles
   and thorns.
The luxury of former times—now all destroyed and buried;
A dreary waste as far as the eye can see—not a single familiar
   thing there.
The Imperial Treasury was burned to the very ash of its
   brocades and embroideries,
On the Street of Heaven were trampled to dust the bones of
   State Officials.

(lines 135–46)

When the lady of Ch'in finally leaves Ch'ang-an, now become a wasteland of famine as well as rebellion (lines 147–216), she finds that the surrounding country has suffered as much as the city, and more—an old man tells her that his family and lands were first pillaged by the rebels and then by the imperial troops to which he had looked for salvation (lines 189–216). He gives words to the lady's realization of the true nature and extent of this disaster:

> ". . . But that one person should suffer—alas!—How should
>   that be my only lament?
> For in the mountains are ever more, thousands and
>   thousands of families:
> By day hunger gnaws them as they hunt wild raspberries on
>   the hillsides,
> By night they shelter with the frost, sleeping on reeds and
>   flowers."
> I heard this poor old father's heart-rending words;
> For the rest of the day I cried and cried, my tears flowed
>   down like rain.

> (lines 213–18)

The lady finally asks the poet to tell her story to "the marquis of Chin-ling," with whom she hopes to find refuge: perhaps a compliment to Chou Pao, the commander of the naval forces on the lower Yangtze at the time of the rebellion, with whom Wei Chuang himself is said to have found safety.[28] Wei Chuang's lady is a survivor, clear-eyed and unsentimental in her account of events, sensitive in her observations of others, bitterly vivid in her description of the collapse of the power which ordered her whole world. The poem, however, is ultimately not centered on an individual consciousness; Wei Chuang has made the tale of one unnamed individual a lament for the whole empire. While the lady of Ch'in may be regarded as a mouthpiece for the poet in recording his own experience, through imagery and action his vision is extended to embrace the whole northern region of China. By evoking the tradition of Ts'ai Yen, Wei Chuang gives his poem almost a fin-de-siècle consciousness; and his vision indeed presents the end of Ch'ang-an as a capital in Chinese history.[29]

The techniques of description and direct discourse necessary to characterization in narrative *shih* were also present in personal *fu*, where they were used to convey the poet's particular, not universalized, concerns. In narrative *shih* these techniques are carried further, to develop individuals whose personal identity is not necessarily that of the poet. The use of character types and character roles helps to ensure that the poet, as well as the reader, will be separated from the experience of the text. Character thus imparts to narrative a kind of experience which is distinct from lyric, where the tendency is to suppress the particular source of the emotions inspired. Furthermore, a distinctive character such as Ts'ai Yen as narrator rather than poet invokes the lyrical convention of apprehending a poet's personality through a poem and redirects it to shed light on *her* self, as an independent figure in her own right. Thus, the convention of reading to reveal the self of the poet can be considered an essential aspect of characterization in the Chinese tradition, co-opting this critical convention to refer not to the poet but to the narrator or other characters in the poem. The personality of the *narrator*, rather than that of the poet, is central to "Poem of Affliction" and "Eighteen Songs of a Nomad Flute." This is true also of explicitly autobiographical poems such as Po Chü-yi's "Ballad of the *p'i-p'a*," where the sub-prefect of Chiang-chou—the poet as he sees himself in exile—asserts his centrality throughout. In the case of "Song of the Lady of Ch'in," the poet's use of the narrative frame removes him from center stage and refocuses the reader's attention on the lady as she narrates the traumatic experience of the poet's entire generation.

The methods of characterization in Chinese narrative poetry, however, must also depend upon a strong sense of specific temporal context for characters as individuals—not just generalized archetypes. Without a sense of temporal context and development, the most detailed description, the most passionate speech, will be detached from the sense of particular experience which is the essence of narrative experience. To have a sense of a "whole" character is to have a sense of the individual development of that character, which implies a process of development over time. Relying on the power of narrative archetypes, character development in Chinese narrative poetry may indeed become schematic; however, even if a character type or role is evoked merely by allusion, the recollection of the archetype provides a sense of character fully developed in another context. Whether character development is a process which depends on a sense of objective time or temporal progression, realization of a character is founded on that individual's existence in time, and as such must be analyzable over time. The sequential structures of narrative *shih* reflect these concerns, and their methods of presentation adapt meter and syntax to accommodate these peculiar expressive needs.

4

Narrative Structure
Temporal and Other Sequences

We have seen how the presence of explicit points of view reinforces the essentially vicarious nature of narrative, and how description may enhance the particularity of events, characters, and temporal context. To these subjective features we may add the order in which a reader encounters the elements of experience presented in a poem. It follows, therefore, that techniques of sequencing on a large scale are vital to narrative. This chapter will consider how the ordering of experience influences the structure of Chinese narrative poems, and what this means for the way we read them. In chapter 1 it was suggested that enumeration may serve the demands of narrative expression when the units or elements to be enumerated involve actions, events, or temporal references. The order of events as related by the narrator determines the underlying structure of a narrative poem. The most obvious structure for a persuasively logical sequence of events is one based on objective time, and indeed

Chinese and Western critics have recognized temporal sequence as an essential aspect of narrative composition.[1] A narrative structure based on temporal sequence provides a framework for events apart from the personal experience of the reader. Depending upon the aims of the composition, the framework of objective time can be manipulated for different effects.[2] In the simplest form a strictly chronological organization recounts events in the order in which they supposedly occurred, as in Ts'ai Yen's "Poem of Affliction." While the author of this poem did not place equal emphasis on all events, the events are ordered chronologically from the point of view of the narrator. The reader assumes that the events are related from hindsight, rather than as they occur, but there is minimal internal evidence beyond the naming of Tung Cho's rebellion as the cause of the lady's displacement. Shih Ch'ung employed a variation of this structure by including a prose preface with his "Song of Wang Ming-chün." The preface, in the poet's voice, stands outside the poem, which is in the voice of the lady. The preface gives a brief synopsis of the background of the exile, then the temporal context of Shih Ch'ung's composition of his poem in the style of the "original": "she composed a poem full of sounds of sadness. I have subsequently composed one like it, thus . . . ." The lady as narrator then relates her sorrows in the order in which they occurred, ending in the present tense, still in hopeless exile.

A more complex temporal structure in narrative *shih* employs the technique of framing to organize events in a poem. Po Chü-yi included a prose preface giving the precise date and context of the composition of "Ballad of the *p'i-p'a*," then organized the events of that night in three narrative tableaux. These reflect the chronology of the experience from the narrator's point of view, but in terms of objective time they move from the present of the party on the river to the sad events of the past, and back again. The musician's tale of her past life is interpolated by indirect quotation into the body of the narrative, and then the narrator-poet himself reaches back in time in order to explain his present affinity with her.

Shen Ch'üan-ch'i employs a less elaborate version of this system of narrative tableaux in "My Reply to the Troll: A Letter to Send to My Family." The contextual frame provides the poet with a questioner to whom he can unburden himself with an exile's lament. In this case the frame of the exchange with the troll (lines 1–12) gives the poet an excuse for a detailed autobiographical narrative, relating chronologically the events which led him to this desolate place. While a temporal sequence based on objective time, chronological or not, may seem to be the most logical—even the only possible—structure for a narrative poem, we have seen that in the Chinese tradition it is enumeration, not plot or temporality in themselves, which provides a basis for the organization of events in a poem. In other words, while temporal sequence may emerge from sequences of other kinds, the primary motive of organization in a Chinese poem may be some other kind of sequence or progression entirely. This is not to say that temporal sequence is devoid of interest or significance; rather, it is simply not conceived to be the primary focus of poetic composition and execution. For instance, in the stanzaically organized "Hsia Wu," from the *Shih Ching*, each stanza contains an event from the king's career, and the sense of progression from one event to the next is achieved by organizing the stanzas linked by catenation. The order of events does happen to be chronological, but the effect of this order of events is to bring each event to bear with equal weight on the people's relation to the political order as established by King Wu, rather than to recount his deeds for their own sake. "Wen Wang yu sheng" is also divided into stanzas, which are unified by the use of a variable refrain as much as by the order of the deeds of the kings. In this case the movement of events is actually chronologically *backward*, again to explain "the way we are now" from the point of view of the people. In this sense both of these poems from the *Shih Ching* manipulate a narrative of events to describe the background of a present tradition rather than to enshrine the deeds of the past. The main interest of these poems is not in the *narrative*, but in contemporary social patterns and conventions; not in the myth behind these patterns, but in the rituals said to have been the results of these events.[3] Temporal sequence as the generator of plot or story is therefore not of primary interest in these poems. Their underlying sequential structure either manipulates temporal references as partial means to an end, or perhaps produces the temporal sequence as a by-product of their expressive intent. Although this use of the stanzaic form is rare in long, unified, narrative *shih*, catenation and the repetition of characters and key phrases as seen in the stanzaic poems of the *Shih Ching* are used to enforce a sense of connection between events. More particularly, these techniques are crucial to the impression of narrative in a style of *shih* which employs many of these stanzaic techniques, the poem sequence.

Other major genres suggest patterns of organization which are not strictly temporal in themselves, but which may enforce a sense of temporal progression in a text. The poems of the *Ch'u Tz'u*, especially those termed *itineraria*, are structured by patterns that are supposed to be more dependent on the ritual movements associated with shamanism than on strictly temporal progressions. The speaker's "journey" through the cosmos, because of its ritualistic intent, is not so much temporal as accretive, in the sense that by following the conventions of this ritual the shaman accrues potency to meet his or her divine "lover," and the flights through the cosmos detailed in the poems occur under this accumulated spiritual power. Time enters into these compositions explicitly only when the communion is over and the earthbound poet laments that the experience was of too short a duration.[4]

Patterns other than time may be inferred from natural phenomena and used as the structural basis for poetic sequence. Compass directions or astronomical patterns may complement or even dominate temporal sequence in narrative *shih*.[5] This type of order is also frequently used in *fu*, especially of the "capital city" type, in which the four corners of the empire are encompassed and united under the harmonious rule of the emperor in his proper place in the cosmos.

It is clear that there are many kinds of sequences in Chinese literature. While narrative seems to emerge from certain sequences, it does not necessarily emerge from every kind.[6] Let us consider first the case of poem sequences, which display aspects of the principle of enumeration (as noted in the case of the stanzaic poems of the *Shih Ching*) in combination with the requirements of the prosody of *shih* as they developed in the later Han dynasty. Poem sequences, while by no means always narrative, may have an underlying structure which evokes progression over objective time. A poem *sequence* is a group of poems by a single author or by two or even more poets intended to be read together in a specified order. The integrity of a poem sequence is dependent on this prescribed order of presentation. A poem sequence by a single author is sustained throughout by a single voice or point of view, as in the sequence "Poems Presented to Prince Piao of Pai-ma" ("*Tseng Pai-ma Wang Piao*"), by Ts'ao Chih, or Tu Fu's "Autumn Meditations" ("*Ch'iu hsing*").[7] Those with two or more authors vary in point of view as the pen changes hands, as in the exchange between Wang Wei and his friend P'ei Ti (b. 716), the "Wang Stream Collection" ("*Wang ch'üan chi*"). A framework of objective time may be implied in a composition because poem sequences are usually based on a particular experience. In the case of a single author this experience is presented as a set of observations from a single point of view, while in sequences with two or more authors the variety of points of view is unified by the context of shared experience.[8]

It is important to note the difference between a poem sequence and a poem *series*. A series is not conceived in terms of an underlying unified *structure*, but rather in terms of a unifying *theme*. In contrast with a sequence, the poems in a series may be reordered without detriment to the integrity of the composition as a whole. Poems collected under a single heading, such as "Poems on Historical Subjects" ("*Yung-shih shih*"), by Wang Ts'an (177–217), and *Poems Expressing My Feelings* ("*Yung-huai shih*"), by Juan Chi (210–263), were not conceived in terms of a prescribed sequence.[9] These series are groups of poems on various subjects which reflect a general theme, usually suggested by the title. Juan Chi's poems are bound by a general expressive purpose, but the individual poems vary widely in subject matter and tone, and also in length and diction. Tu Fu's "Thoughts on Ancient Sites" ("*Yung-huai ku-yi wu shou*") have a more unified purpose. They follow the poet's visits to a variety of places of historical interest, which are described in terms of the significance these sites and the people associated with them have for the poet himself. While this series is unified in terms of subject matter (touring the ancient monuments) and theme (the evocative power of these places for the poet's evaluation of his own plight), their order of presentation is not significant: neither the chronology of the poet's journey nor the

relative dates of the sites suggest an underlying sequential structure for these poems. They function as an anthology on a single
theme or group of related themes, bound together by expressive
purpose but not by formal or sequential structure.[10]

A poem sequence shows consistency in style and purpose
from one poem to the next. The same meter is employed throughout, even if all the poems in the sequence are not of the same
length. It is a crucial technical feature of the poem sequence that,
while the poems in their set order function as an artistic whole and
convey a logical progression of events, each poem must have its
own value and integrity as a lyric. Poem sequences lay out a chain
of events not by integrating the individual units into a single, narrative poem, but by presenting a set sequence of lyric vignettes,
which considered as an integrated composition convey sequential
unity.[11] On the level of poetic diction the individual lyrics may be
firmly set in the desired order of experience by interlocking characters, catenation, rhymes, or other kinds of repetition, which in
turn reinforce the logic of the temporal sequence implied by their
order.

I say "implied" because the specific context of the experience
of a poem sequence is not always included in the sequence itself.
In the case of Ts'ao Chih's "Poems Presented to Prince Piao of Pai-
ma," the precise date and context of the events described in the
composition are recorded in an attached prose preface. The preface,
though written in the first person, almost certainly was not written
by Ts'ao Chih himself. It does not appear in the earliest extant
text and has been identified as a fourth-century editor's addition.[12]
The fact that the preface was attached, however, suggests that the
editor was impressed by the particularizing details of the sequence
describing a well-known personal crisis in the colorful life of Ts'ao
Chih, and I quote it here as the best synopsis:

> In the fourth month of the fourth year of the Huang-chu reign
> period (223), the Prince of Pai-ma, the Prince of Jen-ch'eng
> (Ts'ao Chang), and I went together to the Imperial Court in
> the capital. When we met to celebrate the seasonal festival, the
> Prince of Jen-ch'eng died. In the seventh month, the Prince of
> Pai-ma and I were to return to our fiefs, but later an officer in-

formed us that we two princes should lodge separately while traveling to our domains. We deeply resented these insinuations, especially because our great parting was but a few days away. I seized the opportunity to open my heart as we said our farewells, and wrote these pieces in frustration.[13]

The poem sequence contains seven five-character-line poems in the *shih* meter. The number of lines in the poems varies from ten to fourteen, each poem sustaining a single rhyme in the even-numbered lines.[14] With the exception of the first two, all the poems are linked by the repetition of the last two characters of one poem as the first two characters of the next. All the poems consistently have an implicit first-person speaker (the preface uses a first-person pronoun but there are none in the poems), and the continuity of the point of view is reinforced by catenation. The linking characters indicate the necessary order of the poems in the sequence. Each poem describes the poet's feelings and responses to the landscape at a different stage in his journey, a chronological sequence which corresponds to the formal order of the poems.

The first poem, which is not linked to the others by catenation, is also distinct in its treatment of the subject matter. Here Ts'ao Chih gives a swift overview of his predicament, then describes his last, heartbroken look at the capital:

> When visiting the Emperor I lodged in the Ch'eng-ming
>   quarters,
> Then forthwith returned from the capital to my former
>   domains.
> In the clear dawn I set out from the Imperial City;
> When the sun was setting, I passed by Shou-yang
>   Mountain . . .
> I turn back my head and gaze, yearning for the city's towers,
> I crane my neck for one last glance, my feelings within me are
>   wounded.
>
> (poem 1, lines 1–4, 9–10)

The first poem deals with the cause of the poet's unhappiness and reveals his inmost wishes: to stay in the capital with his family united. Because of the jealous suspicions of his elder brother, the emperor Wei Wen-ti, the other princes of the blood were only allowed to congregate in the presence of the emperor, and otherwise were distributed in fiefs well separated all over the empire. In the first poem, therefore, Ts'ao Chih casts one last look on all his hopes, then in the next poem turns to the journey into exile. The landscape of his travels reflects the poet's unhappiness: it is all hardship and obstacles. While the cause of his misery is established in the first poem, it is subsequently amplified and compounded by the rigors of the road. Having turned his back on his last fantasy of family reconciliation, the poet concentrates on the road ahead.

The journey from this turning point to the point of his final parting from his brother gives the poems their underlying sequential structure. This sequence is further enforced as each poem, while representing progress on the journey, also reflects the progress of the poet's emotions. In the first poem he regrets his departure from the capital and all that this implies for his family. In poem 2, with only one brother as companion and knowing they too must part, Ts'ao Chih confronts the hard and lonely road leading away from their proper home:

> How vast the Great Valley seems!
> Dense and deep green are the trees on the mountains.
> Unceasing rains have turned my road to mud,
> The draining waters wash out the land in all directions.
>
> (poem 2, lines 1–4)

They are entering unknown territory: "At the crossroads, the tracks of the carts leave off" (poem 2, line 5). His fellowship with the prince of Pai-ma is threatened from this point, as the ill-omened images of poem 3 suggest: "Tufted-ear owls cry on our crossbars / Wolves bar our way at the crossroads" (poem 3, lines 7–8). As the sun sets in poem 4, the poet observes the animals in the landscape returning to their rightful place, in sad contrast with the two princes:

> How lonely and barren are the plains—
> The white sun is suddenly hidden in the west.
> Returning birds head for their lofty treetops,
> With a flurry of feathers they urge on their wings,

A lone beast chases in search of its herd,
Its mouth full of grass, it will not take time to eat.

(poem 4, lines 5–10)

Facing the inevitability of their parting in poem 5, the poet reflects on the hopeless separation between them and their brother who died in the capital. Since such a final separation is inevitable, why not accept this one? Yet the poet is unable to extinguish his longing: "Is this not the sentimental nonsense of our childhood? / But all in a rush, my yearning for my flesh and blood inspires me" (poem 6, lines 10–11). He tries to comfort himself with the thought that as long as the prince of Pai-ma is still alive there will be someone in the world who cares for him and understands his mind. But even this gleam of comfort is overshadowed by their foreboding that this is in fact their last meeting: "We part, never to meet again, / Now we clasp hands, where shall we have another chance?" (poem 7, lines 7–8).

Poems 1–4 make extensive use of visual imagery drawn from the harsh landscape to reflect the emotional state of the poet. Poems 5–7 are more discursive, as the poet abandons landscape description and meditates on the inevitability of death (poem 5), the intimation of death in the loneliness of exile (poem 6), and finally addresses his brother directly, "My prince, take care to cherish your jade body / We may yet enjoy a time together when our hair is yellow with age" (poem 7, lines 9–10). The poem sequence culminates in its own composition: "I check my tears, then turn to the long road / And taking out my pen, write out these verses of farewell" (poem 7, lines 11–12). With such a reference to the act of composition itself, the poet asserts his intent to preserve the integrity of this particular experience, with all the details of his individual feelings. The sequence not only records the emotions of the poet but sets them in a specific and personal context. The temporal progression of the elements of the experience is stressed by the poet's reflections on the joys and sorrows of the past, his indignation and frustration in the present, and his fears for the future. These poems are not meant to stand as discrete laments, but to reveal a most particular poetic moment and poetic consciousness.

In terms of the style of treatment of their subject matter, the poem sequences written by individual authors seem to provide a satisfying balance between the unified sequential structure of a longer narrative poem and the concentrated expression of emotion typical of shorter, individual lyrics.[15] The form allows the poet to treat elements of particularized experience in sustained and unified form, while avoiding some of the technical difficulties of a long, explicitly narrative composition. Each poem in a sequence focuses on a different moment or aspect of an experience, allowing the poet to express a complex range of emotions in a unified context. While inviting the audience to sympathize with the particular experience, the sequence retains a sense of intimacy.

By contrast, the cumulative force of the sequential structure of long narrative poems like "Poem of Affliction," "Song of Everlasting Sorrow," and "Song of the Lady of Ch'in" presents a totally different kind of experience. Even an "intimate" experience like the night of music in "Ballad of the *p'i-p'a*" enforces the reader's separation from the experience by the poet's assertion of his centrality and uniqueness. In my discussion of "Ballad of the *p'i-p'a*," I divided the poem into three parts, based on the poet's manipulation of point of view, to show how the mode of description so vital to lyric poetry could be adapted to serve the needs of narrative expression. By virtue of their sequential relation and the intent of the poet, those three sections—the poet's initial encounter with the lady and her first performance, the lady's tale of her life, and the poet's response to her experience by telling his own feelings—form three narrative tableaux. By identifying a shift in point of view or focus of action, rather than a shift in rhyme or language, we may recognize the main divisions of the experience and understand the purpose of their organization. Po Chü-yi's "Song of Everlasting Sorrow" is organized according to the same principle, using narrative tableaux to focus on the three main phases of the emperor T'ang Hsüan-tsung's romance. This device balances the demands of a plot or sense of narrative progression with the features dearest to the virtuoso of *shih* lyrics, such as imagery, allusion, and description. Any sense of dynamism or action is secondary to the demands of atmosphere and emotion, and so the technique of narrative tableaux is ideal for adapting *shih* poetics to the narrative mode.

Technical considerations of meter and diction, parallelism,

and rhyme do not always work against the dynamic sequence of events. There are examples of narrative *shih* in which action provides the underlying structure, which the traditional devices of lyric serve primarily to reinforce. Most impressive in this regard is Wei Chuang's "Song of the Lady of Ch'in." It is not only the longest (238 seven-character lines) of the T'ang narrative *shih*, it is also a virtual showcase of the techniques of T'ang lyricism adapted to the demands of a unified, fully integrated narrative.[16] The structure of the poem may be analyzed according to the use of framing devices to present various points of view (there are four explicit speakers in this poem), and also according to poetic units identified by rhyme and syntax, including the style of quatrains and octets so dear to T'ang lyrics. As a result, while for the purposes of this analysis I have divided "Song of the Lady of Ch'in" into twelve main units according to subject matter, these units may be subdivided into smaller units, identified by parallelism or rhyme, each demonstrating its own internal logic. While we might think of the larger units of subject matter as narrative tableaux, the divisions between the units are not as obvious as the divisions in poems like "Song of Everlasting Sorrow." Indeed, these larger units of subject matter may be linked by rhyme, for instance, to the next section, resulting in a far more dynamic and tightly integrated structure than the poems organized into narrative tableaux that we have examined. Wei Chuang evidently took great pains to make his narrative units within the larger tableaux evoke standard T'ang quatrains and octets, with occasional striking couplets to vary the rhythm. This represents an important innovation in the adaptation of *shih* poetics to narrative expression, one that potentially combines features of both poem sequences and unified narrative *shih* from earlier periods. In "Song of the Lady of Ch'in" the poetic structure and the sequential structure of events are more completely integrated than in the other poems we have studied, suggesting a new awareness on the part of the poet of the importance of an underlying sense of structural as well as thematic unity for achieving narrative effects.

The first section (lines 1–16) is the poet's introduction of the lady who will relate the main body of the tale, and may be divided into four quatrains: lines 1–4 sketch the pastoral setting outside of peaceful Loyang; lines 5–8 describe the appearance of the lady; in lines 9–12 the poet and the lady exchange greetings; in lines 13–16 the lady invites the poet to hear her story. The story proper begins in the second section (lines 17–32), in which the lady provides the precise date of the arrival of the rebels in Ch'ang-an (line 17). The first quatrain (lines 17–20) describes the lady at her toilette as an image of the calm before the storm; then the dust rises for a moment of uncertainty (lines 21–28) before the full extent of the disaster is known:

> But an instant later my husband came galloping up, stopped
> at the house,
> Dismounted, then entered the gate and stood stunned like a
> drunken man.
> By chance he had met the Purple Imperial Coach in flight,
> covered with the dust of exile;
> Already he saw the rebels' white flags stream in from the
> land all around.
>
> (lines 29–32)

Section 3 (lines 33–84) describes the initial sack of Ch'ang-an. The stampede of the population of the city (lines 33–42) is mirrored by the stars stampeding in the heavens (lines 43–48), which in turn symbolize the rout of the court and imperial house, who have deserted the capital to save their own lives. The lady then turns back to the city as the slaughter of the civilians begins, first in general terms (lines 49–52), then more particularized, as the next four octets describe the fates of four of the lady's young neighbors, organized according to the four directions: the daughter of the eastern neighbor (lines 53–60), the daughter of the neighbor to the west (lines 61–68), the two daughters of the southern neighbor (lines 69–76), and the wife of the northern neighbor (lines 77–84). Each octet has an internal rhyme scheme, but the relation of the four units is reinforced by the nontemporal pattern of the four directions as well as the headlong rush of the rebels' onslaught. In section 4 (lines 85–108) the lady goes out to meet the rebels willingly, in order to preserve her life (lines 85–88), then in vignettes which strongly recall Ts'ai Yen she laments the loss of her home (lines 89–92) and describes her life among the rebels with her new "husband" (lines 93–100). This marriage, however, is only part of the larger, and far more serious, desecration perpetrated by the rebels on the state. In attempting to conduct the affairs of the imperial government, the ignorant rebels invert the proper order of their conduct in a way that is chilling, yet hilarious:

> On the Cypress Terrace, the "Censorate Scholars" had all
>   become fox spirits,
> At the Orchid Bureau the "Official Recorders" were all rat
>   demons;
> They kept trying to wear ornate hairpins in their short hair,
> But without taking off their robes of state, rolled themselves
>   in embroidered quilts.
> With ivory tablets held upside down, some aped the Three
>   Lords of State,
> Golden fish tail up and turned wrong way 'round, some
>   became "Historians of the Left and Right."
> In the morning I could hear them report to the Throne and
>   enter the audience chamber,
> In the evening I could see them go to the wine shops in a
>   brawl.
>
>   (lines 101–8)

This octet is particularly densely packed with action on the literal level and symbols of larger problems on the level of imagery. The description of the new imperial government is a series of parallel couplets forming two rhyming quatrains. The effect is brisk in pace and underlines the irony of the efforts of the rebels by reeling off their consistent inversion of their roles and even the symbols they have unlawfully adopted. The men who present themselves as the new "Censorate Scholars" and other ministers have no qualifications but their empty titles, and this is evident even in the way they carry the symbols of their usurped offices. The fact that the "Three Lords of State" carry their ivory tablets upside down is the final symbol of their perverse inversion of the proper order of the state: the rebels seem not to know that the round end (for heaven) should go up, the square (earth) end down—no wonder the empire is topsy-turvy!

Section 5 (lines 109–26) is an interlude in which a rumor of rescue by the imperial troops (lines 109–12) briefly exhilarates the captives and disconcerts their cowardly tyrants (lines 113–22), but hopes are dashed when the vanguard of the army meets with disaster (lines 123–26). Section 6 (lines 127–46) then proves that matters can indeed get worse, as Huang Ch'ao wreaks vengeance on the captive populace for their disaffection, and famine comes to the city. The description of the desolation of Ch'ang-an again recalls Ts'ai Yen's return to her home village, but with the added impact that the lady of Ch'in has been present all through the time her home has been transformed into a desert.

A new kind of temporal progress is established in section 7 (lines 147–54), as rebels and captives are forced by the famine to abandon the capital completely. On the first day out, their progress suggests that because of the ravages of the rebellion the boundaries between city and country have broken down; what distinction is there between the wasteland Ch'ang-an and the wastes outside its walls? On the second day out (section 8, lines 155–78), the desolation of the countryside extends farther (lines 155–58), but the lady begins to encounter others who have suffered from the rebellion. The lady, acting as questioner, provides a frame (lines 159–63) for the "speech" of an abandoned and impotent village idol, who laments that because he was powerless to save his people from the "nightmare demons" (*yen-kuei*) the times are lean for him (lines 163–74). The lady then begins to reflect on the larger implications of this spirit's impotence:

> When I heard this speech, my melancholy deepened—
> Heaven sends down calamity in due season, not of its own
> accord.
> If this spirit runs to the mountains in order to flee his danger,
> How can we turn accusing looks to the nobles of the East?
>   (lines 175–78)

In section 9 (lines 179–88) the refugees finally emerge from the Shensi plateau and begin the descent to Loyang. Seeing the peaceful landscape lifts their hopes of finding a virtuous government under which to live again. The lady then encounters another victim of the rebellion and hears his tale (section 10, lines 189–216), which reveals that the common people suffered as much at the hands of the imperial troops they expected to protect them as from the outrages of the rebels. The lady then turns her hopes to news of other provinces (section 11, lines 217–36); while the provinces to the east and west of the imperial domain have been devastated (lines 217–24), the news from a traveler from Chin-ling (Nan-ching) to the south holds some promise of peace (lines 225–36). The lady's final remark to the poet (lines 237–38) is also the poet's "dedication" of the poem to the marquis of Chin-ling. The poet's intent, however, is not just to compliment one patron. Wei Chuang has taken the tale of one individual and made it the basis of a lament for the whole empire. While the lady of Ch'in may be considered a mouthpiece for the poet in recording his own experience, through imagery and action he has extended his experience at least through the whole northern region of China. While the poet draws on autobiographical material, the ultimate purpose of "Song of the Lady of Ch'in" is to display that personal and highly individualized experience to the general public. The final dedicatory couplet suggests that the poem was intended to present the topical material to someone perhaps capable of bringing relief, but the direct appeal to the marquis of Chin-ling, rather than to the emperor, would not have been lost on his contemporary audience.

If the principle of enumeration is considered as it obtains in Wei Chuang's "Song of the Lady of Ch'in," it is possible to analyze the sequential structure of the poem on several levels that operate simultaneously as the poem is read. The kinds of sequences vary according to what we identify as the units to be enumerated. We have seen that the smallest units of action or description correspond to the units of lyrical expression, like the quatrains and octets of T'ang regulated verse. While there are units of six or as many as ten lines, so identified by their rhyme scheme, patterns of four- or eight-line units dominate the body of the poem. Occasionally a rhyme will carry over from one unit of subject matter to the next, as in the shift from the second to the third quatrain of the poem, the introduction of the lady (line 10 rhymes with lines 6 and 8, but there is a shift from description to dialogue at line 9). This has the effect of intensifying our sense of the flow of action, as the rhyme carries the reader over from one vignette of action to the next. This is a step beyond the effect of catenation in the poem sequences which, while enforcing a sense of sequence of action, also enforced the sense of separation between the units by calling attention overtly to the transition from one poem to the next.

These small units of metrical coherence make up the larger units based on a place or scene of action corresponding to the twelve narrative tableaux detailed above. The tableaux may in turn demonstrate an organization that is sequential but nontemporal. Progress in the narrative tableaux, or parts of them, may follow patterns such as the four directions; for instance, in section 3 the sack of the city is told by telling the fates of the neighbors to the east, west, south, and north (lines 53–84). Another kind of sequential structure is provided by the four narrative frames, two of which do correspond to two of the tableaux (section 8, the encounter with the local deity, the "Golden Spirit," lines 155–78; and section 10, the tale of the elderly householder, lines 189–216). The other two are the larger frames of the "autobiographical" account of the lady, detailing the events in nearly chronological order from the point of view of an eyewitness, and finally the frame of the poet-narrator, telling of how he came to hear this tale. This largest frame provides, as it were, a historical overview, or at least a view of events with poetic if not personal hindsight. It is Wei Chuang's only concession to the convention of presenting political criticism allusively, and a highly ironic one at that—why, after all this, should he bother to disguise himself? Before his own eyes the imperial government has proved to have no power to defend its very roots in the capital against unrighteous rebels and savages; how could it raise a hand against one insignificant poet?

Wei Chuang's "Song of the Lady of Ch'in" actually contains examples of all the styles of sequencing mentioned in this study, and thus should have posed a challenge to later poets adapting the conventions of lyrical expression to narrative. But Wei Chuang's sense of the risk of such a blatant piece of political criticism caught up with him. He did not include the poem in his own anthology of his *shih*, *Hua-chien chi*, and while known by reputation and one vivid couplet, the text was lost to the tradition until this century, when the excavations at Tun-huang uncovered the five manuscripts which form the basis of our reconstructions of the text.[17] "Song of the Lady of Ch'in" stands now as perhaps the crowning achievement of narrative *shih;* had the poem been preserved throughout the intervening centuries, narrative poetry after the T'ang might have taken a different course.

Epilogue

This model of the methods and properties of narrative expression in Chinese poetry is intended to shed light on the relation of lyrical expression to narrative expression, and to bring an important and previously neglected area of Chinese literature within the scope of comparative poetics. Whereas European narrative poetry displays distinctive generic features as well as the expressive concerns associated with narrative in general, the poems in the *shih* form discussed in this book cannot be identified as narrative by form or meter alone. The Chinese tradition allows us to recognize the extent to which European narrative theory depends upon these formal distinctions, and thus raises a possibility with wide-ranging implications for literary theory: that the narrative mode of expression can be analyzed without primary recourse to the demands of a particular poetic genre.

Central to the study of narrative poetry in China is the recognition that the dominant aesthetics of Chinese poetry are lyrical. From the Chinese critical tradition we have seen that lyrical expression is intended to be integrative, not only fostering the impression of affinity with the experience of a poem, but also with the personality of the poet who wrote it. Narrative, on the other hand, offers a kind of experience which, however enthralling or sympathetic, is essentially vicarious. Through the mediation of a narrator with an explicitly identified voice, the poet arouses curiosity for the significance of an experience which the reader cannot expect to reproduce. The affinity that is felt for the poet through the experience of lyric is in narrative turned to the narrator, who may be far removed from the poet. Considering the conventions of Chinese poetic language, this may be the most difficult of all illusions to maintain. The highly personalized, specific details of context necessary to preserve the experience of a poem as vicarious rather than integrative must be rigorously emphasized lest the tendency to a more universalized sense of experience compromise the specificity of narrative. The conventions of Chinese poetic language simply will not support the narrative mode of expression unless the poet displays through his use of language an intent to unify the poem as a particular and irreproducible experience. The expressive nature of Chinese poetic language may be adapted to the needs of narrative poetry, but only within the conventions of lyric. It may be only in prose fiction, where the poetic genres are fully integrated into a much larger narrative structure, that this tension ceases to be a major issue for the composition of poetry itself.

The features of narrative expression that have been described as they appear in and apply to *shih*, but whose implications transcend a single genre, are point of view, characterization, and sequence. Point of view as a feature of narrative *shih* has two vital components. The first is the identification of particular speakers to enforce the separation of the reader from the experience of the text. This explicit presence sets a specific context for the experience of the poem, which by virtue of its particularity is vicarious, resisting the reader's attempts to assume the experience personally. The second component of point of view is a logical consequence of establishing particular speakers and contexts, for its specificity allows the techniques of description so dear to Chinese poetry to be adapted from the objective mode of lyric to the subjective contexts of narrative. The passion for detail and description exhibited in all genres in Chinese literature is at least as important as temporal sequence in narrative *shih*, both for the sheer enjoyment of language and as a technique of enforcing narrative point of view and even narrative progression.

Characterization extends the technique of narrative point of view to refer unequivocally to a particular speaker or actor in a poem. Encouraging the reader to bring the knowledge acquired from the text to bear on these speakers or actors as individuals, rather than on the personality of the poet, enforces the specificity and vicarious nature of the experience. The creation of "unique" individuals in narrative also exploits the evocative power of Chinese poetic language in the creation and manipulation of archetypes, either as character "types" (distinctive traits which come to be associated with a particular individual) or as character "roles" (distinctive configurations of events which are recognizable even if applied to a variety of contexts). The same principles also allow the adaptation of literary allusion with all its evocative power to the needs of narrative.

Finally, a sense of logical, sequential relation of the elements of experience is essential in narrative *shih*. This is a feature not just of the genre of *shih* as it comes into its own from the late Han through T'ang dynasties, but of earlier forms as well. The stanzaic poems from the *Shih Ching* are unified by such linking devices as catenation as well as by subject matter, and these poetic devices enhance the sense of progression of events in time and space. The genre of *fu* provides other models of sequence by virtue of the principle *fu*, "enumeration," which is said to have given the genre its name. Within the *fu* genre the kinds of sequences established may make the difference in generic designations, as between "descriptive" *fu* and "personal" *fu*. From the roots of sequence in the principle of enumeration, it is clear that temporal sequences are but a subset of the larger category of poetic sequences. Other features of sequential structure besides temporal references, like catenation, rhyme, and larger metrical units, may contribute as much to the dynamism of a poem as a sense of temporal progression could. While a poem like "Song of the Lady of Ch'in" has a definite temporal sequence according to the historical relation of events, the narrative *progression* is carried along as much by the sequence of small metrical units such as quatrains and octets as by a sense of objective time. Indeed, within the lady's lament the sense of objective time is often eclipsed by other patterns, such as the order of celestial bodies or compass directions. All of these kinds of sequences are in play simultaneously in the experience of the text, giving a sense of complexity which a more straightforward, chronological structure could never impart alone. Indeed, the use of a structure which relies on the resonance of so many kinds of sequences is a challenge to the very idea of objective time as the basis of narrative.

By delineating the fundamental expressive qualities of lyric and narrative compositions, and identifying the techniques whereby narrative expression is achieved in a tradition of lyrical aesthetics, I have attempted to provide a theoretical basis for a literary history of Chinese narrative poetry. Such a history would otherwise be difficult to imagine, though not because the narrative mode of expression in *shih* was not recognized. It is the growth of concern for narrative theory that raises the question of the "narrativity" of these works, whose properties were previously recognized more intuitively than analytically, and whose qualities were happily taken for granted in their native tradition. When considered in a comparative context, the peculiarity of the Chinese model is so striking as to baffle the methods and principles of analysis which have served for the European traditions. This should justify, even demand, a search for an approach to narrative that is truly cross-cultural, one that recognizes underlying principles which transcend the formal and generic considerations familiar from traditional Western criticism.

Appendix

Four Translations

Poem of Affliction (Ts'ai Yen?, late second–early third century)

In the later phases of the Han, when it lost hold of its power,
Tung Cho rebelled against the abiding principles of Heaven:[1]
He had a perverted ambition to usurp his ruler's place,
But first he murdered all the worthy men and the wise and noble
    lords.
He forced a migration to the old imperial capital,[2]   5
He got control of his lord and exploited him to make himself
    strong.
The empire rose up with forces of resistance,

---

1 Tung Cho assassinated the emperor Han Shao-ti in 189, after he had reigned only
  four months.
2 Tung Cho forced his puppet emperor, Han Hsien-ti, to move the capital from
  Loyang to Ch'ang-an in 190.

Intending to launch a punitive campaign against the evil.
Tung Cho's horde appeared and swarmed down upon the East,
Golden armor glittering in the rays of the sun.   10
The men of the plains were easily broken
For the soldiers who came were all Hu and Chiang barbarians:[3]
They surrounded the cities as if they were hunters in the fields,
And where they struck, there wasn't a thing left alive.
They killed people wherever they turned until no one was left,   15
Corpses and dry bones propped each other up.
On their horses' sides they suspended the heads of the men,
Behind them on their horses' backs they carried off the women.
Long we rode to the west and entered the passes,
A twisting road, perilous and impassable.   20
I gazed back into the dark and blurry distance;
My vitals were crushed with anguish.
Although those they had captured numbered tens of thousands,
We were not allowed to camp or meet together.
There were times when we might be near our next of kin,   25
But though we wished to speak, we dared not say a word.
If they felt displeased at the least little thing
They'd bark out, "Kill the captives!
Anyone who holds back his blade
Will not be left alive."   30
How could we even wish to go on living?
We could not endure their cursing;
Sometimes they would just pick up and start beating us
So bitterness and pain were mixed as the blows came down.
By day we wailed and cried as we trudged along,   35
By night we grieved and groaned as we sat down.
If we wished to die, we were unable to manage it;
If we wished to live, we were hardly able to do that, either.
What crime had we committed against Heaven
To meet with such suffering and misfortune?   40

---

3 Tung Cho employed mercenaries from the western nomadic tribes to fight the
  imperial forces; it was during one of their raids that Ts'ai Yen was captured.

The frontier wastes are not at all like China,
The customs have little righteousness or order.
Everywhere there is plenty of frost and snow
And the nomads' wind begins to blow in spring and summer.
Whipping up, the wind whistled through my clothes,   45
Wailing, it entered my ears.
Moved by the passing of time, I thought of my parents:
My grieving sighs were endless.
When a traveler came from the outside world
I always felt happy to hear of it;   50
I would welcome him, ask him for the news,
And yet again discover he was not from my native place.
Unexpectedly, my wishes for help were finally granted,
An envoy from my family came to take me home.
But though I was able to have myself released,   55
When I returned, I still had to abandon my sons.
There were natural ties which bound our hearts together,
I brooded that I would be parted from them, without hope of
      meeting again.
In life or death we would always be separated,
And I could not bear to take my leave of them.   60
My children came forward and hung around my neck,
Crying, "Mother, where are you going?
They say you have to go away,
But how will we ever be reunited?
Mother, you have always been so loving, so indulgent,   65
How can you now be so unkind to us?
We have not yet grown to manhood,
How could you not look back and long for us?"
To see them this way crushed my very vitals,
Distressed as I was, I became as one demented.   70
Wailing and crying, hands clutching, caressing,
As I was about to go, I turned back yet again.
Some women who had been taken at the same time I was
Came out to send me off and say farewell.
They envied me as the only one able to go home,   75
The sound of their wails and cries was shattering;

Even the horses stood, hesitating to leave,
And the carts would not roll forward in their tracks.
All of the onlookers were sighing,
And travelers on the road were sobbing, too.   80

Go, Go! My lingering ties were cut.
Marching fast, as days rolled by we were farther and farther
    away;
With the vastness of three thousand *li* between us,
When would I again meet with those I loved?
I thought of the sons who were born from my womb;   85
My spirit for life was crushed in defeat.
When I arrived, my family was all gone;
Again I was without even a distant relative.
The city walls had become a mountain forest,
The courtyards and pavilions sprouted brambles,   90
There were white bones of who knows whom
In all directions with no one to cover them up;
I went outside the gates, but not a human sound—
Just the wolves howling and yelping;
Desolate, I faced my orphan shadow;   95
Grief and anger swelled in my entrails.
I climbed a hill to look off into the distance,
And my spirit seemed suddenly to fly from me;
But just when I seemed to be at my last breath,
Some people near me acted with great kindness.   100
So again I forced myself to go on living,
But though I lived, what had I to depend on?
I entrusted my life to yet another husband,[4]
I did my utmost to force myself to go on.
My homeless life completes my suffering;   105
My constant fear is to be cast off again.
How long can one person's life endure?
I shall harbor my grief to the very end of my days!

4 Tung Ssu.

Song of Everlasting Sorrow (Po Chü-yi, 772–846)

The Emperor prized beauty, and longed for a woman to topple a
    kingdom,
Through a reign of many years he searched without obtaining
    her.
There was a girl of the Yang family, just about grown,
Who had been reared in the inner chambers—no one knew of her
    yet,
She had beauty and charms granted by Heaven, difficult to
    conceal,   5
And so one day was chosen to be the concubine of her sovereign.
A glance exchanged, a single smile; she showed a hundred
    charms,
The painted beauties of his Six Palaces seemed to have no allure.
In the cold of early spring she bathed in the Flower-Clear Pool,
The warm spring's water polished her skin translucent white and
    glossy smooth.[1]   10
A servant helped her up; she was graceful, so helplessly
    languid—
That was the first time the emperor bestowed his favor on her.
Her clouds of hair, her lovely face, her swaying, gold-shod steps,
Within hibiscus canopies they passed their spring nights in
    warmth.
The spring nights seemed very short, the sun would rise high;   15
But from that time His Majesty would not attend the early court.
They took their pleasure at feasts and entertainments without
    pause,
The spring came, and passed on as night followed night.
There were three thousand other beauties in the women's palace;
For him, all their three thousand charms were combined in one
    body.   20
In the golden room, her toilette complete, she seductively
    attended him all night,

---

1 In the original Chinese her skin is compared to the whiteness of rendered mutton
  fat.

In the jade tower, the feasting finished, she harmonized with
    spring delights.
Her sisters and brothers were all given rank and titles;
To the dismay of many, her glory reflected on her family,
And so throughout the empire the hearts of mothers and fathers   25
Did not value the birth of a boy, but valued that of a girl.
In the upper stories of Li Palace, piercing the blue sky,
Fairy music wafted on the wind, to be heard everywhere,
Slow-paced songs and languorous dances were played by strings
    and flutes:
Though he gaze all day, His Majesty could not gaze on her
    enough.   30
Then the war-drums from Yü-yang came, shaking the earth,[2]
Abruptly breaking off the songs of the "Rainbow Skirt" and the
    "Robe of Feathers."
The Nine Rings of the Forbidden City threw up smoke and dust,
Thousands mounted, ten thousand in carts moved off to the
    southwest.
The Imperial banner fluttered, then its movement stopped   35
West of the city gates more than a hundred *li*.
There the six armies refused to budge, no matter what the cost,
Until he yielded his moth-browed beauty to die before the horses.
Hairpins like flowers flung to the ground, with no one to catch
    them,
A kingfisher crown, golden birds and hair-tassels of jade.   40
The Emperor could only cover his face; he was unable to save her.
Looking back, the blood and tears were flowing together.
The yellow dust dispersed, the wind blew cold,
The trail in the clouds twisted around to climb the Chien-ko Pass.[3]

Under O-mei Mountain a few people passed,[4]   45
Without light, the day-bright colors of flags and pennants faded.
The water of the Shu River is green, Shu Mountain is blue:
The Emperor, day after day, night after night, grieved.

2 The forces of the rebel general An Lu-Shan.
3 Into Ssu-ch'uan.
4 One of the five sacred mountains of China, near Ch'eng-tu.

Pacing the palace, he looked at the moon, his wounded heart full
    of longing,
In the night rain he heard bells, but his feelings cut off their
    sounds.   50
Heaven and Earth swung 'round again, and the dragon-cart
    returned,
When they came to that spot he hesitated, and could not go on.
She was in the earth under the Ma-wei Slope,
He could not see her jade face—the place where she died was
    empty.
Lord and courtier, when they met, would soak their clothes with
    tears,   55
Looking east to the city gates, they trusted their horses to know
    the way back.
When they returned, the pools and parks were as in the olden
    days,
Hibiscus from Lake T'ai-yi, and Wei-yang Palace willows.
The hibiscus were like her face, the willows like her brows,
So when he looked at them, how could he help but weep?   60
In the spring wind the peaches and plums blossomed with the
    days,
In the autumn rains the *wu-t'ung* trees shed their leaves in season.
The West Palace and the Southern Enclosure were full of autumn
    grasses,
Falling leaves covered the stairs with red, and were not swept
    away.
The attendants of the Pear Garden, their white hair was new,   65
The Pepper House eunuchs' young eyebrows began to show their
    age.
Fireflies flew in the evening halls; he thought quietly of her,
The wick in his lonely lamp burnt out, and yet he would not
    sleep.
Slowly, slowly, the bells and drums began each long night,
Brighter, brighter the Milky Way, urging the sky to dawn.   70
The roof-tile mandarin ducks were cold, the frost was bright and
    thick,
His kingfisher-feather covers were cold, for who was to be with
    him?

His thoughts were on the distance between life and death, year
    after year without end,
But her spirit would not return, or come to enter his dreams.

A Taoist adept of Ling-chün was a voyager in the heavens   75
Able because of his devout conviction to contact spirits.
Moved by their sovereign's constant torment of longing,
Some sought out this adept to search diligently for her.
He marshalled the clouds and drove ether before him, quick as
    lightning,
Up in the sky, down into the earth, he looked for her everywhere.   80
He rose to the ends of the jade-green sky, he plumbed the Yellow
    Springs,[5]
In both places, look as he might, he did not see her.
Suddenly he heard of a mountain of immortals in the sea,
The mountain was in the misty realm of emptiness.
Splendid towers and gates rose up from the five-color clouds,   85
And in the midst of these delights there were many immortals.
Among them was one called "Most Genuine,"
With snowy skin, a flower face, who could be compared with her?
At the gold towers on the west side he knocked on the jade door,
And asked a little jade attendant to inform the one of the paired
    perfections.   90
When she heard the Chinese court had sent an envoy from the
    Emperor,
She was awakened from her dreams in her nine-flowered
    canopied bed.
Pushing aside her pillow, she dressed and rose like a flying
    swallow,
Rushed over to open the pearly door and the silver screen.
New-wakened from sleep, her cloud of hair tilted to one side,   95
Her flower cap was not set straight when she came down to the
    courtyard.
The wind sighed in her immortal sleeves and raised them up in
    dancing,

5 The underworld.

As if this were the dance of the "Rainbow Skirt" and the "Robe of
    Feathers."
On her jade face from loneliness the tears trickled down,
Like pear blossoms on a branch when the spring brings down the
    rain.   100
She restrained her emotions, calmed her eyes and thanked the
    emperor:
"Since we parted our voices and faces are dim to one another,
Cut off was our happy love in the Court of the Bright Sun,
And the long days and nights in P'eng-lai Palace.
But when I turn my head to gaze down at the mortal world,   105
I can never see Ch'ang-an, but only fog and dust."
She gave the envoy the old things that were pledges of their love,
A golden hairpin in its case she gave him to take away;
But of the hairpin she kept one branch, of the box she kept one
    half,
Breaking the hairpin's yellow gold and the hinge of the box.   110
"Tell him our love should be as whole as this hairpin and its
    case—
In heaven or in the world of men we will meet again."
About to part, she charged him further to take these words,
In these words was meaning only their two hearts knew:
"On the seventh day of the seventh month, in the Palace of Long
    Life,   115
At midnight, with no one else there, we exchanged a secret vow:
That in the heavens we wished to fly, two birds with joined
    wings,
And on the earth we wished to grow, two trees with branches
    entwined."
Heaven endures, earth's span is long, but sometime both will
    end—
This sorrow everlasting will go on forever.   120

Ballad of the *p'i-p'a* (Po Chü-yi)

In the tenth year of the Yüan-ho reign (815) I was degraded in
rank to the post of deputy prefect in the Chiu-chiang prefecture.
In the autumn of the next year I was seeing off a guest beside the

P'en River, and we heard from a boat in the night the playing of a
p'i-p'a. As I listened to its notes, its jingling had the sound of the
music of the capital. I asked after this person: originally she had
been a singing-girl in Ch'ang-an, and had studied the *p'i-p'a* with
the two eminent masters Mu and Ts'ao. When she grew older and
her charms were fading, she gave herself as wife to a merchant. I
ordered wine and asked her to play some songs right away. When
the songs were finished she dwelt on her story pathetically, speaking a bit of the happy times when she was younger, and of how
she now drifted, haggard with grief, constantly moving around the
rivers and lakes. I became a provincial official and was sent out
two years ago. I had been tranquil and at peace with myself, but
affected by this woman's words, this evening I finally began to feel
what it meant to be degraded and banished. Therefore I composed
a long poem, a song which I could present to her in 616 characters,
called "Ballad of the *p'i-p'a*."

On the banks of the Hsün-yang River, I was seeing off a guest one
    night,
The autumn wind sighing in the maple leaves and reed-flowers.
As host, I dismounted and joined my guest on the boat,
Where we raised up our wine and were ready to drink, but had
    no music of pipes or strings.
Though tipsy, we could not stir up feelings of joy, and were on
    the point of parting;   5
As we said farewell, the moon seemed half-submerged in the
    boundless river.
Suddenly I heard coming over the water the sound of a *p'i-p'a*;
I forgot all about going home, and my friend did not set out.
We followed the sound and discreetly asked who the player might
    be.
The sound of the *p'i-p'a* halted, reluctantly she answered   10
We moved our boat to the side of hers and invited her to meet us.
We ordered more wine, renewed the lanterns, and again began
    the feast.
A thousand calls, ten thousand pleas, before she emerged
Still holding the *p'i-p'a* in such a way as half to hide her face.
She turned the pegs and plucked the strings for several notes;   15

Even before they became a song, they began to reveal her
    emotion.
With every string she pressed or released, each note was full of
    memories,
As if to complain that throughout her life she had never fulfilled
    her desires.
She lowered her brows, let her hands go and played continuously,
Expressing all that was in her heart without keeping anything
    back.   20
Pressing lightly, vibrating slowly, alternately strumming and
    plucking,
First she played "The Rainbow Skirt," then "Sixes in Dice." [1]
The large strings drummed with a noise like the rush of rain,
The small strings whispered as if they told a secret,
Drumming and whispering mingled in her playing   25
Like big pearls and small pearls pouring into a dish of jade.
There was the call of a hidden oriole, rolling out from under the
    flowers,
And the muffled sob of a flowing spring as its water poured down
    the bank.
The water of the spring seemed cold, as if the strings were
    freezing,
Their freezing kept the spring from flowing; the sound gradually
    choked to a halt.   30
The music ceased in deep melancholy, then hidden griefs came
    forth;
Those moments of silence were more powerful than those with
    sounds of music.
A silver pitcher suddenly broke, the liquid burst out,
Armored cavalry rushed forth with the ringing of blades and
    spears,
At the end of the piece she paused with her plectrum, then struck
    right across the heart;   35

---

1 Tunes composed by the emperor T'ang Hsüan-tsung in honor of the dancing
talents of his favorite concubine, Yang Kuei-fei.

All four strings gave one sound like the tearing of silk.
The boats around us east and west were silent, without a word,
Just the white light of the autumn moon was seen in the heart of
    the river.

As if deep in thought, she put the pick in its place under the
    strings,
Then she arranged her clothes, sat up and composed her face.   40
She told us that originally she was the daughter of a family in the
    capital,
She lived in a house at Ha-ma, at the foot of the ridge,[2]
At the age of thirteen her studies of the *p'i-p'a* had been perfected;
Her name belonged among the names of the Imperial musicians.
Whenever she played, she was always admired by those with real
    talent,   45
Whenever she was all dressed up, she was envied by the girls of
    the season,
Wu-ling's youths vied with each other for her attentions,[3]
For just one song, who knows how many rolls of red silk they
    offered,
Silver combs with gold inlay were broken keeping time to her
    playing,
Blood-red silk skirts were soaked by wine cups overturned,   50
One year's happiness and laughter were followed by next year's,
Autumn moons and spring breezes passed unheeded.
Then her little brother went into the army, and her aunt (on her
    mother's side) died,
The evenings went, the mornings came, and her beauty faded;
Her gateway grew desolate, carriages and horses few,   55
As she grew older she made a match, to be a merchant's wife.
The merchant valued his profits, and made light of being
    separated from her—
Last month he went out to Fu-liang to buy tea.
Since he had gone, at the river's mouth she kept watch in the
    empty boat;

2 Near the pleasure quarters of Ch'ang-an.
3 The young men of the capital city.

Surrounding the boat the bright moon and the river water were
    cold.   60
Deep in the night she would suddenly dream of the doings of her
    youth,
In her dream she cried out, her face streaming with tears and
    rouge.[4]

When I heard the *p'i-p'a* I was already sighing,
When I had heard her words as well, I sighed once again.
"We are both lost wanderers at the ends of the earth;   65
Meeting here, what need have we to have known each other
    before?
Last year I bade farewell to the imperial capital;
In exile I live, pining away in the city of Hsün-yang.
Hsün-yang is a place so remote that there is no music—
For a whole year I have not heard the sound of strings or flutes.   70
I live near P'en-ch'eng, where the ground is low and damp,
Yellow rushes and bitter bamboos press in around my dwelling,
In such a place, morning and evening, what sort of thing do I
    hear?
The cuckoo cries its bloody cry, and the apes wail mournfully.[5]
In spring on the river are flowery mornings, in autumn are
    moonlit nights,   75
But any time I go to fetch wine, I must always drink alone.
Oh, I'm not without 'mountain songs' and 'village pipes,'
But they do sound uncouth and shrill, and grate on my ears.
This evening, when I heard the voice of your *p'i-p'a*,
It was like hearing immortals' music, and my ears became clear
    again.   80
Don't refuse me! Sit down for a while and play another song,

4 Literally, "streaming with 'red balustrade' tears." It suggests a double meaning:
    that her tears were for the old days "at the red balustrade" (in the pleasure quar-
    ters waiting for patrons), and that her "red balustrade" makeup (the makeup
    typical of an entertainer) was streaming down her face, dissolved by her tears.
5 The cuckoo's unhappy cry is attributed to the regret of the adulterous Emperor
    Wang, who seduced the wife of his prime minister and in his shame abdicated in
    the minister's favor. When he died he was transformed into a cuckoo, which is
    said to spit blood to show the emperor's continuing remorse.

And I will in return compose a 'Ballad of the *p'i-p'a'* for you."
Moved by these words of mine, she stood for a long while,
But finally sat and hurried the strings' tempo even faster;
In their forlorn emotion not the same as she played before;   85
The whole company listened again, and everyone hid their tears.
Of those among the company, who wept most of all?
I, sub-prefect of Chiang-chou; I soaked my blue sleeve through.

Song of the Lady of Ch'in (Wei Chuang, c. 834–910)

In the third year of the Chung-ho reign, the third month of the
   spring,
Outside Loyang's city walls the blossoms massed like snow;
East, west, south, north the people on the road had vanished,
The green willows were quiet and still, the fragrant dust had
   settled.
At the roadside I suddenly came upon a lady like a flower—   5
Alone she had gone to the green willows, and sat down to rest in
   the shade.
Her phoenix clasp was tilted, bell-bird hairpins askew, lock-ends
   falling every which way,
Her rouge smeared off, her brow paint beaded, the line of her
   eyebrows broken.
"Young lady, where have you come from?" I asked.
She composed her features and started to speak, but her voice
   first broke into a sob,   10
So she turned her head to adjust her sleeves, then courteously
   answered me.
"Swept along by the waves of rebellion, how can I bear to speak
   of it?
Three years I remained in the rebels' hands, detained in the land
   of Ch'in,[1]
Blurred and obscured in my memory are the things that
   happened there.

---

1 The old name for the country surrounding the imperial capital.

Sir, if you have the time to loosen your golden saddle for me,   15
I likewise will rest my jade foot to keep you company.

The year before last, which was *keng-tzu*,[2] on the fifth day of the
    last month,
Just as I was closing the golden cage of my parrot after its lesson,
I reached over to take up my bell-bird mirror, lazily combed my
    hair,
And peacefully leaned on the carved balustrade, still idle and
    without speaking,   20
I suddenly saw that outside the gates of the house red dust was
    rising,
Already I glimpsed in the street men frantically beating on metal
    drums.
The inhabitants then rushed out to them, breathless and terrified;
Courtiers, returning, stood incredulous.
But just then from the west end government troops marched into
    the city,   25
Ready to march to T'ung Pass, thus confirming disaster.[3]
Everyone said that the Po-yeh troops could hold the enemy back, [4]
Everyone said that the rebels were coming, but could never get
    this far!
An instant later my husband came galloping up and arrived at
    home,
Dismounting, he entered the gate and stood stunned like a
    drunken man.   30
By chance he had met the Purple Imperial Coach in flight,
    covered with the dust of exile;
Already he saw the rebels' white flags stream in from the land all
    around.

2 The name of the year according to a sixty-year calendar.
3 Of great strategic importance throughout Chinese history, T'ung Pass was located
    at the bend of the Yellow River where the borders of the ancient states of Ch'in,
    Chin, and Yü met. Enemy troops who could penetrate this point had a clear walk
    through the valley to Ch'ang-an.
4 A group of local reinforcements.

Supporting the weak, leading children by the hand, shouting to
    make themselves heard,
Some climb to the roofs, others flee by the walls, with no trace of
    decorum or order,
Neighbors run to their northern friends' hiding places,   35
Neighbors east escape to their neighbors in the west.
The women of our northern neighbor's household come out like a
    herd together,
Bursting their gate like a hurricane, stampeding as if they were
    cattle.
Rumbling, rumbling, a rolling roar! Heaven and earth both shake.
The thunder of ten thousand horses wells up from the earth.   40
Fires burst out with golden sparks which fly up to the Ninth
    Heaven,
The Twelve Municipal Thoroughfares fill up with flames and
    smoke.
The sun's wheel descends to the west, its cold rays are white,
The Lord of Heaven still speaks no word—in vain the mind
    throbs with horror!
Dark clouds ring the sun with a halo of haze, like troops in
    formation for siege,   45
The Minister Stars fall from their paths, tinged with blood,
Purple vapors stealthily follow the Royal Throne as it shifts
    position,
Weird rays of light shoot through the darkness, to destroy the
    Three T'ai Lords' stars.[5]
Every household flows with blood, bubbling like a spring,
Everywhere screams of atrocity; the screams shake the earth.   50
The dancers and the singing girls are all despoiled,
Infants and young girls are cast aside to lose their lives.
Our eastern neighbor had a girl just beginning to paint her
    eyebrows,
A beauty to overthrow city or state; her qualities yet unknown.

---

5 These four lines refer to various constellations whose political symbolism indicates that the chaos in the heavens reflects the chaos in the world below.

Long spears forced her to climb up into a warrior's chariot,   55
Turning her head to her fragrant boudoir, her tears filled her
    handkerchief.
Now she pulls out golden threads, learning to mend their
    banners,
And climbs up to a carved saddle, to be taught how to ride a
    horse.
Sometimes from her own horse she may catch a glimpse of her
    'husband';
She dares not turn away her eyes, but helpless her tears fall.   60
Our western neighbor had a girl; truly, a fairy spirit!
Sidelong glances flashed like waves from her large, bewitching
    eyes.
Her toilette complete, she was gazing at her spring beauty in the
    mirror,
Still young, she did not know what went on outside her gate.
Some scoundrel jumped in over the wall and leaped up the
    golden steps,   65
Pulling her clothes half off her shoulders, he tried to rape her;
Dragged by her gown, she was unwilling to leave her vermilion
    gate—
So rouge, fragrant ointments, and all, she perished under the
    knife.
Our southern neighbor had a girl whose name I do not recall,
Just the day before a good matchmaker had exchanged betrothal
    gifts for her;   70
On the shimmering tiles of the staircase she did not hear
    footsteps coming,
Through her shades of kingfisher blue she saw their shadows too
    late.
Suddenly we saw her at the courtyard's edge, but a swordblade
    rang;
Her head and body were severed in an instant.
Looking to Heaven, then covering their faces with a single cry,   75
Her younger and elder sisters together threw themselves into the
    well.
The young wife of our northern neighbor was hurrying to depart,

Just shaking out her cloudlike hair and wiping green pigment
   from her brows;[6]
Already she heard battering sounds at her tall gate,
Without thinking, she climbed out onto the eaves and up to her
   second storey.   80
Soon from all sides the blaze of fires came;
When she tried to come down the spiral stairs, the stairs had
   already collapsed.
While her loud screams from the midst of the smoke still begged
   for her rescue,
Her corpse hanging on the rafters was already burned to cinders.

I by some chance had been preserved intact from the rebels'
   deadly weapons,   85
I did not dare to hesitate, to linger or look back,
But combed out my hairstyle's 'cicada wings' to follow the path of
   the troops,
And forcing my brows to a cheerful look, I went out from my
   gate.
From that time on I could never again return to my old ward,
From that time on there was no place I might look to find my
   kinfolk;   90
It has been three years since the time I first fell into the rebels'
   hands,
Each day long I have trembled and grieved, my heart and courage
   broken.
At night when I rested a thousand ranks of swords and spears
   surrounded me;
At the morning meal, each taste seemed like slivered human
   livers.
Although I 'entered the curtains of marriage,' how could I enjoy
   'marital bliss'?   95
Although I had plenty of precious goods, they were not things I
   could enjoy.

6 She lets down her elaborate hairstyle and wipes off her cosmetics to make herself
   seem less attractive. Dark green was a popular color for painting the eyebrows; it
   was thought to give a youthful appearance.

His hair unkempt, his face filthy, his eyebrows bright red!
If I gave my man even a sidelong glance, I still could not bear the
    sight.
His clothing was put on inside out, the language he spoke was
    uncouth,
On his face there were boasts of his deeds—the words being
    tattooed there![7]   100
On the Cypress Terrace, the 'Censorate Scholars' had all become
    fox spirits,
At the Orchid Bureau the 'Official Recorders' were all rat
    demons;[8]
They kept trying to wear ornate hairpins in their short hair,
Without taking off their robes of state, they rolled up in
    embroidered quilts.
With ivory tablets held upside down, some aped the Three Lords
    of State,   105
Golden fish tail up and turned wrong way 'round, some became
    'Historians of the Left and Right.'[9]
In the morning I could hear them report to the Throne and enter
    the audience chamber,
In the evening I could see them go to the wine shops in a brawl.

One morning in the fifth watch everyone rose up in alarm
With shouting and clamor conflicting, there seemed to be secret
    tidings.   110
During the night a mounted scout had entered the Imperial city—
Yesterday government troops had taken the town of Ch'ih-shui.
The distance from Ch'ih-shui to the city is only a hundred *li*,
If they set out at daybreak, ah! by evening they ought to arrive!
The big, fierce men on their horses now silently gulp back sighs, 115
While their female companions in their chambers secretly vent
    their delight.

7 Convicted criminals often were punished by having the character for their crime
  branded or tattooed on their faces.
8 The Cypress Terrace and the Orchid Assembly were parts of the Imperial Censorate.
9 The ivory tablets and golden fish are symbols of the empire's highest-ranking
  ministers.

All say that outrage and injustice this time will be avenged,
Surely, we say, these monstrous troops will die this very day!
They gallop their horses in full retreat, really frightened by the
    rumors,
At last they say the army advances, to enter in full force!   120
Now Big P'eng and Little P'eng may well look at each other and
    worry,
This fine fellow and that fine fellow may cling to their saddles and
    weep.[10]
But for several days we drift on and on, without any news at all,
This must mean that the vanguard troops already 'have jade
    tablets in their mouths.'[11]
Waving standards and brandishing swords, the rebels then came
    back   125
To tell us the government's forces were all completely defeated.

From this time on, on every side, our suffering grew more dire:
A peck of yellow gold bought but a single pint of grain,
In Shang Jang's kitchen they prepared the bark of trees to eat,
On Huang Ch'ao's table they carved the meat of men.[12]   130
The Southeast was cut off from us, no roads would bring
    supplies,
The moat 'round the city gradually filled, while the people grew
    fewer and fewer.
Outside the Gates of the Six Armies lay heaps of stiffened
    corpses,
Inside, the Ch'i-chia camp was filled with those who starved to
    death.
Ch'ang-an lies so still, so still; what is left there now?   135
Ruined markets, desolate streets where shoots of wheat are
    sprouting,

10 Literally, "Big P'eng and Little P'eng . . . Gentleman II and Gentleman IV"—a
   contemptuous way of referring to their captors.
11 As tokens of submission.
12 At the time of the sack of Ch'ang-an, Shang Jang acted as Huang Ch'ao's lieu-
   tenant; however, after the rebels' later retreat from the city he defected to the
   imperial cause and dealt his former chief a final, deadly blow in 884.

For firewood they chopped down the last of the trees that
      bloomed in the Apricot Gardens,
For building their fortress they doomed the willows along the
      Imperial Canal.
Splendid coaches with paint-patterned wheels were all smashed
      and scattered,
Of the mansions with their vermilion gates, not even half survive.   140
On the floor of the Han-yüan Audience Hall foxes and rabbits
      roam,
The approach to the Hua O Tower is filled up with brambles and
      thorns.
The luxury of former times—now destroyed and buried;
A dreary waste as far as the eye can see—not a single familiar
      thing there.
The Imperial Treasury was burned to the very ash of its brocades
      and embroideries,   145
On the Street of Heaven were trampled to dust the bones of State
      Officials.

So we set out on the road east of the city, when day was breaking,
The wind-borne smoke made the land outside the city look like
      the frontiers.
At the roadside we sometimes came upon wandering parties of
      soldiers,
At the foot of the slope, no guests were welcomed or sent off as
      they used to be.   150
Gazing off to the east at Pa-ling, all signs of men's dwellings were
      gone,
Tree-clouded Li Shan's gold and kingfisher blue had all been
      destroyed.[13]
The great highroads had all become forests of brambles,
And travelers had to pass the night in a roofless house under the
      moon.

Next morning at dawn we arrived at the highway to San-feng,   155

13 A complex of temples and pavilions that had been a major resort for the imperial
   family.

In hundreds and thousands of homes, not a single family
   remained.
In the barren, deserted fields and gardens only punk-weeds were
   left,
The bamboos and trees were completely destroyed, and all was
   derelict.
By the roadside was Hua Shan's Golden Spirit, whom I tried to
   question,[14]
But the Golden Spirit would not speak; he was even more grieved
   than we.   160
Of the ancient cypresses before the shrine, only shattered stumps
   were left,
From the temple's golden incense burners, only some dark dust
   rose.
'Ever since that frenzied bandit laid waste to the heartland,
Heaven and earth have been clouded with gloom, and the wind
   and rain are black.
The holy water before the altar failed in its protective spell,   165
The underworld warriors on the wall were unable to drive back
   the rebels.
In the days of peace I falsely accepted kind libations and
   offerings,
For in times of danger I could bring no aid, nor exert any divine
   power.
Now I am filled with shame for my ineptness as a god;
I should flee deep into the mountains and hide myself away!   170
Within my domains, no sound of flutes and pipes,
No place for me to look for a sacrificial victim on its bamboo mat.
The marauding nightmare demons came from all sides around my
   village,
And slaughtered all living beings before a day was done.'
When I heard this speech, my melancholy deepened—   175
Heaven sends down calamity in due season, not of its own
   accord.

---

14 The mountain's genius loci, to whom the surrounding population would offer
   seasonal sacrifices.

If this spirit runs to the mountains in order to flee his danger,
How can we turn accusing looks to the nobles of the East?

Year before last, I finally emerged to see the Yang-chen Pass,
Raising my head to view Mount Ching at the borders of the
    clouds;   180
It was like coming out of a world of darkness and reaching the
    human world,
I immediately felt that the times were clear and Heaven and Earth
    at peace.
The governor of Shen Chou is a loyal and virtuous man,
He does not rise up in rebellion, but only guards his city.
The Governor of P'u-chin is able to keep down fighting there,   185
A thousand *li* of tranquility, without the sound of weapons.
One can carry precious goods by day without anyone molesting,
At night wearing golden hairpins one can travel alone.

The next morning we again went on, passing east of Hsin-an,
And on the road we came upon an old man begging gruel.   190
Hoary and old, his careworn face the color of moss and lichens,
He tried to conceal himself in a tangled mass of rushes.
I asked the old man, 'In former times, what was your native
    place?
What forced you under the cold sky, to lodge with frost and
    dew?'
The old man gradually stood erect, wanting to tell his story,   195
But sank back hiding his face in his hands and wept aloud to
    Heaven.
'My native fields originally were part of Tung-chi province,
Year after year my mulberry groves adjoined crown lands,
Each year I would sow two hundred *ch'an* of fertile fields,[15]
The household tax I paid each year was thirty million cash.   200
My daughters were expert weavers of heavy damask robes.
My daughters-in-law were able to cook red millet for their meals.
I had a thousand granaries! Ten thousand chests as well!

---

15 A *ch'an* is a unit of land covering one hundred *mou*, or acres.

Even after Huang Ch'ao came through, only half had been
    destroyed.
But ever since, from around Loyang, where the armies are
    encamped,   205
Day and night patrolling soldiers enter the village walls,
The swords they draw are "Green Serpents," glittering like
    autumn waters in their scabbards,
The high winds on their banners blow out the symbol of the
    White Tiger.[16]
Entering the gates, they dismount and swoop down like a
    whirlwind,
Despoil the houses, emptying purses in piles as if they were
    heaping up earth.   210
Once my household goods were all gone, my flesh and blood
    were torn from me,
So now in my declining years I am all alone, bitter and wretched.
But that one person should suffer—alas!—How should that be my
    only lament?
For in the mountains are ever more, thousands and thousands of
    families:
By day hunger gnaws them as they hunt wild raspberries on the
    hillsides,   215
By night they shelter with the frost, sleeping on reeds and
    flowers.'

I heard this poor old father's heartrending words;
For the rest of the day I cried and cried, my tears flowed down
    like rain.
I left my home only to hear the cry of the owl, signifying
    rebellion,
Even more do I wish now to hasten east, but where shall I find to
    live?   220
Yet again I hear that traffic is cut off on the road to Pien,[17]

16 These symbols indicate that these are troops loyal to the empire, not the troops
  of the rebels.
17 K'ai-feng.

And they say on the road west to P'eng-men they are
    slaughtering one another.
Facing that wilderness warriors' ghosts flee from their bodies,
At the fords, the waters mingle with the blood of murdered men.
I have just now heard of a traveler who has come here from
    Chin-ling,   225
Hearing him speak of Chiang-nan, it seems the scenery there is
    different.
For there, though the frenzied bandit subjugated the central plain,
No muster of war horses overflows that land's four borders.[18]
There they feel destroying criminals is work of divine merit,
They treat all people with mercy and love, just as if they were
    children.   230
The walls and moats are a secure protection of metal and boiling
    water,
The taxes levied are like clouds, and are sent straight on to the
    fortresses.
How can it be helped that all within the four seas is in violent
    flux?
Yet this one district is clear as a mirror and life there smooth as a
    whetstone!
We who have lived by the royal palace must flee to escape
    disaster   235
And in our yearning for peace must envy Chiang-nan's very
    ghosts.

I pray you, Sir, to raise your oars and go farther and farther
    east
And chant this long song as an offering to His Excellency of
    Chin-ling."

---

18 An allusion to the *Tao te ching*, signifying that a virtuous ruler need not fear
    attack from outside.

Notes

Introduction

1 See Murasaki Shikibu, *The Tale of Genji*, trans. Edward G. Seidensticker (New York: Knopf, 1976), pp. 430–40. For discussion of the influence of "The Song of Everlasting Sorrow" on *The Tale of Genji*, see Endō Toshio, *Chōhonka Kenkyu* (Tokyo: Kensetsusha, 1934); Lin Wen-yüeh, *"The Tale of Genji* and 'A Song of Unending Sorrow,'" *Tamkang Review* 6.2 and 7.1 (October 1975–April 1976): 281–85. For the more general influence of the poetry of Po Chü-yi in Japan, see Robert H. Brower and Earl Miner, *Japanese Court Poetry* (Palo Alto: Stanford University Press, 1961), pp. 18off.; and David Pollack, *The Fracture of Meaning: Japan's Synthesis of China from the Eighth to the Eighteenth Century* (Princeton: Princeton University Press, 1986).

2 See Earl Miner, "On the Genesis and Development of Literary Systems," *Critical Inquiry* 5, pt. 1 (Winter 1978): 339–53, and pt. 2 (Spring 1979): 553–68, on the fundamental features of traditions based on lyrical

poetics, and their influence on the development of literary forms and aesthetics.

3 The term *hsü-shih shih* is adapted from *hsü-shih wen*, which refers to prose narrative, especially historiography. It is used in too restricted a sense to be translated with such a broad term as "narrative." Liu Chih-chi (661–721) used the term in his discussions of the features of historiography; see *Shih t'ung hsiao-fan chu* (reprint, Taipei: Kuang-wen, 1963), pp. 64–72. For the critical application of the term *hsü-shih wen* beyond historiography, see Andrew H. Plaks, "Issues in Chinese Narrative Theory in the Perspective of the Western Tradition," *PTL: A Journal for Descriptive Poetics and Theory of Literature* 2 (1977): 341. See also Hu Ying-lin (1551–1607), *Ssu pu cheng wei*, in *Wei shu k'ao wu chung* (reprint, Taipei: Shih-chieh, 1965). Hu Shih (1891–1962) uses both the terms *hsü-shih shih* and *ku-shih shih* in *Pai hua wen-hsüeh shih* (Shanghai: Shang-wu, 1928). Chiu Hsieh-yu goes so far as to define *ku-shih shih* as a subcategory of *hsü-shih shih*, and translates the term as "epic." See *Chung-kuo li-tai ku-shih shih* (Taipei: San-min, 1969).

4 For the primacy of historiography in the evolution of narrative in the Chinese tradition, see Jaroslav Průšek, "History and Epics in China and the West: A Study of Differences in the Conception of the Human Story," in Průšek, *Chinese History and Literature: A Collection of Essays* (Dordrecht, Holland: Reidel, 1970), pp. 17–34; John C. Y. Wang, "The Nature of Chinese Narrative: A Preliminary Statement of Methodology," *Tamkang Review* 6.2 and 7.1 (October 1975–April 1976): 229–45; Andrew H. Plaks, "Towards a Critical Theory of Chinese Narrative," in Plaks, ed., *Chinese Narrative: Critical and Theoretical Essays* (Princeton: Princeton University Press, 1977), pp. 309–52; and Plaks, "Conceptual Models of Chinese Narrative Theory," *Journal of Chinese Philosophy* 4.1 (June 1977): 25–47.

Another important source for narrative technique and method is *pien-wen*, or "transformation texts." These are prosimetric compositions from the popular Buddhist story-telling traditions. In "The Narrative Revolution in Chinese Literature: Ontological Perspectives," *CLEAR* 5.1 (July 1985): 1–27, Mair focuses on *pien-wen* in "an attempt to assess the overall impact of Buddhism on the Chinese narrative tradition" (p. 1). In the same issue of *CLEAR*, Kenneth Dewoskin and W. L. Idema take up the debate in "On Narrative Revolutions" (pp. 29–45) and "The Illusion of Fiction" (pp. 47–51), respectively. Idema does mention narrative poetry (p. 51), but all three essays focus on the origins of the *pien-wen* form rather than on the techniques whereby the form achieves a narrative mode of expression. See also Pai Hua-wen, trans. Victor H.

Mair, "What is *Pien-wen?" Harvard Journal of Asiatic Studies* 44.2 (1984): 493–514.

5 I use the terms *genre* and *generic* here in the sense of a critical division based on rhetorical structure or "radical of presentation," as defined by Northrop Frye in *Anatomy of Criticism: Four Essays* (Princeton: Princeton University Press, 1957). According to Frye, the "radical of presentation" determines "the conditions established between the poet and his public" (p. 247), a concept essential to my analysis of the distinctions between narrative and lyrical tendencies in artistic expression in Chinese poetry.

In this study I will use the term *mode* when referring to narrative or lyrical tendencies in the expressive intent underlying a work of art, and *genre* when referring to distinctions based on rhetorical structure or formal features of composition. For representative studies of Chinese genre theory, see James Robert Hightower, "The *Wen Hsüan* and Genre Theory," *Harvard Journal of Asiatic Studies* 20 (1957): 512–33; Ferenc Tőkei, *Genre Theory in China in the Third through Sixth Centuries (Liu Hsieh's Theory on Poetic Genres)* (Budapest: Akadémiai Kiadó, 1971); and David R. Knechtges, *Wen xuan, or Selections of Refined Literature*, vol. 1: *Rhapsodies on Metropolises and Capitals* (Princeton: Princeton University Press, 1982), introduction.

6 James J. Y. Liu, *The Interlingual Critic* (Bloomington: Indiana University Press, 1982), pp. 16–21.

7 For a discussion of Hu Shih's "dissatisfaction" with traditional Chinese narrative, see Lin Shuen-fu, "Ritual and Narrative Structure in *Ju-lin Wai-shih*," in Plaks, ed., *Chinese Narrative*, pp. 245–49.

8 See Kao Yu-kung, "Lyric Vision in Chinese Narrative Tradition: A Reading of *Hung-lou Meng* and *Ju-lin Wai-shih*," in Plaks, ed., *Chinese Narrative*, pp. 228–33; James J. Y. Liu, *Chinese Theories of Literature* (Chicago: University of Chicago Press, 1975), especially pp. 63–87; and Pauline Yu, "The Poetics of Discontinuity: East-West Correspondences in Lyric Poetry," *Publication of the Modern Language Association* 94.2 (March 1979): 261–74. For a study focusing on this issue in Chinese aesthetics, see Hsü Fu-kuan, "*Chung-kuo yi-shu ching-shen chu-t'i chih chen hsien*," in *Chung-kuo yi-shu ching-shen* (Taichung: Tunghai University Press, 1966), pp. 45–143.

9 For a general discussion of the fundamental properties of narrative in the Western tradition, including the importance of generic characteristics, see Robert Scholes and Robert Kellogg, *The Nature of Narrative* (New York: Oxford University Press, 1966). A structuralist analysis of

this problem, which focuses upon generic quality, may be found in Gérard Genette, *Figures III* (Paris: Editions de Seuil, 1972). A helpful analysis of the issues raised by *Figures III* is Shlomith Rimmon, "A Comprehensive Theory of Narrative: *Figures III* and the Structuralist Study of Fiction," *PTL: A Journal for Descriptive Poetics and Theory of Literature* 1 (1976): 33–62. Alastair Fowler provides a comprehensive historical and critical study in *Kinds of Literature: An Introduction to the Theory of Modes and Genres* (Cambridge: Harvard University Press, 1982); see also William Elford Rogers, *The Three Genres and the Interpretation of Lyric* (Princeton: Princeton University Press, 1983), pp. 9–76.

10 I have been consistent throughout this study in translating the terms *hsing* as "ballad," *ko* as "song," and *shih* as "poem" when they appear in titles, unless otherwise indicated. There is much speculation as to the original significance of these terms for musical or metrical references; however, I have found no consistent use of any one term which would indicate whether the composition so titled was intended to be narrative or lyric, or to adhere to any particular metrical convention.

11 Viktor Pöschl, *The Art of Vergil: Image and Symbol in the Aeneid* (Ann Arbor: University of Michigan Press, 1962), pp. 13–24.

12 D. W. Fokkema, "Cultural Relativism and Comparative Literature," *Tamkang Review* 3.2 (1972): 59–71, focuses on this issue in relation to the Chinese tradition. The dependence of European literary theory on the fundamental interrelations of the European linguistic traditions is often overlooked. In a sense, linguistic scholarship has fueled the study of cultural interrelations; cf. the influential Antoine Meillet, *L'Introduction à l'étude comparative des langues indo-européennes* (1903; reprint, University, Ala.: University of Alabama Press, 1964). I have especially consulted Georges Dumézil, *Mythe et epopée I. L'ideologie des trois fonctions dans les epopées des peuples indo-europeens* (Paris: Gallimard, first ed., 1968, third ed. with additional notes, 1979); *Mythe et epopée II. Types epiques indo-européens: un héros, un sorcier, un roi* (Paris: Gallimard, 1971); and *Mythes et epopées III. Histoires romaines* (Paris: Gallimard, 1973); and W. B. Lockwood, *Indo-European Philology. Historical and Comparative* (London: Hutchinson University Library, 1969).

13 On Ezra Pound and the influence of his interpretation of Chinese poetics on European poetry, see Wai-lim Yip, *Ezra Pound's Cathay* (Princeton: Princeton University Press, 1969); and Hugh Kenner, *The Pound Era* (Berkeley: University of California Press, 1971). For critical considerations of European images of Chinese poetics as interpreted by Pound and others, see Zhang Longxi, "The *Tao* and the *Logos*: Notes on Der-

rida's Critic of Logocentrism," *Critical Inquiry* 11 (March 1985): 385–98; and Hugh Kenner, "The Poetics of Error," *Tamkang Review* 6.2 and 7.1 (October 1975–April 1976): 89–97. See also chap. 1, note 4.

14 For a description of the metrical properties of *ku-shih*, see Hugh M. Stimson, *Fifty-five T'ang Poems* (New Haven: Far Eastern Publications, 1976), pp. 23–51; Hans H. Frankel, *The Flowering Plum and the Palace Lady* (New Haven: Yale University Press, 1976), p. 213; Kang-i Sun Chang, *The Evolution of Chinese Tz'u Poetry from Late T'ang to Northern Sung* (Princeton: Princeton University Press, 1980), pp. 210–11.

15 Stimson, *Fifty-five T'ang Poems*, pp. 23–49.

16 See the entry by C. Bradford Langly in William Nienhauser, Jr., ed., *The Indiana Companion to Traditional Chinese Literature* (Bloomington: Indiana University Press, 1986), pp. 656–60. See also James Robert Hightower, "Some Characteristics of Parallel Prose," in Søren Egerod and Else Glahn, eds., *Studia Serica Bernhard Karlgren Dedicata* (Copenhagen: Munksgaard, 1959), pp. 60–91; and Hsieh Hung-hsien, *P'ien-wen henglun* (Taipei: Kuang-wen, 1973).

17 See Lo Ken-tse, *Yüeh-fu wen-hsüeh shih* (Peking: Wen-hua, 1931); Hsiao Ti-fei, *Han Wei liu-ch'ao yüeh-fu wen-hsüeh shih* (1944; reprint, Taipei: Ch'ang-an, 1976); Jean-Pierre Diény, *Aux origines de la poésie classique en Chine (T'oung Pao Monographie VI)* (Leiden: Brill, 1968), pp. 81–100; and Hans H. Frankel, "*Yüeh-fu* Poetry," in Cyril Birch, ed., *Studies in Chinese Literary Genres* (Berkeley: University of California Press, 1974), pp. 69–107.

18 Stimson goes so far as to term *yüeh-fu* a "subset" of the genre of *ku-shih;* see *Fifty-five T'ang Poems*, p. 51. Frankel analyzes the development of *yüeh-fu* as a literary rather than folk genre in "The Legacy of the Han, Wei, and Six Dynasties *Yüeh-fu* Tradition and Its Fuller Development in T'ang Poetry," in Shuen-fu Lin and Stephen Owen, eds., *The Vitality of the Lyric Voice: Shih Poetry from the Late Han to T'ang* (Princeton: Princeton University Press, 1986), stating that "During the second phase [of its development]—from the 190s to the end of the Wei dynasty in 266—*yüeh-fu* becomes a major poetic genre in the hands of Ts'ao Ts'ao, his sons Ts'ao P'i and Ts'ao Chih, Ts'ao P'i's son Ts'ao Jui, and some of their contemporaries" (p. 287). For a discussion of the relation of *yüeh-fu* to T'ang narrative poetry, see C. H. Wang, "The Nature of Narrative in T'ang Poetry," in Lin and Owen, *The Vitality of the Lyric Voice*, pp. 217–52, especially sect. 1, "Origins."

19 Hu Ying-lin, *Shih sou* (Shanghai: Chung-hua, 1958), pp. 1–55.

20 A recent study that surveys the folk origins of Chinese narrative poetry,

with emphasis on the *Shih Ching* and *yüeh-fu*, is Joseph Roe Allen III, "Early Chinese Narrative Poetry: The Definition of a Tradition" (Ph.D. diss., University of Washington, 1982).

21 Ch'en Yin-k'o, "*T'ao-hua yüan chi p'ang cheng,*" in Ch'en Yin-k'o, *Ch'en Yin-k'o hsien-sheng wen-shih lun-chi*, 1:183–93.

22 Chang Wei-ch'i, "*T'ao-hua yüan chi shih yi,*" *Kuo-hsüeh yüeh-pao hui-k'an* 1 (1924): 201–20; Meishi Ts'ai, "Peach Blossom Spring: A Mythic Arcadia," *Tamkang Review* 11.1 (Fall 1980): 1–22.

23 This occurs in both Chinese anthologies and in English translations; cf. Wu Ch'eng-ch'üan (fl. 1711) et al., *Ku-wen kuan-chih* (Hong Kong: Hua-mei, 1951). The translation in Robert F. Fang, *Gleanings from T'ao Yüan-ming* (Hong Kong: Commercial Press, 1980), pp. 178–83, omits the poem, as does Burton Watson, in *The Columbia Book of Chinese Poetry: From Early Times to the Thirteenth Century* (New York: Columbia University Press, 1984), pp. 142–43. I have followed the work of James Robert Hightower, which includes a complete translation of preface and poem as a united composition, with commentary, in *The Poetry of T'ao Ch'ien* (Oxford: Clarendon Press, 1970), pp. 254–58. Another complete translation has recently appeared in A. R. Davis, *T'ao Yüan-ming*, 2 vols. (Cambridge: Cambridge University Press, 1983), 1:195–201, and 2:139–43. For a treatment of preface (with partial translation) and poem (complete) together as autobiography, see Kang-i Sun Chang, *Six Dynasties Poetry* (Princeton: Princeton University Press, 1986), pp. 16–20.

24 Text from Ting Fu-pao, *T'ao Yüan-ming shih chien chu* (1927; reprint, Taipei: Yi-wen, 1964); translation by Hightower, *The Poetry of T'ao Ch'ien*, p. 255.

25 For the biography of Liu Tzu-chi, see Fang Hsüan-ling, ed., *Chin Shu* (Peking: Chung-hua, 1974), 8:2460–66; for T'ao Ch'ien's interest in this legend, see Ch'en Yin-k'o, "Notes on the 'Account of Peach Blossom Spring,'" *Ch'ing-hua hsüeh-pao* 2 (1936), reprinted in *T'ao Yüan-ming yen-chiu tzu-liao hui-p'ien* (Peking: Chung-hua, 1962), pp. 338–47; and Pei-ching ta-hsüeh, Chung-kuo yü yen wen-hsüeh hsi, ed., *T'ao Yüan-ming shih-wen hui-p'ing* (Peking: Chung-hua, 1961), pp. 339–62.

26 Hightower, *The Poetry of T'ao Ch'ien*, p. 257.

27 Stephen Owen, *The Great Age of Chinese Poetry: The High T'ang* (New Haven: Yale University Press, 1981), p. 28.

28 I have chosen to use my own translation of "Poem of Peach Blossom Spring" because of my interpretative emphasis on the narrative qualities of the poem. It has seemed most appropriate to me to use the first person for the text in translation, as I feel that the narrator and the fisherman are meant to represent the same person. In assuming this

"autobiographical" stance, Wang Wei's poetic persona and his relation to T'ao Ch'ien are emphasized. The text is from Chao Tien-ch'eng, ed., *Wang Yu-ch'eng chi chien-chu*, 2 vols. (Peking: Chung-hua, 1961), 1:98–99.

Other translations include Witter Bynner and Kiang Kang-hu, *The Jade Mountain: A Chinese Anthology Being Three Hundred Poems of the T'ang Dynasty* (New York: Knopf, 1929), pp. 203–4; Wai-lim Yip, *Hiding the Universe: Poems by Wang Wei* (New York: Grossman, 1972), pp. 62–67; G. W. Robinson, *Poems of Wang Wei* (Baltimore: Penguin, 1973), pp. 34–37; and a translation with commentary by Pauline Yu, *The Poetry of Wang Wei: New Translations and Commentary* (Bloomington: Indiana University Press, 1980), pp. 59–61. All of these translations use the third person except for Yip, who carefully avoids the use of any pronouns at all.

29 Hightower, *The Poetry of T'ao Ch'ien*, p. 256.

30 The process followed by the artist for the choice of internalization or externalization of approach to subject matter has been described from the artist's point of view by Joyce Cary, *Art and Reality: Ways of the Creative Process* (Garden City, N.Y.: Doubleday, 1958). See also Jacques Maritain, *Creative Intuition in Art and Poetry* (New York: Pantheon Books, 1953).

31 On the role of stanzaic composition in European ballads, see Francis James Child, ed., *The English and Scottish Popular Ballads*, 5 vols. (Boston: Little, 1886–98), 5:469–502; Gordon Hall Gerould, *The Ballad of Tradition* (Oxford: Oxford University Press, 1932); and William J. Entwhistle, *European Balladry* (Oxford: Oxford University Press, 1939). In *Japanese Linked Poetry: An Account with Translations of Renga and Haikai Sequences* (Princeton: Princeton University Press, 1979), Earl Miner discusses the role of stanzaic units in long compositions in Japanese literature in detail; see especially pp. 58–85, 132–59; and Jin'ichi Konishi, "Association and Progression: Principles of Integration in Anthologies and Sequences of Japanese Court Poetry, A.D. 900–1350," *Harvard Journal of Asiatic Studies* 21 (1958): 67–127.

32 Miner, *Japanese Linked Poetry*, pp. 140–59.

33 Diény, *Aux origines de la poésie classique en Chine*. The importance of formulaic language and the possible folk origins of the *Shih Ching* is the focus of C. H. Wang, *The Bell and the Drum: A Study of the Shih Ching as Formulaic Poetry* (Berkeley: University of California Press, 1974). For such considerations in *yüeh-fu*, see Hans H. Frankel, "The Formulaic Language in the Chinese Ballad 'Southeast Fly the Peacocks,' " *Bulletin of the Institute of History and Philology* (Academia Sinica) 39, pt. 2 (1969): 219–44; and "Some Characteristics of Oral Narrative Poetry in China,"

Etudes d'histoire et de littérature chinoises offertes à Professeur Jaroslav Průšek,
Bibliothèque de l'Institute des Hautes Etudes Chinoises 24 (Paris: Presses
universitaires de France, 1976), pp. 97–106.

34 Cary, *Art and Reality*, pp. 15–20, 37–50.

35 I have dealt with the distinctive features of early Chinese techniques
of characterization at greater length in "The Trojan and the Hegemon;
or, The Culture Hero as Slave of Duty," *Comparative Literature Studies*
22.1 (Spring 1985): 136–46. See also C. H. Wang, "Towards Defining a
Chinese Heroism," *Journal of the American Oriental Society* 95.1 (January–
March 1975): 25–35.

1 Narrative Elements in Traditional Chinese Poetics

1 Adapting the terms used by Scholes and Kellogg in *The Nature of Narra-*
tive. Instead of "sequence," their analysis of narrative sequence focuses
on "plot" (pp. 207–49), in accordance with their teleological analysis of
the development of European narrative forms culminating in the novel.
For the category of "sequence" in preference to "plot," applied to East
Asian models, see Miner, *Japanese Linked Poetry*, pp. 3–159.

2 During the discussion of C. H. Wang's "The Nature of Narrative in
T'ang Poetry," at the A.C.L.S. Conference on the Evolution of *Shih*
Poetry (York, Maine, June 9–12, 1982), François Cheng observed that
"in the semiological definition of narrativity, there are three distinctive characteristics in Chinese poetry," which he describes as image,
speaker, and sequence. Cheng's theory of the function of images, which
can partake of lyric and narrative modes, is developed in detail in his
L'écriture poétique chinoise (Paris: Editions de Seuile, 1977), translated
by Donald A. Riggs and Jerome P. Seaton as *Chinese Poetic Writing*
(Bloomington: Indiana University Press, 1982). Cheng's description of
"active procedures" and "passive procedures" in Chinese poetic language is contrasted with procedures of poetic language in European
models.

3 Chow Tze-tsung suggests that the poems in which the word *shih* first
appeared were composed as early as the eleventh century B.C. See Chow
Tze-tsung, "The Early History of the Chinese Word *Shih* (Poetry),"
in Chow Tze-tsung, ed., *Wen Lin: Studies in the Chinese Humanities*
(Madison: University of Wisconsin Press, 1968), p. 155. More recently,
Chow has also discussed the relation of the practices of ancient Chinese
shamanism to the evolution of concepts of poetry, dance, and music;
see "Ancient Chinese *Wu* Shamanism and Its Relationship to Sacrifices,

History, Dance Music, and Poetry" ("*Chung-kuo ku-tai ti wu-yi yü chi-ssu, li-shih, yüeh-wu, chi shih ti kuan-hsi*"), pts. 1–3, *Ch'ing-hua hsüeh-pao*, n.s. 12.1–2 (December 1979): 1–59, and n.s. 13.1–2 (December 1981): 1–25. Part 3 is of most direct interest to this study.

4 This is an aspect of Chinese poetics that has intrigued European artists and critics, most influentially Ernst Fenellosa and Ezra Pound. Unfortunately, they focused their attention on the *orthography* of the Chinese language, especially the so-called pictographs, which led them into erroneous assumptions as to the nature of the Chinese poetic language. The peculiar characteristics of Chinese critical terminology and poetic language are by no means the product of pictographs, which comprise, after all, only a small minority of characters. Indeed pictographs, ideographs, and compound ideographs, according to Yuen Ren Chao's classifications, "represent words (or rather morphemes) and do not directly represent meanings. They are not therefore strictly pictographs or ideographs, but, to follow Peter A. Boodberg's terminology, *logographs*, that is, written forms to represent spoken words." Yuen Ren Chao, *Language and Symbolic Systems* (London: Cambridge University Press, 1968), pp. 102–5.

While *The Chinese Written Character as a Medium for Poetry* relies heavily on the models from the *Shih Ching*, it should be remembered that these poems come down to the present time through Han dynasty redactions of texts transmitted orally, preserved by memory from the ravages of the Ch'in dynasty (221–206 B.C.). Furthermore, it has been argued convincingly by Chinese and European scholars that the *Shih Ching* is in fact what Chinese literary history makes it; namely, an anthology based on orally composed songs from the folk tradition, and Chou state and local rituals. See C. H. Wang, *The Bell and the Drum*. Emphasizing the "pictorial" quality of the written language provides a fantastical notion of whence Chinese poetic language derives its expressive power. See also Zhang Longxi, "The *Tao* and the *Logos*." George A. Kennedy criticized Fenellosa's essay in "Fenellosa, Pound, and the Chinese Character," in Li Tien-yi, ed., *Selected Works of George A. Kennedy* (New Haven: Yale University Press, 1964), pp. 443–62. Perhaps more useful are his two essays dealing with the most persistent clichés about the nature of Chinese language; see "The Monosyllabic Myth," pp. 104–18; and "The Fate of Chinese Pictographs," pp. 238–41.

5 James J. Y. Liu, *Chinese Theories of Literature*, pp. 69–70; Chow Tze-tsung, "Ancient Chinese Views on Literature, the Tao, and Their Relationship," *CLEAR* 1.1 (January 1979): 3–29; and Donald Holzman, "Con-

fucius and Ancient Chinese Criticism," in Adele Austin Rickett, ed., *Chinese Approaches to Literature from Confucius to Liang Ch'i-ch'ao* (Princeton: Princeton University Press, 1978), pp. 21–41.

6 James J. Y. Liu, *Chinese Theories of Literature*, pp. 63–81, 106–16.

7 *Shu Ching*, pt. 2, book 1, sec. 5.24, translation by Chow Tze-tsung, "The Early History of the Chinese Word *Shih* (Poetry)," pp. 152–53. See also James Legge, *The Shoo King*, in *The Chinese Classics*, rev. ed. (Shanghai: Mer Seng Press, 1935), 3:48: "Poetry is the expression of earnest thought; singing is the prolonged utterance of that expression." James J. Y. Liu remarks, "The attribution of this statement to the legendary sage Emperor Shun cannot be accepted" (*Chinese Theories of Literature*, p. 118). Again, it is symptomatic of the importance given to this statement that such apocryphal material concerning the nature and proper function of literature should be recorded and considered with the greatest seriousness by literary scholars.

8 The date of composition of the "Great Preface" is by no means fixed. A case for a date as early as the third century B.C. is made by Chu Tzu-ch'ing, *Shih yen chih pien* (Taipei: K'ai-ming, 1964), sec. 3:19–20. For an overview of the problem, see Ch'u Wan-li, *Shih ching shih yi*, facsimile ed. (Taipei: K'ai-ming, 1964), introduction, pp. 20–21.

9 For a text and complete translation see James Legge, *The She King or the Book of Poetry*, in *The Chinese Classics*, rev. ed. (Shanghai: Mer Seng Press, 1935), 4:34–36. His text is based on that of the *Mao shih chu shu*, in Juan Yüan, ed., *Shih-san ching chu shu* (1815). This text was also the basis for the annotated edition of Kuo Shao-yü, *Chung-kuo wen-hsüeh p'i-p'ing wen-hsüan* (reprint, Tainan: P'ing-p'ing, 1975), on which I have based my translation of the text. See also Chow Tze-tsung, "The Early History of the Chinese Word *Shih* (Poetry)," p. 157; and James J. Y. Liu, *Chinese Theories of Literature*, pp. 63–64, 69, 119–20.

10 Some Han scholars even went so far as to equate *shih* with *chih*, by definition: see Hsü Shen (30?–124?), *Shuo wen chieh tzu*, in Ting Fu-pao, ed., *Shuo wen chieh tzu ku lin*, 12 vols. (Taipei: Shang-wu, 1966), pp. 968a–b.

11 See, for example, Kao Yu-kung, "The Aesthetics of Regulated Verse," in Lin and Owen, eds., *The Vitality of the Lyric Voice*, p. 348: "Many have pointed out that this simple maxim [*shih yen chih*] is indeed the cornerstone of Chinese poetic theory, which prescribes an 'expressive theory' of poetry by all accounts."

12 Kao Yu-kung, "Lyric Vision in Chinese Narrative Tradition: A Reading of *Hung-lou Meng* and *Ju-lin Wai-shih*," in Plaks, ed., *Chinese Narrative*, pp. 228–29.

13 Kao Yu-kung and Mei Tsu-lin, "Syntax, Diction, and Imagery in T'ang Poetry," *Harvard Journal of Asiatic Studies* 31 (1971): 49–136.

14 Kao and Mei, "Syntax, Diction, and Imagery in T'ang Poetry," pp. 58–59; see also Ernst Cassirer, *Language and Myth*, trans. Suzanne K. Langer (New York: Dover, 1946), especially pp. 32–33; and François Recanati, "Some Remarks on Explicit Perfomatives, Indirect Speech Acts, Locutionary Meaning, and Truth Value," in John R. Searle, Fernec Kieffer, and Manfred Bierwisch, eds., *Speech Act Theory and Pragmatics* (Dordrecht: Reidel, 1980), pp. 205–20.

15 See Kao and Mei, "Syntax, Diction, and Imagery in T'ang Poetry," pp. 58–60 ("Preview of Some Basic Ideas").

16 Kao and Mei, "Syntax, Diction, and Imagery in T'ang Poetry," pp. 98–112; see also W. A. C. H. Dobson, *Late Archaic Chinese: A Grammatical Study* (Toronto: University of Toronto Press, 1959), p. 76; and Yuen Ren Chao, *Mandarin Primer* (Cambridge: Harvard University Press, 1948), introduction. In my interpretation I have relied greatly upon Chou Fa-kao's historical grammar of classical Chinese; see Chou Fa-kao, *Chung-kuo ku-tai yü-fa*, 4 vols. (Taipei: Academia Sinica, 1959, 1961).

17 Kao, "Lyric Vision in Chinese Narrative Tradition," pp. 227–31.

18 James J. Y. Liu, *The Interlingual Critic*, pp. 17–18. See also Achilles Fang, "Some Reflections on the Difficulty of Translation," in Reuben Brower, ed., *On Translation* (Cambridge: Harvard University Press, 1959); and Eugene Eoyang, "The Tone of the Poet and the Tone of the Translator," *Yearbook of Comparative and General Literature* 24 (1975): 75–83.

19 George A. Kennedy, "The Monosyllabic Myth," pp. 110–13; see also his "A Note on Ode 220," in *Studia Serica Berhard Karlgren Dedicata*, pp. 190–98.

20 Chou Fa-kao, "Reduplicatives in the Book of Odes," *Bulletin of the Institute of History and Philology* (Academia Sinica) 34.2 (1963): 661.

21 Chou Fa-kao, "Reduplicatives in the Book of Odes," p. 669: "*Kuan kuan* is an identical reduplicative, while *ts'en tz'u* is an alliterative reduplicative, and *yao t'iao*, a rhyming reduplicative." It should be noted that while most of the reduplicatives in the *Shih Ching* are qualitative verbs, or "descriptives," there are some nouns and a few instances of interjections and intransitive verbs used in this fashion. See pp. 664–65. For my analysis of the function of reduplicatives and imagistic language in the *Shih Ching* I am indebted to conversations with David Lattimore and to his notes, "Verbal Repetition in *The Canon of Songs*."

22 James Legge, *The She King*, p. 1.

23 Bernhard Karlgren, *The Book of Odes* (Stockholm: Museum of Far Eastern Antiquities, 1950), p. 2.

24 Arthur Waley, *The Book of Songs* (London: Allen and Unwin, 1937), no. 87, p. 81.

25 Bernhard Karlgren, *Grammata Serica Recensa, Bulletin of the Museum of Far Eastern Antiquities*, no. 29 (1957; reprint, Stockholm: Museum of Far Eastern Antiquities, 1972), no. 187, p. 69.

26 Legge, *The She King*, p. 8.

27 Waley, *The Book of Songs*, no. 40, p. 45. Chou Fa-kao agrees that Waley is correct in treating this compound as a descriptive. He goes further to state that no transitive verbs are used reduplicatively in the *Shih Ching*, or perhaps more precisely, no reduplicatives function as transitive verbs here. See "Reduplicatives in the Book of Odes," p. 665, note 3.

28 Kao and Mei, "Syntax, Diction, and Imagery in T'ang Poetry," pp. 93–94.

29 W. A. C. H. Dobson, "Studies in the Grammar of Early Archaic Chinese," *T'oung Pao* 46, livr. 3–5 (1955): 342.

30 Kao and Mei discuss these verbs under their category of "static verbs," in "Syntax, Diction, and Imagery in T'ang Poetry," pp. 98–103.

31 James Robert Hightower, "Allusion in the Poetry of T'ao Ch'ien," *Harvard Journal of Asiatic Studies* 31 (1971): 5–27; reprinted in Birch, ed., *Studies in Chinese Literary Genres*, pp. 108–32; David Lattimore, "Allusion in T'ang Poetry," in Denis Twitchett and Arthur Wright, eds., *Perspectives on the T'ang* (New Haven: Yale University Press, 1973), pp. 405–39; Chou Shan, "Allusion and Periphrasis as Modes of Poetry in Tu Fu's 'Eight Laments,'" *Harvard Journal of Asiatic Studies* 45.1 (1985): 77–128.

32 This issue has been analyzed in great detail, with reference to many European critics, in the discussion of the principle of "manifold meaning" in Kao Yu-kung and Mei Tsu-lin, "Meaning, Metaphor, and Allusion in T'ang Poetry," *Harvard Journal of Asiatic Studies* 38.2 (December 1978): 281–356.

33 Chen Shih-hsiang, "The *Shih Ching*: Its Generic Significance in Chinese Literary History and Poetics," *Bulletin of the Institute of History and Philology* (Academia Sinica) 39.1 (1968): 371–413: reprinted in Birch, ed., *Studies in Chinese Literary Genres*, pp. 23–24.

34 This preface has recently been completely translated and annotated by David R. Knechtges, along with the "Two Capitals *Fu*," in *Wen xuan, or Selections of Refined Literature*, vol. 1: *Rhapsodies on Metropolises and Capitals* (Princeton: Princeton University Press, 1982), pp. 93–180. Knechtges has rendered this sentence: "Someone has said, 'The rhapsody is a genre of the ancient Songs'" (p. 94). I have translated it differently above in order to avoid the equation of the term "genre" with *liu*. It is interesting to note that the anthologist Chih Yu (d. c. 310),

a contemporary of Lu Chi, also asserted that *fu* were derived from the *Book of Songs*, using exactly the same phrase. It is quoted in Ou-yang Hsün (557–641) (Wang Shao-ying, ed.), *Yi wen lei-chü* (Peking: Chunghua, 1965), p. 56. For a translation, with notes, see Joseph Roe Allen III, "Chih Yü's *Discussions of Different Types of Literature*: A Translation and Brief Comment," in *Two Studies in Chinese Literary Criticism* (*Parerga* 3) (Seattle: Institute for Foreign Area Studies, 1976), pp. 3–36.

35 Interestingly enough, this seems not to apply to the other five principles outside the context of the *Shih Ching. Feng, ya,* and *sung* have often been assumed to designate generic categories in the *Shih Ching* itself, although these terms are not applied to examples of similar genres outside of this anthology. For another perspective, the role of the six principles in the development of Japanese poetics and genre theory in relation to Chinese critical theory is discussed in John T. Wixted, "The *Kokinshu* Prefaces: Another Perspective," *Harvard Journal of Asiatic Studies* 43.1 (1983): 215–38. For line-by-line correspondences between the "Great Preface" and the two *Kokinshu* prefaces, see E. B. Ceadel, "The Two Prefaces of the *Kokinshu*," *Asia Major*, n.s. 7.1–2 (1959): 40–51.

36 All poems from the *Shih Ching* will be cited according to their number in the Mao edition, with particular reference to the commentaries of Mao Heng, Cheng Hsüan (117–200), and K'ung Ying-ta (574–648). K'ung Ying-ta's edition and commentary, *Mao shih cheng yi*, relies upon the Mao edition and Cheng Hsüan's textual notes. I have used *Mao shih chu shu*, 3 vols., from the series *Kuo-hsüeh chi-pen ts'ung shu* (Taipei: Shang-wu, 1968). For later studies, the Sung commentaries of Chu Hsi (1130–1200) are most influential, although his interests are not primarily in the realm of literary theory or aesthetics. See *Shih chi chuan* (reprint, Shanghai: Chung-hua, 1958). In the classification of poems according to technique, Chu Hsi follows K'ung Ying-ta, but while K'ung Ying-ta remarks on particular phrases or lines he regards as characteristic of given techniques, Chu Hsi assumes that the characteristics of a particular passage apply to the poem as a whole. Chu Hsi's approach can be explained in other than literary critical or theoretical terms. For a discussion of his principles and aesthetics of canonical commentary, see Daniel K. Gardner, "Principle and Pedagogy: Chu Hsi and the Four Books," *Harvard Journal of Asiatic Studies* 44.1 (1984): 57–81.

37 David Hawkes, "The Quest of the Goddess," *Asia Major*, n.s. 13.1–2 (1967): 71–94; reprinted in Birch, ed., *Studies in Chinese Literary Genres*, pp. 42–68. The etymology cited is from Cheng Hsüan's commentary on the *Chou li* 6.13a (*Shih-san ching* ed.): "*fu chih yen p'u.*"

38 This etymology is a very ancient one, and seems the most promising

for reconciling the critical term with the poetic form, designated by the same character in Chinese. See the entry on *fu* in Karlgren, *Grammata Serica Recensa*, no. 104g–h, pp. 47–48. David R. Knechtges also discusses possible etymologies for the term in *The Han Rhapsody: A Study of the Fu of Yang Hsiung (53 B.C.–A.D. 18)* (Cambridge: Cambridge University Press, 1976), pp. 12–14, but is more concerned with the significance of *fu* as a poetic form than as a principle of composition. For a discussion of *fu* as a military tax, see Yang Lien-sheng, *Studies in Chinese Institutional History* (Cambridge: Harvard University Press, 1961), pp. 104–7.

39 Georges Margouliès, *Evolution de la prose artistique chinoise* (Munich: Encyclopädie-Verlag, 1929), p. 36.

40 James Legge, *The She King*, passim. In his notes on the "Great Preface," Legge first tends to define *fu* in terms of its effects rather than its technical function: "The term *Foo* needs little explanation. It is descriptive of a narrative piece, in which the poet says what he has to say right out, writing it down in a simple straightforward manner, without any hidden object. There is no meaning intended beyond what the words express, excepting in so far as we may infer from what is said the state of mind or the circumstances of the writer or subject" ("Prolegomena," p. 35).

41 Knechtges, *Wen xuan*, p. 92.

42 Chen Shih-hsiang, "The *Shih Ching*," p. 17.

43 Chen Shih-hsiang suggests the terms "poetic usage" and "poetic corporality" for K'ung Ying-ta's terms. What is important to our understanding of the terms is that *"shih chih suo yung"* refers to the means whereby certain poetic effects may be achieved, while *"shih chih ch'eng hsing"* indicates formal distinctions in this context. See K'ung Ying-ta, *Mao shih cheng yi*, preface.

44 James J. Y. Liu, *Chinese Theories of Literature*, p. 64.

45 C. H. Wang, "The Nature of Narrative in T'ang Poetry," pp. 218–19.

46 Pauline Yu, "Metaphor and Chinese Poetry," *CLEAR* 3.2 (July 1981): 214, 216.

47 Mao no. 35, *"Ku feng,"* is regarded as representing all three principles in action. See *Mao shih chu shu*, 1:205–7; *Shih chi chuan*, pp. 21–22; see also Legge, *The She King*, pp. 55–58.

48 Karlgren, *Grammata Serica Recensa*, entry 566g–h, p. 150.

49 For the translation of *pi* as "similes," see Chen, "The *Shih Ching*," p. 17; as "comparison" or "simile," see Yu, "Metaphor and Chinese Poetry," p. 214. Legge is unusual in assigning the term "metaphor" to *pi*; see *The She King*, "Prolegomena," pp. 35, passim.

50 *Mao shih chu shu*, 1:324–26; *Shih chi chuan*, pp. 40–41; Legge, *The She King*, pp. 106–8.

51 *Mao shih chu shu*, 1:554–56; *Shih chi chuan*, p. 73; Legge, *The She King*, pp. 186–87.

52 Chung Jung, in Ch'en Yen-chieh, ed., *Shih p'in chu* (Taipei: K'ai-ming, 1958), p. 4; also cited in this context by Chen Shih-hsiang, "The *Shih Ching*," p. 18. In "Theory, Standards, and Practice of Criticizing Poetry in Chung Jung's *Shih-p'in*," Yeh Chia-ying and Jan Walls translate the term *fu* as "direct description," *pi* as "comparison," and *hsing* as "evocative image": "The evocative image yields a meaning beyond words; comparison reveals internal feelings by means of external objects; description is the direct recounting of events and the depiction of objects through words"; in Ronald C. Miao, ed., *Studies in Chinese Poetry and Poetics* (San Francisco: Chinese Materials Center, 1978), 1:43–80, 52.

53 Karlgren, *Grammata Serica Recensa*, entry 889a–d, p. 237.

54 Chen, "The *Shih Ching*," pp. 22–23. For this etymology Chen cites the works of Shang Ch'eng-tso and Kuo Mo-jo on oracle bone inscriptions. See Shang Ch'eng-tso, *Yin ch'i i ts'un*, 2 vols. (Nan-ching: Chung-kuo wen-hua yen-chiu suo, 1933), p. 62; and Kuo Mo-jo, *Pu tz'u t'ung tsuan* (1933; reprint, Tokyo: Meiyu, 1977), p. 34.

55 Legge, *The She King*, "Prolegomena," pp. 35, passim; Yu, "Metaphor and Chinese Poetry," p. 214; Chen, "The *Shih Ching*," p. 16.

56 Translations by Legge, *The She King*, pp. 91, 103, 200–201.

57 By the time of the composition of the "Great Preface," the term which previous to the Han had been used for a certain style of chanting had become more frequently applied to the literary genre, probably in reference to its intended context of public declamation. See Knechtges, *The Han Rhapsody*, pp. 14–43.

58 C. H. Wang, *The Bell and the Drum*; Frankel, "Some Characteristics of Oral Narrative Poetry in China," pp. 97–106.

59 Chu Hsi, *Shih chi chuan*, pp. 43–44; Legge, *The She King*, pp. 112–13.

60 Some notable exceptions occur among the *sung* (hymns) in Chu Hsi's commentary, twenty-one of which are not divided into stanzas at all. Chu Hsi labels several of these as demonstrating the principle *fu*, in which the people count their blessings, as it were. This strongly suggests that the original applications of the principle as enumeration were still considered valid in Sung literary criticism, even if commentators tended to stress sequences of action over other kinds.

61 Translations of Mao nos. 243 and 244 by Legge, *The She King*, pp. 458–64.

62 Legge, *The She King*, p. 460.

63 For the origins of the genre *fu* in the poems of the *Ch'u Tz'u*, see Ch'eng T'ing-tso, "*Sao fu lun*," in *Wan shu ting yi* (Taipei: Chin-ling, 1970), pp. 169–71.

64 David Hawkes, "The Quest of the Goddess," *Asia Major*, n.s. 13.1–2 (1967): 79–94; reprinted in Birch, ed., *Studies in Chinese Literary Genres*, pp. 42–68. See also Arthur Waley, *The Nine Songs: A Study of Shamanism in Ancient China* (London: Allen and Unwin, 1953); and L. C. Hopkins, "The Shaman or Chinese *Wu*: His Inspired Dancing and Versatile Character," *Journal of the Royal Asiatic Society* (1945, pts. 1–2): 3–16.

65 Hawkes, "The Quest of the Goddess," p. 63.

66 Ch'en Yüan-lung (1652–1736), ed., *Yü-ting li-tai fu-hui*, reprint, with introduction by Yoshikawa Kōjirō (Tokyo: Chubun, 1974).

67 For translations and commentary on Hsiao T'ung's preface, see James R. Hightower, "The *Wen Hsüan* and Genre Theory," pp. 512–33; and Knechtges, *Wen xuan*, 1:73–91.

68 See Ch'en Yüan-lung, *Yü-ting li-tai fu-hui*, preface, and the introduction by Yoshikawa Kōjirō; and Nakashima Chiaki, *Fu no seiritsu to tenkai* (Matsuyama: Kankosei, 1963).

69 The terms for the basic categories of *fu* vary from anthology to anthology, and critical studies of individual poets are perhaps more helpful for developing a sense of the distinctions between "descriptive" and "personal" *fu*. For general discussions of the different classifications, see Nakashima Chiaki, *Fu no seiritsu to tenkai*; Chin Chu-hsiang, *Han tai tz'u fu chih fa-ta* (Shanghai: Commercial Press, 1931); T'ao Chiu-ying, *Han fu chih shih ti yen-chiu* (Shanghai: Chung-hua, 1939); and Wang Kuo-ying, "*Han fu chung ti shan-shui ching-wu*," *Chung wai wen-hsüeh* 9.5 (1980): 4–34.

70 Ch'eng T'ing-tso, "*Sao fu lun*," p. 170. Hsiao T'ung regards Chia Yi as the heir of Sung Yü (third century B.C.), to whom the "*Chiu pien*" are attributed, and these poems are classified as "*sao*" in *Wen Hsüan* 33. The fact that Ssu-ma Ch'ien included Chia Yi's biography with the biography of Ch'ü Yüan points to a far earlier association of the two (*Shih Chi* 84), and Chia Yi's earliest extant poem, "*Tiao Ch'ü Yüan fu*," suggests that he drew this comparison himself. See Hightower, "The *Wen Hsüan* and Genre Theory," p. 519; Knechtges, *Wen xuan*, 1:75.

For a complete translation of the "Owl *fu*" with analysis and notes, see James Robert Hightower, "Chia Yi's 'Owl *Fu*,'" *Asia Major*, n.s. 7.1–2 (1959): 125–30.

71 Ch'eng T'ing-tso, "*Sao fu lun*," p. 170. For a study of the problem of

genre in early Chinese literature focusing on *sao* see Ferenc Tőkei: *A kínai elégia születése. K'iu Juan és kora* (Budapest: Akadémiai Kiadó, 1959). Tőkei renders *"sao"* as "elegy," and explores the relation between the elegiac quality of Chinese poetry in general and the representative quality of the genre of elegy (*sao*) in particular. He sees the emergence of the elegy as a natural outgrowth of the social conditions of Ch'ü Yüan's era. A revised edition appears in French under the title *Naissance de l'élégie chinoise. K'iu Yuan et son époque. Les Essais CXXV* (Paris: Gallimard, 1967).

72 Knechtges, *The Han Rhapsody*, pp. 21–43. See also Waley, *The Nine Songs*; and Hellmut Wilhelm, "The Scholar's Frustration: Notes on a Type of *Fu*," in John K. Fairbank, ed., *Chinese Thought and Institutions* (Chicago: University of Chicago Press, 1957), pp. 310–19. Wilhelm emphasizes the importance of persuasive purpose in both descriptive and personal *fu*, a feature of the essential unity of the genre. F. A. Bischoff also emphasizes the aspect of persuasive rhetoric: see *Interpreting the Fu: A Study in Chinese Literary Rhetoric*. Münchener ostasiatische Studien, no. 13 (Wiesbaden: Franz Steiner, 1976).

73 David Knechtges and Jerry Swanson, "Seven Stimuli for the Prince: The *Ch'i-Fa* of Mei Ch'eng," *Monumenta Serica* 29 (1970–71): 99–116; and Frankel, *The Flowering Plum and the Palace Lady*, pp. 186–211.

74 In "Hsieh Ling-yun: The Making of a New Descriptive Mode," in *Six Dynasties Poetry*, pp. 68–70, Kang-i Sun Chang suggests a special style of "lyrical" *fu*, whose development paralleled that of landscape poetry in the *shih* form, in spite of the preponderence of descriptive (or as Chang terms them, "epideictic") *fu*. Her purpose is to consider the possibility of reciprocal influences between *shih* and *fu* as the use of description in lyric *shih* intensified.

75 Ch'en Yüan-lung, *Yü-ting li-tai fu-hui*, vol. 4 (*wai-chi*), pp. 1910–14.

76 Beginning with the *Shu Ching*, as mentioned above, the significance of the phrase "*yen-chih*" is of great importance in Chinese poetics. My translation here of *yen-chih*, "to speak of one's true self," is used here for the particular purpose of describing this category in the poetic anthologies cited, and is not meant to be adequate to the term's implications in all of Chinese poetic theory. See Chu Tzu-ch'ing, *Shih yen chih pien*.

77 See William T. Graham, Jr., *"The Lament for the South": Yü Hsin's "Ai Chiang-nan Fu"* (Cambridge: Cambridge University Press, 1980). Graham's study includes an exhaustive commentary with his complete translation, as well as analyses of the literary and historical sources of the material of the poem. All references to the poem's text and transla-

tions in this study are taken from this work. For the expressive qualities of Yü Hsin's masterpiece, see Ch'en Yin-k'o, "*Tu Ai Chiang-nan fu*," in *Ch'en Yin-k'o hsien-sheng wen-shih lun-chi*, 2:339–45.

78 Graham, "*The Lament for the South*," pp. 43–44, 134–35.
79 Graham, "*The Lament for the South*," p. 111.
80 Graham, "*The Lament for the South*," p. 67.
81 Graham, "*The Lament for the South*," p. 77.
82 Graham, "*The Lament for the South*," p. 89.

2 Setting Specific Contexts

1 Point of view is a well-explored concept in theory of narrative, but studies show a persistent bias toward prose fiction. This should be kept in mind when applying the concept to poetry. I have tried to qualify the term according to the requirements of narrative poetry whenever necessary.

  A comprehensive discussion of point of view in literature, based on European models and especially prose fiction, is Scholes and Kellogg, *The Nature of Narrative*, pp. 240–82; see also Wayne C. Booth, "Distance and Point of View," in Philip Stevick, ed., *The Theory of the Novel* (New York: Free Press, 1967), pp. 87–107. For a historical and bibliographical survey of the concept during the period of the establishment of the primacy of the novel, see Norman Friedman, "Point of View in Fiction: The Development of a Critical Concept," *Publication of the Modern Language Association* 70 (December 1955): 1160–84. For a study of Chinese fiction that deals specifically with this question, see Wong Kam-ming, "Point of View, Norms, and Structure," in Plaks, ed., *Chinese Narrative*, pp. 203–26.

2 Norman Friedman emphasizes the importance of point of view for critical interpretation and, suggestively, compares its function in fiction to the choice of poetic genre in poetry; however, he fails to make a connection between the functions of point of view in narrative prose and poetry: "Thus the choice of a point of view in the writing of fiction is at least as crucial as the choice of a verse form in the composing of a poem; just as there are certain things which cannot get said [*sic*] in a sonnet, so each of the categories we have detailed has a probable range of functions it can perform within its limits. The question of effectiveness, therefore, is one of the suitability of a given technique for the achievement of certain kinds of effects, for each story requires the establishment of a particular kind of illusion to sustain it ("Point of View in Fiction," p. 1180).

These applications of point of view do not preclude its use in other narrative genres, as works of structuralist poetics have attempted to elucidate. See, for example, Tzvetan Todorov, "Poétique," in Oswald Ducrot et al., *Qu'est-ce que le structuralisme?* (Paris: Seuil, 1968); and Gérard Genette, *Figures III*. Certainly point of view is of great concern to artists themselves; see Henry James, *The Art of the Novel*, R. P. Blackmur, ed. (New York: Charles Scribner's Sons, 1934); and Joyce Cary, *Art and Reality*, pp. 15–20, 37–50. In Cary's discussion point of view is seen as the controlling device through which artists present their intuitions about the chosen subject matter to their audience. Cary reflects that determining point of view is vital because it is the agency which determines the reader's access to and appreciation of the content of the author's intuition and interpretation of events. This formulation is particularly interesting in view of the Chinese critical tradition of "reading" a poet's character through his literary work (see discussion below).

3 See Kao Yu-kung, "Lyric Vision in Chinese Narrative Tradition," pp. 227–43. Two studies which deal with the nature of lyricism in *tz'u* are Shuen-fu Lin, *The Transformation of the Chinese Lyrical Tradition: Chiang K'uei and Southern Sung Tz'u Poetry* (Princeton: Princeton University Press, 1978); and Kang-i Sun Chang, *The Evolution of Chinese Tz'u Poetry*. For a study focusing on T'ang *shih*, see Stephen Owen, "Transparencies: Reading the T'ang Lyric," *Harvard Journal of Asiatic Studies* 39.2 (1979): 231–51. A more general theoretical discussion appears in Hsü Fu-kuan, "*Chung-kuo yi-shu ching-shen chu-t'i chih chen hsien,*" pp. 43–143.

4 Northrop Frye, *Anatomy of Criticism*, pp. 246–51, 270–81.

5 The Confucian emphasis on purposive creation and criticism, mentioned in the previous chapter, helps to explain this attitude and its pervasiveness in the Chinese tradition. The assumption forms the basis of innumerable critical studies, especially commentaries, and enforces a methodology of interpreting a poem in terms of what is known of a poet's biography, or extrapolating biographical detail of an individual poet based on interpretations of particular poems. Even Western scholars take these assumptions into account in their critical and particularly biographical studies of Chinese poets. For instance, Arthur Waley's lives of Po Chü-yi, Li Po, and Yüan Mei (first published in 1949, 1950, and 1956, respectively) are all based on this premise, and scholars continue to emulate his method. It lends itself perhaps most easily to literary biography. William Hung begins the final paragraph of his study, *Tu Fu: China's Greatest Poet* (Cambridge: Harvard University Press, 1952), with these remarks: "I cannot claim to have fully understood Tu Fu, the poet. I believe I have a fairly accurate understanding of Tu Fu,

the man" (p. 282). For more recent works of literary history which follow the same tendency, although their critical approaches to the poets studied are distinctive, see Stephen Owen, *The Poetry of Meng Chiao and Han Yü* (New Haven: Yale University Press, 1975); and Ronald C. Egan, *The Literary Works of Ou-yang Hsiu* (Cambridge: Cambridge University Press, 1984), to name only two examples. Stephen Owen takes up the issue of "reading the poet" in its own right in "Transparencies: Reading the T'ang Lyric," and *Traditional Chinese Poetics: The Omen of the World* (Madison: University of Wisconsin Press, 1985), pp. 63–68.

6 In "The Concept of Creative Personality in Traditional Chinese Criticism," *Oriens Extremus* 27.2 (1980): 183–202, Marian Galik stresses this concept as it applies to the notion of the creative personality in Chinese culture in general: "[Chinese literary theories] accentuate the components of relations and affinities that lie between 'reality,' the author, and the work" (p. 183). See also Maureen Robertson, ". . . 'To Convey What is Precious': Ssu-k'ung T'u's Poetics and the *Erh-shih-ssu Shih P'in*," in D. C. Buxbaum and F. W. Mote, eds., *Transition and Permanence: Chinese History and Culture* (Hong Kong: Cathay Press, 1972), pp. 323–57.

7 For a discussion of the memorial on "The Buddha's Finger Bone," and its biographical consequences for Han Yü, see Homer H. Dubs, "Han Yü and the Buddha's Relic: An Episode in Medieval Chinese Religion," *The Review of Religion* 11 (November 1946): 5–17; and Charles Hartman, *Han Yü and the T'ang Search for Unity* (Princeton: Princeton University Press, 1986), pp. 84–93. "The Officer at the Rapids" is mentioned in passing on p. 89, as one of many poems, in many styles, written by the disgraced statesman on his exile. The Chinese text I have consulted is from Chu Yi-tsun (1629–1709), ed., and Ku Ssu-li (1669–1722), annot., *Ch'ang-li hsien-sheng shih chi chu* (reprint, Taipei: Hsüeh-sheng, 1967), sec. 6, pp. 351–53. A translation by Charles Hartman, "The Officer at the Rapids," appears in *Sunflower Splendor*, pp. 188-89.

8 Another analysis of "The Officer at Lung River," focusing on the biographical implications of the poem, may be found in Stephen Owen, *The Poetry of Meng Chiao and Han Yü*, p. 271. Emphasizing the perspective of literary biography, Owen describes "The Officer at Lung River" (which he translates as "Clerk at the Rapids") as possibly Han Yü's "finest personal narrative." Owen assumes that the shift from implicit to explicit point of view constitutes a shift from lyric to narrative mode; see his discussion of the three categories of "personal narratives," pp. 73–89.

9 For texts, see *Ch'üan T'ang shih*, 7:2265–66, 2275–76. For the relation

of these poems to Tu Fu's biography and complete translations, see
William Hung, *Tu Fu*, pp. 87–89, 115–18. For translations with critical
analyses emphasizing the expressive process and purpose of Tu Fu,
see David Lattimore, "The Journey North" (in manuscript), and "From
the Capital to Feng-hsien: Five Hundred Words to Chant My Feelings,"
Ironwood 17 (also known as vol. 9, no. 1) (Spring 1981): 52–54. I am grateful to Professor Lattimore for sharing these materials with me and for
discussions about them. For a translation of "Journey North" focusing
on its linguistic peculiarities, see Hugh Stimson, "The Rimes of 'Northward Journey,' by Duh-Fuu, 712–770," *Journal of the American Oriental
Society* 93 (1973): 129–35; for a complete transcription of its T'ang pro-
nunciation and lexicography, with textual notes, see his *Fifty-five T'ang
Poems*, pp. 91–111.

10 Mark Schorer, "Technique as Discovery," *The Hudson Review* 1.1 (Spring
1948): 67–87; Herman M. Weisman, "An Investigation of Methods and
Techniques in the Dramatization of Fiction," *Speech Monographs* 19 (1952):
48–59; Frye, *Anatomy of Criticism*, pp. 282–93; Rogers, *The Three Genres
and the Interpretation of Lyric*, pp. 77–120.

11 This description of the function of point of view stems from a common-
sense interpretation of the process of reading. For discussions of this
problem in "reader-response" criticism, with implications sufficiently
broad for application to the Chinese models, see I. A. Richards, *Practical Criticism: A Study of Literary Judgement* (New York: Harcourt, Brace,
1935); James F. Ross, "On the Concepts of Reading," *Philosophical Forum*
6 (Fall 1972): 93–141; Wolfgang Iser, *The Implied Reader: Patterns of Communication from Bunyan to Beckett* (Baltimore: Johns Hopkins University
Press, 1978), pp. 274–94; and Earl Miner, "The Objective Fallacy and
the Real Existence of Literature," *PTL: A Journal for Descriptive Poetics and
Theory of Literature* 1 (January 1976): 11–31. For the relation of "speaker"
to experience and expression, see Paul Friedrich, *The Language Parallax:
Linguistic Relativism and Poetic Indeterminacy* (Austin: University of Texas
Press, 1986), pp. 137–62; and Wolfgang Motsch, "Situational Context
and Illusionary Force," in Searle et al., *Speech Act Theory and Pragmatics*,
pp. 155–68.

12 In *Jen chien tz'u-hua*, Wang Kuo-wei draws a distinction between the *k'o-
kuan shih-jen*, or "objective" poet, and the *chu-kuan shih-jen*, or "subjective" poet. Wang's analysis of the distinction between these two types
is based on their different modes of presentation of subject matter, as
determined by their level of experience and intent in composition: "Objective poets must observe the world as much as possible. The more

profound their observation, the richer and more varied will be their material. . . . Subjective poets, on the other hand, do not need to observe the world to any great extent. The more superficial their observation the more genuine will be their expression of their own natural feelings." Translation by Adele Austin Rickett, *Wang Kuo-wei's Jen-chien Tz'u-hua: A Study in Chinese Literary Criticism* (Hong Kong: Hong Kong University Press, 1977), p. 46. As they reflect the underlying expressive intent of the poet, the terms are suggestive of the distinctions I would like to draw between lyrical and narrative tendencies in poetic expression. See *Jen-chien tz'u-hua*, in Hsü Tiao-fu, ed., *Hai-ning Wang Ching-an hsien sheng yi-shu* (Peking: n.p., 1927–28). On the topic of description as a literary mode, see Jeffrey Kittay, ed., *Towards a Theory of Description*. Yale French Studies, no. 61 (New Haven: Yale University Press, 1981). See also Kang-i Sun Chang, "Description of Landscape in Early Six Dynasties Poetry," in Lin and Owen, eds., *The Vitality of the Lyric Voice*, pp. 105–29; and *Six Dynasties Poetry*, pp. 47–78.

13 See my introduction, p. 14; and Pauline Yu: *The Poetry of Wang Wei*, pp. 59–61.

14 For text see Shen Te-ch'ien (1675–1769), ed., *Ku-shih yüan*, pp. 76–77. For a complete translation, with analysis focusing on the orphan's movement in time and space within the poem, see Frankel, *The Flowering Plum and the Palace Lady*, pp. 62–66.

15 For a complete text, translation, and analysis of this poem, see Hans H. Frankel, "The Chinese Ballad 'Southeast Fly the Peacocks,'" *Harvard Journal of Asiatic Studies* 34 (1974): 249–71. For an analysis focusing on the characteristics of the poetic language of the piece, see Frankel, "The Formulaic Language in the Chinese Ballad 'Southeast Fly the Peacocks,'" *Bulletin of the Institute of History and Philology* 39.2 (1969): 219–44. Another translation appears in Watson, *The Columbia Book of Chinese Poetry*, pp. 82–92.

16 Couplets 59, 186–87; text from Wang Yi (second century A.D.), ed., *Ch'u tz'u chang-chu* (reprint, Taipei: Shih-chieh, 1965); translation by David Hawkes, *Ch'u Tz'u: The Songs of the South* (Oxford: Oxford University Press, 1959), pp. 25, 34 (italics added to emphasize the presence of personal references in the Chinese text).

17 For text see *Ch'üan T'ang shih*, vol. 4, sec. 97 (Shen Ch'üan-ch'i 3), pp. 1051–52. For a brief discussion of the career of Shen Ch'üan-ch'i and a translation of the first ten lines of this poem, see Stephen Owen, *The Poetry of the Early T'ang* (New Haven: Yale University Press, 1977), pp. 359–60. The term *chih-mei* is an example of a translator's nightmare, as English terms for supernatural creatures (in this case, a creature indige-

nous to hills and rocks) often have specific connotations from Western folklore which can be misleading when applied to Chinese folklore. I have chosen to use "troll" because of the association of trolls with rocky terrain, as per *chih-mei* in China and as borne out by Shen Ch'üan-ch'i's description of the landscape in his poem. For a detailed study of the work of Shen Ch'üan-ch'i in exile, see Suzanne Cahill, "Shen Ch'üan-ch'i; Poems in Exile" (M.A. thesis, University of California at Berkeley, 1978).

18 Hsiao T'ung, *Wen Hsüan* 19.

19 Arthur Waley, *The Life and Times of Po Chü-yi* (London: Allen and Unwin, 1949), pp. 117–18. My complete translation appears in the appendix. For other complete translations with interpretative analyses, see Howard S. Levy, "Lute Song," *Literature East and West* 11.3 (September 1967): 223–35; and Watson, *The Columbia Book of Chinese Poetry*, pp. 249–52.

20 The "chance meeting" inspired Ma Chih-yüan (c. 1210–1280) to write a play in the *tza-chu* form about Po Chü-yi's romance with the musician. *Ch'ing-shan lei* (*Tears on the Blue Sleeve*) transforms the autobiographical encounter of the poet and the musician, here given the name Pei Hsing-nu, into a full-blown romance with its origins in the capital, reuniting them in exile in Hsün-yang on this fateful night. It seems ironic that the poet who made such a romance of the story of Emperor Hsüan-tsung and his favorite concubine should have received similar treatment himself. Many later plays were based on Ma Chih-yüan's version of the story, including a *ch'uan-ch'i* by the Ming dramatist Ku Ta-tien (*chin-shih* 1568), *Ch'ing-shan chi* (*The Tale of the Blue Sleeve*). For an analysis of *Ch'ing-shan chi*, see Cyril Birch, "Some Concerns and Methods of Ming Ch'uan-ch'i Drama," in Birch, ed., *Studies in Chinese Literary Genres*, pp. 220–58. For a study of five plays about Po Chü-yi's romance, including *Ch'ing-shan chi*, see Kubo Tenzui (1875–1935), "*Biwaku no gokyoku*," in *Shina gikyoku kenkyū* (Tokyo: Jinbun, 1928).

21 "Ballad of the *p'i-p'a*," preface. Text from Ku Chao-ts'ang and Chou Ju-ch'ang, eds., *Po Chü-yi shih hsüan* (Peking: Tso-chia, 1962), pp. 125–29. I am grateful to Professor Anthony C. Yu for his meticulous critique of my draft translation.

22 The locus classicus for this allusion and the topos of mutual recognition and affinity is the story of the friendship of Po Ya and Chung Tzu-ch'i, from *Lieh Tzu* 5, "T'ang-wen" (see *Chung-hsü chih-te chen ching* 5.7a, *Ssu-pu tsung-k'an* ed.). When Po Ya played his lute, Chung Tzu-ch'i could divine his friend's thoughts with unerring accuracy and perfect sympathy. For a translation of this anecdote, see Angus Graham, *Lieh-tzu: A New Translation* (London: John Murray, 1960). My translation of

the phrase *"chih-yin,"* literally, "to understand the sound," is meant to evoke the underlying allusion, which is particularly appropriate to this meeting. For the theme of *chih-chi* or *chih-jen* as it influences characterization in Chinese fiction, see Plaks, "Towards a Critical Theory of Chinese Narrative," p. 343.

23 Cary, *Art and Reality*, pp. 15–20. While Po Chü-yi's image of his participation as an artist in the experience of the reader is of course founded on entirely different cultural assumptions, his concept of the creative process as it affects point of view is strikingly like Cary's notion of the role of intuition. See Waley's discussion of Po Chü-yi's "Letter to Yüan Chen" (*"Yü Yüan Chiu shu"*) in *The Life and Times of Po Chü-yi*, pp. 107–13; and the letter itself, in Ku Hsüeh-hsieh, ed., *Po Chü-yi chi*, 4 vols. (Peking: Chung-hua, 1979), chap. 45, 3: 959–67.

24 On the characteristics of *yüeh-fu* prosody and the conventions of *yüeh-fu* representations of storytellers' performances, see Frankel, *"Yüeh-fu* Poetry," in Birch, ed., *Studies in Chinese Literary Genres*, pp. 69–107; see also Huang Chieh, ed., *Han Wei yüeh-fu feng chien* (Hong Kong: Commercial Press, 1961), preface (dated 1923).

25 Frankel, *"Yüeh-fu* Poetry," and "The Formulaic Language in the Chinese Ballad 'Southeast Fly the Peacocks.' "

26 Text from Ku Chao-ts'ang and Chou Ju-ch'ang, eds., *Po Chü-yi shih hsüan*, pp. 14–27. My complete translation appears in the appendix. There are many translations of this poem into English. Arthur Waley, author of *The Life and Times of Po Chü-yi*, did not translate Po Chü-yi's most famous poem himself, but rather refers the reader of the biography to the translation by Witter Bynner and Kiang Kang-hu, in *The Jade Mountain*, pp. 120–25. Other translations include Howard S. Levy, *Lament Everlasting: The Death of Yang Kuei-fei* (Tokyo: n.p., 1962), see also his *Translations from Po Chü-yi's Collected Works*, 2 vols. (New York: Paragon, 1971), 1:131–40, for additional analyses; and Mimi Chan and Piers Grey, "Three Poems on Yang Kuei-fei," *Renditions* 14 (Autumn 1980): 79–84. For an analysis with reference to the relation of Po Chü-yi's poetry with that of his friend Yüan Chen, see Ch'en Yin-k'o, *"Ch'ang-hen ko chien-cheng"* (*"Yüan Po shih chien-cheng kao chih yi"*), *Ch'ing-hua hsüeh-pao* 14.1 (October 1947): 1–34.

27 For historical accounts of Emperor Hsüan-tsung's reign, see E. G. Pulleyblank, *The Background of the Rebellion of An Lu-shan* (London: Oxford University Press, 1955); and Denis Twitchett, ed., *The Cambridge History of China*, vol. 3: *Sui and T'ang China, 589–906* (Cambridge: Cambridge University Press, 1979), pt. 1, pp. 427ff. For a more subjective account from the perspective of the career of the poet Tu Fu, with

translations of his poems written during this period, see Hung, *Tu Fu*, chaps. 6–11, pp. 90–254. Howard S. Levy has made the emperor's infatuation with Yang Kuei-fei a special topic of study; see "The Career of Yang Kuei-fei," *T'oung Pao* 45 (1957): 101–18; "The Selection of Yang Kuei-fei," *Oriens* 15 (1962): 411–22. Two biographies of Yang Kuei-fei and studies of the political influence of her family appear in the dynastic histories; see Liu Hsu, ed., *Chiu T'ang shu* (Peking: Chung-hua, 1975), 7:2178–81; Ou-yang Hsiu, ed., *Hsin T'ang shu* (Peking: Chung-hua, 1975), 12:3493–96.

28 For Tu Fu's poem about the emperor's romance, "Lament by the Riverside" (*"Ai-chiang t'ou"*), see Hung, *Tu Fu*, pp. 106–7; David Hawkes, *A Little Primer of Tu Fu* (Oxford: Clarendon Press, 1967), pp. 49–59.

29 Hans H. Frankel, "The Contemplation of the Past in T'ang Poetry," in Wright and Twitchett, eds., *Perspectives on the T'ang*, pp. 345–64; David Lattimore, "Allusion in T'ang Poetry," pp. 405–39; James J. Y. Liu, *Chinese Theories of Literature*, pp. 106–16.

30 For text, see Feng Chih, *Tu Fu shih hsüan* (Hong Kong: Ta-kuang, 1961), pp. 48–49.

31 Text from Feng Chih, *Tu Fu shih hsüan*, pp. 77–78; see also Hung, *Tu Fu*, p. 141; Stimson, *Fifty-five T'ang Poems*, pp. 112–14.

32 Text from Feng Chih, *Tu Fu shih hsüan*, pp. 78–80; see also Hung, *Tu Fu*, pp. 141–42.

3 Character Types and Character Roles

1 Levy, "The Trojan and the Hegemon," p. 136.

2 The role of character in European narrative, like its Chinese counterpart, focuses more on prose fiction than on other genres. For a general survey of the properties of characterization, see Scholes and Kellogg, *The Nature of Narrative*, pp. 160–208. For other studies of character useful for comparison to the Chinese models, see E. M. Forster, *Aspects of the Novel* (New York: Harcourt, 1950), pp. 69–125; Henry James, "The Art of Fiction"; Lionel Trilling, "Manners, Morals, and the Novel"; and Northrop Frye, "Fictional Modes," all in Robert Scholes, ed., *Approaches to the Novel* (San Francisco: Chandler, 1961), pp. 289–312, 231–47, and 31–39, respectively. For more technical considerations, see E. M. Forster, "Flat and Round Characters," and W. J. Harvey, "The Human Context," in Philip Stevick, ed., *The Theory of the Novel*, pp. 223–30 and 231–52, respectively. Forster's essay is particularly suggestive for the distinction between "types" and "individuals" (see discussion below). Characterization in European literary theory is seen as a dynamic process, which

has greatly affected critics' perception of the function of character in Chinese narrative. See, for example, Marvin Mudrick, "Character and Event in Fiction," *Yale Review* 50.1 (Winter 1961): 202–18.

3 Andrew H. Plaks, "Towards a Critical Theory of Chinese Narrative," in Plaks, ed., *Chinese Narrative*, p. 344.

4 Plaks devotes a section of his essay, "Towards a Critical Theory of Chinese Narrative," to the problem of characterization; see pp. 339–48. On pp. 343–44, Plaks mentions that Ch'ien Mu deals with the problem of expressing authorial intent through characterization in narrative, stressing that the creation of "unique" individuals is actually a matter of the coherent and persuasive combination of recognizable attributes in a given character, which he terms a balancing of *pieh-hsiang* (distinctive attributes) and *kung-hsiang* (common attributes); see *Chung-kuo wen-hsüeh chiang-yen chi* (Kowloon: Jen-sheng, 1963), pp. 27–31. The distinction between exemplary and mimetic characters as they relate to a larger narrative framework in the European traditions is discussed in Scholes and Kellogg, *The Nature of Narrative*, pp. 204–6.

5 See Andrew H. Plaks, *Archetype and Allegory in the Dream of the Red Chamber* (Princeton: Princeton University Press, 1976), pp. 11–26. Plaks defines the notion of archetypes to refer to "patterns of more generalized structure" (p. 12). His concern is with the properties of narrative in general and prose fiction in particular: "The abiding patterns of literary *form* to which we apply the term 'archetype,' then, stand out as the synchronic underpinnings that set off and render intelligible the diachronic dimension of historical modification within the system. . . . Just as the spectrum of colors in painting and the tonal scales in music provide internal orders within the materials of artistic creation, so do archetypes of literary structure provide the ground of coherence, the aesthetic expectations, that may be fulfilled, subtly varied, or negatively negatively transformed in a given work" (pp. 12–13).

My discussion of narrative archetypes as they apply to the concept of character and techniques of characterization essentially describes a special category within the more general scope of Plaks's "archetype." While character archetypes make up a subset of archetypal patterns in general, a distinctive character has the potential to generate these larger patterns of narrative form and structure. My separation of archetypal patterns of character into "types" and "roles" below recognizes this potential and provides an approach to the analysis of the relation of character to larger narrative structures.

6 In "The Wang Chao-chün Legend: Configurations of the Classic," *CLEAR* 4.1 (1983): 3–22, Eugene Eoyang uses these terms in slightly

different senses. He analyzes the story of Wang Chao-chün in terms of character "roles," which evoke symbolic associations ("The Cinderella figure, the proud and haughty beauty, the political hostage, the patriotic heroine, the beauty despoiled"), then assigns these to "types" that are aspects of human concerns ("ambition, pride, power, loyalty, sexuality"); in other words, here "types" indicate the human themes underlying the "roles." He also refers to these categories as "motifs" (pp. 5–6). Eoyang's terms reflect his concern with the multiple layers of significance acquired by the story of Wang Chao-chün over the course of its evolution. My use of these terms focuses rather on aspects of structure and techniques of character presentation.

7 For text and commentary of the "Poem of Mu-lan" (*Mu-lan shih*), see Pei-ching ta-hsüeh, Chung-kuo yü yen wen-hsüeh hsi, ed., *Wei Chin Nan-pei ch'ao wen-hsüeh shih ts'an-k'ao tz'e-liao* (Peking: Chung-hua, 1962), pp. 379–82. In *The Flowering Plum and the Palace Lady*, pp. 68–72, Hans H. Frankel provides a complete translation with analysis of its relation to the *yüeh-fu* tradition. For other translations which take the poem's narrative features into special consideration, see J. D. Frodsham and Ch'eng Hsi, *An Anthology of Chinese Verse: Han Wei Chin and the Northern and Southern Dynasties* (Oxford: Clarendon Press, 1967), pp. 104–6; Wong T'ong-wen and Jean-Pierre Diény, in Paul Demiéville, ed., *Anthologie de la poésie chinoise classique* (Paris: Gallimard, 1962), pp. 189–91; and Arthur Waley, *Chinese Poems* (London: Allen and Unwin, 1946), pp. 113–15.

8 Wang Yi, *Ch'u Tz'u chang-chu*, sec. 7, pp. 239–44; translation in Hawkes, *Ch'u Tz'u*, pp. 90–91.

9 See chap. 2, note 22. This approach to the analysis of character in terms of types and roles, especially in terms of understanding the transmission of archetypes and the interplay of types and roles, owes much to Vladimir Propp's *The Morphology of the Folk Tale*, 2d ed. (Austin: University of Texas Press, 1968), especially pp. 19–65.

10 Fan Yeh (398–445), ed., "Tung Ssu chi chuan," in *Hou Han Shu* 84 (Peking: Chung-hua, 1965), pp. 2800–2806.

11 The authenticity of the attribution of "Poem of Affliction" has been a matter of debate since the eleventh century, when the poet Su Shih expressed his skepticism because of the denunciation of Tung Cho in the first lines, and because of the sophistication of the treatment of the five-character meter, which suggested to him a later date than the early third century. The most recent and comprehensive study of Ts'ai Yen's work is by Hans H. Frankel ("Cai Yen and the Poems Attributed to Her," *CLEAR* 5.2 [1985]: 133–56), which includes texts and translation of

the three compositions associated with Ts'ai Yen (including "Eighteen Songs of a Nomad Flute," which will be discussed below), a survey of the textual problems, and an up-to-date bibliography. The first "edition" of the "Poem of Affliction" studied here appears in the *Hou Han Shu*, which was compiled between 424 and 445. Frankel suggests that this poem dates from the third, fourth, or fifth century, but feels that it almost certainly was not composed by Ts'ai Yen herself.

It should be noted, however, that other recent critics have upheld Ts'ai Yen's authorship of at least "Poem of Affliction"; see especially Yü Kuan-ying, "*Lun* Ts'ai Yen *Pei-fen shih*," in *Han Wei Chin Liu-ch'ao shih lun-tsung* (Shanghai: T'ang-ti, 1953). The Japanese scholar Okamura Sadao has gone so far as to assert that all three compositions are genuine—at least, genuinely composed by the historical Ts'ai Yen—see "Sai En no sakuhin no shugi," *Nihon Chugoku gakkai hō* 23 (1971): 20–35. For the historical background of this poem, see Wang Yi-t'ung, "The Lamentation of Ts'ai Yen (c. A.D. 200)," *Delta* (January–March 1960): 11–14. For other studies of the authenticity of Ts'ai Yen's authorship, see Kuo Mo-jo et al., *Hu-chia shih-pa p'ai t'ao-lun chi* (Peking: Chung-hua, 1959). While most of these articles focus on the poem sequence "Eighteen Songs of a Nomad Flute," the problem of "Poem of Affliction" is also treated in considerable detail.

12 On the relation of events to character for the revelation of inner life, see Scholes and Kellogg, *The Nature of Narrative*, pp. 171, 177–94; Erich Kahler, *The Inward Turn of Narrative* (Princeton: Princeton University Press, 1973), pp. 9–66.

13 On the narrator's voice and its powers of persuasion, see Paul Friedrich, *Language, Context, and the Imagination* (Palo Alto: Stanford University Press, 1979), pp. 402–40; also Zeno Vendler, "Telling the Facts," in Searle et al., *Speech Act Theory and Pragmatics*, pp. 273–90. The possibility of autobiographical representation on the part of the author through the narrator or some other character presents special questions on the techniques of characterization for that figure. See Louis D. Rubin, Jr., *The Teller in the Tale* (Seattle: University of Washington Press, 1967); Wayne C. Booth, "Distance and Point of View"; and Erich Kahler, *The Inward Turn of Narrative*.

14 Text from *Wei Chin Nan-pei ch'ao wen-hsüeh shih ts'an-k'ao tz'e-liao*, pp. 161–67. My complete translation appears in the appendix. Other translations include Wang Yi-t'ung, "The Lamentation of Ts'ai Yen" (a revised version appears in *Sunflower Splendor*, pp. 36–39); and Frodsham and Ch'eng Hsi, *An Anthology of Chinese Verse*, pp. 9–13; Frankel, "Cai Yen and the Poems Attributed to Her," pp. 135–37.

15 For the sequence attributed to Ts'ai Yen, with commentary, see *Wei Chin Nan-pei ch'ao wen-hsüeh shih ts'an-k'ao tz'e-liao*, pp. 169–72. See also Kuo Mo-jo et al., *Hu-chia shih-pa p'ai t'ao-lun chi*. This sequence was translated into French by Georges Margouliès under the title "Dix-huit mesures chantées au cornet Hun," in his *Anthologie raisonée de la littérature chinoise* (Paris: Payot, 1948), pp. 267–74; complete English translations are by Rewi Alley, *The Eighteen Laments* (Peking: New World Press, 1963); and Frankel, "Cai Yen and the Poems Attributed to Her."

16 For text, see P'eng Ting-ch'iu et al., *Ch'üan T'ang Shih*, 25 vols. (Peking: Chung-hua, 1960), sec. 303, 10:3450–53. A complete text and translation appear with a study of the Sung handscroll which illustrates Liu Shang's version of Ts'ai Yen's story in Robert A. Rorex and Wen Fong, *Eighteen Songs of a Nomad Flute: The Story of Lady Wen-chi* (New York: Metropolitan Museum of Art, 1974). This study concentrates on the biography of Ts'ai Yen (as presented by Liu Shang), as it influenced Chinese painting. Other studies of the story of Lady Wen-chi in Chinese art include Kōjirō Tomita, "Wen-chi's Captivity in Mongolia and Her Return to China," *Museum of Fine Arts Bulletin* 26 (1928): 40–45; John F. Haskins, "The Pazyryk Felt Screen and the Barbarian Captivity of Ts'ai Wen-chi," *Museum of Far Eastern Antiquities Bulletin* 35 (1963): 141–61; and Wang Chu-fei, "*Kuan-yü Ming mu (Hu-chia shih-pa p'ai) tu-ti yi-hsieh wen-t'i.*" Abstract titled "The Frontier as Seen in a Ming Copy (of the *Eighteen Songs*) and Some Comparisons," *Wen wu* 6 (1959): 36–37.

17 Yen Yü (1180?–1235?), in the second section of *Ts'ang-lang shih-hua*, "Forms of Poetry" ("*Shih-t'i*"), divides the literary history of the T'ang into four major periods: early 618–712 (*ch'u*), high 713–765 (*sheng*), middle 766–835 (*chung*), and late 736–906 (*wan*). See Kuo Shao-yü, ed., *Ts'ang-lang shih hua chiao-shih* (Peking: Jen-min, 1962). Stephen Owen notes that "most traditional literary historians would have the Mid-T'ang begin after the death of Tu Fu or earlier, directly after the An Lu-shan Rebellion" (*The Great Age of Chinese Poetry: The High T'ang*, p. 320).

18 A complete text and translation of Liu Shang's sequence appears in Rorex and Fong, *Eighteen Songs of a Nomad Flute: The Story of Lady Wen-chi* (see note 16, above). The introduction reproduces the "Eighteen Songs" narrative handscroll in the collection of the Metropolitan Museum of Art (accession number 1973.120.3). Other studies of the story of Lady Wen-chi in Chinese art include Robert A. Rorex, "Eighteen Songs of a Nomad Flute: The Story of Ts'ai Wen-chi" (Ph.D. diss., Princeton University, 1975); Kōjirō Tomita, "Wen-chi's Captivity in Mongolia and Her Return to China," pp. 40–45; and John F. Haskins, "The Pazyryk Felt

Screen and the Barbarian Captivity of Ts'ai Wen-chi." Haskins translates several poems from the original sequence often attributed to Ts'ai
Yen, and remarks: "It will be seen that there are no direct links between the verses and the scenes that illustrate them" (p. 148). In fact,
the painting of the final scene from the Wen-chi scroll in Nanjing described by the author (believed to be a Ming copy of a Sung original)
illustrates the ending in the style of Liu Shang, not the poem quoted
in the article. The lady is shown returning to her ancestral home, and
the saplings which flanked the house in the first scene are shown now
grown to full-sized trees. While Haskins posits that the story of Lady
Wen-chi became a favorite subject in painting soon after the original
poem sequence appeared, he admits that no such painting survives
from a period earlier than the Sung dynasty (pp. 145–46); by that time,
of course, the character type of Ts'ai Yen had already been changed
from the original.

.19 Wang An-shih, *Wang An-shih shih-chi* (reprint, Taipei: Kuang-wen,
1974), pp. 243–46.

20 Rorex and Fong, *Eighteen Songs of a Nomad Flute*, introduction; see also
Hsü Pang-ta, " '*Sung-jen hua jen-wu ku-shih ying chi 'Ying luan t'u,' k'ao*"
("A study of the identification of a narrative painting as 'welcoming the
imperial carriages,' " *Wen wu* 8 (1972): 61–63. This scroll is thought to
depict the dowager's actual return from exile. For historical sources of
this event, see T'o T'o et al., *Sung shih* 143 (Peking: Chung-hua, 1977),
11:3439–56; and T'o T'o et al., *Chin shih* 42 (Peking: Chung-hua, 1975),
3:949–59.

21 Eugene Eoyang has taken up the literary evolution of Wang Chao-chün
in several contexts, at least through the T'ang dynasty. For the evocative
power of the figure, see "A Taste for Apricots: Approaches to Chinese
Fiction," in Plaks, ed., *Chinese Narrative*, pp. 65–67. Eoyang has made
a complete translation of a ninth-century T'ang *pien-wen* version; see
"Word of Mouth: Oral Storytelling in the Pien-wen" (Ph.D. diss., Indiana University, 1971), appendix A.5, pp. 275–96. Most recently, "The
Wang Chao-chün Legend" surveys the origins of the story, its literary sources, and its transformations. It should be emphasized that the
historical Wang Chao-chün predates Ts'ai Yen; indeed, besides two
brief accounts in *Han Shu* 9 and 94 (suite), 1:297, and 8:3807–8, and
Homer H. Dubs, *The History of the Former Han Dynasty*, (Baltimore:
Waverley Press, 1944), 2:335, the earliest source for her life appears in
the *Ch'in Ts'ao* of Ts'ai Yung, the father of Ts'ai Yen (Ts'ai Yung, *Ch'in
Ts'ao*, *Ts'ung-shu chi-ch'ang* ed. [Shanghai: Shang-wu, 1937], pp. 23–24).
These accounts focus on Wang Chao-chün's experience as an unappre-

ciated member of the emperor's household—thus her consignment to the Hsiung-nu chieftain. While these established Wang Chao-chün as a character archetype in her own right, certain elements of the character role which seem to originate with the figure of Ts'ai Yen are later attached to the figure of Wang Chao-chün *as an exile*. Shih Ch'ung's poem is perhaps the first to emphasize these aspects, which Eoyang might term "the political hostage" and "the beauty despoiled" ("The Wang Chao-chün Legend," p. 5).

22 Shih Ch'ung's use of the name Wang Ming-chün is in deference to a taboo on the personal name of the emperor Wei Wen-ti (r. 220–27, perhaps better known as Ts'ao P'i): "The woman Wang Ming-chün was originally called Wang Chao-chün, but because of an infringement of the taboo of Emperor Wen-ti the name was changed" ("Song of Wang Ming-chün," preface). Characters occurring in personal names or other titles of members of the royal house were often proscribed for other uses.

Shih Ch'ung himself was probably more notorious for his wealth and luxurious mode of living than for his literary talents. He owned a vast property northeast of Loyang known as the *Chin-ku yüan* (Golden Valley estate). Revels there were described by P'an Yüeh (d. 300) in his poem "*Chin-ku chi tso shih*" ("Poem on the Golden Valley Gathering"). Shih Ch'ung also wrote his own poem about the same literary gathering, "*Chin-ku shih*" ("Poem on the Golden Valley"), whose preface is quoted by Li Shan in his commentary on P'an Yüeh's poem in *Wen Hsüan* 20:439–40. See also Frankel, *The Flowering Plum and the Palace Lady*, p. 223; and Helmut Wilhelm, "Shih Ch'ung and the *Chin-ku-yüan*," *Monumenta Serica* 18 (1959): 314–27.

23 Text from Ting Fu-pao, ed., *Ch'üan Han San-kuo Chin Nan-pei ch'ao shih* (Taipei: Yi-wen, 1968), 1:532–33, translation mine. A complete translation appears in Frodsham and Ch'eng, *An Anthology of Chinese Verse*, pp. 74–75.

24 Plaks, "Towards a Critical Theory of Chinese Narrative," pp. 311–14; John C. Y. Wang, "Early Chinese Narrative: The *Tso Chuan* as Example," pp. 3–20; Ronald C. Egan, "Narrative in the *Tso Chuan*," *Harvard Journal of Asiatic Studies* 37 (1977): 323–52; Levy, "The Trojan and the Hegemon," pp. 144–45.

25 For sources on the varied career of Wei Chuang, see Lionel Giles, "The Lament of the Lady of Ch'in," *T'oung Pao* 24 (1926): 316–25; Hsia Ch'eng-t'ao, *Wei Tuan-yi nien-p'u* (Taipei: Shih-chieh, 1959); Hsin Wen-fang (fl. 1304), *T'ang ts'ai-tzu chuan*, in *Pi-chi hsu-pien* (reprint, Taipei: Kuang-wen, 1969); Chi Yu-kung, ed., *T'ang shih chi shih* 68 (Peking:

Chung-hua, 1975), pp. 1051–52; Sun Kuang-hsien, ed., *Pei-meng suo-yen* 6, in *Ya-yu t'ang ts'ang shu* (Taipei: n.p., 1966), secs. 2–8; Wang Kuo-wei, *Kuo-hsüeh chi-k'an* (Shanghai: Tung-fang, 1924), vol. 1, pt. 4; Lo Chen-yü, *Tun-huang ling-shih* (Shanghai: Tung-fang, 1924). I have been unable to consult a forthcoming study by Robin D. S. Yates, *Washing Silk: The Life and Selected Poetry of Wei Chuang 834?–910* (Cambridge: Harvard University Press, in press).

    For a study of the era of the Huang Ch'ao Rebellion, see Twitchett, *The Cambridge History of China*, vol. 3: *Sui and T'ang China*, pp. 727ff. As a literary figure Wei Chuang has received more recognition for his works in the *tz'u* form than for his *shih;* for his contributions to the development of *tz'u,* see Kang-i Sun Chang, *The Evolution of Chinese Tz'u Poetry*, pp. 33–62; and John T. Wixted, *The Song-Poetry of Wei Chuang (836–910 A.D.).* Occasional Paper no. 12 (Center for Asian Studies, Arizona State University, 1979), introduction. This introduction includes an abbreviated biography of the poet.

26 Giles, "The Lament of the Lady of Ch'in," pp. 316–17. The conventions of political allegory of this kind are discussed in James J. Y. Liu, *Chinese Theories of Literature*, pp. 106–16; see also David Lattimore, "Allusion in T'ang Poetry," pp. 405–39.

27 Text from Ch'en Yin-k'o, *Ch'in-fu yin chiao-chien* (Taipei: Hua-cheng, 1974); see also Chiang Tsung-p'ing, *Wei Tuan-yi shih chiao-chu* (Taipei: Chung-hua, 1968), pp. 272–90. My complete translation appears in the appendix. Other complete translations of "Song of the Lady of Ch'in" are by Lionel Giles, "The Lament of the Lady of Ch'in," with text and commentary; and Robin D. S. Yates, in *Sunflower Splendor*, pp. 267–81.

28 Wang Kuo-wei, *Kuo-hsüeh chi-k'an* (Shanghai: Tung-fang, 1924), vol. 1, pt. 4.

29 See Edward Schafer, "The Last Years of Ch'ang-an," *Oriens Extremus* 10.2 (1963): 133–79. Schafer especially mentions Wei Chuang's eye-witness account of the sack of the city by Huang Ch'ao (pp. 157–58), then Wei's poem on the city's final "death" in the tenth century, "An Old Precinct of Ch'ang-an" (*"Ch'ang-an chiu-li"*), p. 169. For the text of this quatrain, see Chiang Tsung-p'ing, *Wei Tuan-yi shih chiao-chu*, p. 221.

4   Narrative Structure

1 Plaks, "Towards a Critical Theory of Chinese Narrative," pp. 310–16, has a discussion of the problem of defining what constitutes an "event" in Chinese narrative. Plaks focuses on the critical term *shih* (events) as opposed to *yen* (words), citing Pan Ku's seminal distinction of two

types of early narrative in *Han Shu* 30, "*Yi-wen chih*," 4:1715. The association of *shih* with action is emphasized by the later substitution of *tung* (action) for *shih* by Hsun Yüeh (148–208) in *Shen Chien* 2 (*Ssu-pu pei-yao* ed.), p. 6a; and in the *Li Chi*, in Wang Fu-chih (1619–1692), ed., *Li Chi chang-chu* 13 (Taipei: Kuang-wen, 1967), p. 2a. My purpose is to consider how the units of narrative presentation, events or actions, are organized over time, whether the objective time of the experience of the text or the temporal dimension of the reader's experience of the text. For more general discussions of the notion of time in Chinese poetry, see James J. Y. Liu, "Time, Space, and Self in Chinese Poetry," *CLEAR* 1.2 (July 1979): 137–56. For the fundamental quality of temporal structures in Western narrative, see Scholes and Kellogg, *The Nature of Narrative*, pp. 207–8; see also Paul Ricoeur, "Narrative Time," *Critical Inquiry* 7.1 (Autumn 1980): 169–90; and Claude Bremond, "La logique des possibles narratifs," *Communications* 8 (1966): 60–76.

2 Plaks discusses treatment of time as it is manipulated in narrative structure in "Towards a Critical Theory of Chinese Narrative," pp. 329–39. For time as a defining aspect of narrative structure, see Gérard Genette, trans. Jane E. Lewin, *Narrative Discourse: An Essay in Method* (Ithaca: Cornell University Press, 1980); Georges Poulet, *Etudes sur le temps humain* (Paris: Plon, 1976–77), introduction, pp. i–xlvii; Eric Rabkin, *Narrative Suspense* (Ann Arbor: University of Michigan Press, 1973), pp. 71–89; Frank Kermode, "Secrets and Narrative Sequence," *Critical Inquiry* 7.1 (Autumn 1980): 83–101; Nelson Goodman, "Twisted Tales; or Study, Story, Symphony," *Critical Inquiry* 7.1 (Autumn 1980): 103–19; and Barbara Herrnstein Smith, *Poetic Closure; Or, a Study of How Poems End* (Chicago: University of Chicago Press, 1968), p. 137.

3 Levy, "The Trojan and the Hegemon," p. 136.

4 See David Hawkes, "The Quest of the Goddess," pp. 62–63; and Chen Shih-hsiang, "The Genesis of Poetic Time: The Greatness of Ch'ü Yüan, Studied with a New Critical Approach," *Ch'ing-hua hsüeh-pao*, n.s. 10.1 (1973): 1–45.

5 Kang-i Sun Chang, "The Concept of Time in the *Shih Ching*," *Ch'ing-hua hsüeh-pao*, n.s. 12.2 (1979): 73–85.

6 Jin'ichi Konishi, "Association and Progression: Principles of Integration in Anthologies and Sequences of Japanese Court Poetry, A.D. 900–1250," *Harvard Journal of Asiatic Studies* 21 (1958): 67–127; Earl Miner, *Japanese Linked Poetry*, pp. 8–9; see also Claude Bremond, *Logique du récit* (Paris: Seuil, 1973).

7 Stephen Owen comments that Tu Fu's poem sequences were one of his major contributions to the poetic tradition, and sums up his purpose:

"The sequence was the perfect solution to a central problem of Chinese lyric: how to give a topic extended treatment without sacrificing the elliptical density and intensity of the short poem" (*The Great Age of Chinese Poetry: The High T'ang*, p. 218). He compares Tu Fu's techniques of sequencing with Ts'ao Chih's "Poems Presented to Prince Piao of Pai-ma," which will be analyzed in detail below.

8 See n. 7 above. See also Tsu-lin Mei and Yu-kung Kao, "Tu Fu's 'Autumn Meditations': An Exercise in Linguistic Criticism," *Harvard Journal of Asiatic Studies* 28 (1968): 44–80. Owen deals with the structure of the sequence according to theme, Mei and Kao according to formal and linguistic features. Chou Shan, in "Allusion and Periphrasis as Modes of Poetry in Tu Fu's 'Eight Laments,'" brings another element of cohesion to bear on a poem sequence; namely, the potential of allusion as an underpinning of sequential structure. A study emphasizing European theories of semiotics is Tim-hung Ku, "A Semiotic Approach to Wang Wei's *Wang River Sequence*: An Exploration of the Principle of Equivalance and the Principle of Disjunction," *Tamkang Review* 14.1–4 (Autumn 1983–Summer 1984): 339–54. For more general discussions of the nature and aesthetics of poem sequences, see Jin'ichi Konishi, "Association and Progression"; and Earl Miner, *Japanese Linked Poetry*, introduction, pp. 3–159. For a modern English-language response to the problem of poem sequences with a *chinoiserie* twist, see Michael Bernstein, *The Tale of the Tribe: Ezra Pound and the Modern Verse Epic* (Princeton: Princeton University Press, 1980), pp. 3–187.

9 For a study of the life of Juan Chi and his poem series, see Donald Holzman, *Poetry and Politics: The Life and Works of Juan Chi (A.D. 210–263)* (Cambridge: Cambridge University Press, 1976).

10 See Owen, *The Poetry of the Early T'ang*, pp. 256–73. For Tu Fu's poems, see *Tu Fu shih hsüan*, pp. 222–25.

11 Owen, *The Great Age of Chinese Poetry*, p. 218.

12 Hans H. Frankel, "Fifteen Poems by Ts'ao Chih: An Attempt at a New Approach," *Journal of the American Oriental Society* 84 (1964): 1–14; and Lei Chia-chi, "Ts'ao Chih *Tseng Pai-ma Wang Piao shih ping hsü chien-cheng*," *New Asia Journal* 12 (1977): 337–404.

13 Text from *Wei chin Nan-pei ch'ao wen-hsüeh shih ts'an-k'ao tz'e-liao*, pp. 72–78. Other translations include Frodsham and Ch'eng, *An Anthology of Chinese Verse*, pp. 36–39; and George W. Kent, *Worlds of Dust and Jade: 47 Poems and Ballads of the Third Century Chinese Poet Ts'ao Chih* (New York: Philosophical Library, 1969), pp. 52–56. For more detail on the background of Ts'ao Chih's woes, which to some extent may have been

deserved, see Robert Joe Cutter, "The Incident at the Gate: Cao Zhi, the Succession, and Literary Fame," *T'oung Pao* 71 (1985): 228–62.

14 My analysis follows the edition of the text from *Wei Chin Nan-pei ch'ao wen-hsüeh shih ts'an-k'ao tz'e-liao*, pp. 72–78; however, other editions combine poems 1 and 2 into a single composition. I have chosen to follow the edition above because of my interpretation of the subject matter of the two poems (see below), but it should be noted that in addition to the lack of catenated lines between poems 1 and 2, both poems have the same rhyme throughout. For an edition which divides the sequence into six poems, see Shen Te-ch'ien, *Ku-shih yüan*, pp. 121–23. The translation of the sequence by Frodsham and Ch'eng also follows this plan; see *An Anthology of Chinese Verse*, pp. 36–37.

15 Stephen Owen compares the "narrative of personal experience" to the Latin verse epistle, but does not discuss this in terms of poem sequences. See *The Poetry of Meng Chiao and Han Yü*, p. 78.

16 In "The Nature of Narrative in T'ang Poetry," C. H. Wang also treats "Song of the Lady of Ch'in" (or, as he calls it, "Lament of a Ch'in Woman") as the culmination of narrative expression in T'ang *shih* (pp. 245–46).

17 The two lines preserved were 145–46:

> The Imperial Treasury was burned to the very ash of its brocades
>   and embroideries,
> On the Street of Heaven were trampled to dust the bones of State
>   Officials.

The couplet appeared in Sun Kuang-hsien's early Sung work, *Pei-meng suo-yen* 6.7–8, which also includes the comment that Wei found it necessary to suppress the poem, in spite of the fact that its fame was such that he had acquired the nickname "*Ch'in-fu yin* Graduate" (*Ch'in-fu yin hsiu-ts'ai*). For the history of the manuscript, see Lionel Giles, "The Lament of the Lady of Ch'in," pp. 305–23; and Wang Chung-min, *Tun-huang ku-chi hsü-lu* (Shanghai: Shang-wu, 1950), pp. 303–8; Ch'en Yin-k'o, *Ch'in-fu yin chiao-chien.*

Glossary of Chinese Characters

"*Ai Chiang-nan fu*"　　　　　哀江南賦

"*Ai chiang-t'ou*"　　　　　　哀江頭

An Lu-shan (d. 757)　　　　　安祿山

Chang Heng (79–138)　　　　張衡

"*Ch'ang-an chiu li*"　　　　　長安舊里

"*Ch'ang-hen ko*"　　　　　　長恨歌

"*Ch'en feng*"　　　　　　　　晨風

Cheng Hsüan (117–200)　　　鄭玄

"*cheng tsai*"　　　　　　　　烝哉

"*Ch'i ao*"　　　　　　　　　　淇奥

"Ch'i fa"	七發
chia-nü	嫁女
Ch'iang	羌
Chien-k'ang	建康
Ch'ien Mu	錢穆
chih	志
chih-chi (chih-jen, chih-yin)	知己
	(知人，知音)
Chih Yü (d. c. 310)	摯虞
"Ch'in-fu yin"	秦婦吟
Chin-ling	金陵
chin-t'i shih	近體詩
ching fu	京賦
Ch'ing-shan lei	青衫淚
"Ch'iu hsing"	秋興
"Chiu ko"	九歌
Chou li	周禮
Chu Hsi (1130–1200)	朱熹
chu-kuan shih-jen	主觀詩人
Ch'u Tz'u	楚辭
Ch'ü Yüan	屈原
chüan	卷
"Chuan-erh"	卷耳
ch'uan-ch'i	傳奇
chüeh-chü	絕句
"Chün-tzu yang yang"	君子陽陽
"Chün-tzu yü yi"	君子于役

Chung Jung (or Hung, 469–518)	鍾嶸
Chung Tzu-ch'i	鍾子期
feng	風
fu	賦
fu	夫
fu	婦
"*fu chih yen p'u*"	賦之言鋪
"*Fu-niao fu*"	鵬鳥賦
Han Ch'eng-ti (r. 32–7 B.C.)	漢成帝
Han Wu-ti (r. 149–85 B.C.)	漢武帝
Han Yüan-ti (r. 48–32 B.C.)	漢元帝
Hou Ching (fl. 549)	侯景
Hsi-yu chi	西遊記
"*Hsia Wu*"	下武
hsiang-ming	相命
hsiao fu	小賦
Hsiao T'ung (501–531)	蕭統
Hsiao Yi (Liang Yüan-ti, r. 552–554)	蕭繹 （梁元帝）
"*Hsin-hun pieh*"	新婚別
hsing	興
hsü	序
hsü-shih shih	敘事詩
hsü-shih wen	敘事文
Hsün-yang	潯陽
Hu	胡

"Hu-chia shih-pa p'ai"	胡笳十八拍
huang-wang	皇王
Hung-lou meng	紅樓夢
Juan Chi (210–263)	阮籍
ju	如
k'o-kuan shih-jen	客觀詩人
"Ko sheng"	葛生
"Ku-er hsing"	孤兒行
"Ku feng"	谷風
ku-shih	古詩
ku-shih shih	故事詩
ku-t'i shih	古體詩
kuan	關
"K'ung-ch'üeh tung-nan fei"	孔雀東南飛
kung-hsiang	共相
K'ung Ying-ta (574–648)	孔穎達
lao-fu	老婦
lao-yü	老嫗
"Li sao"	離騷
"Liang-tu fu"	兩都賦
lien-mien tzu	連綿字
liu	流
Liu Shang (fl. 770–773)	劉商
liu-shih	六詩
liu-yi	六義
"Lo-shen fu"	洛神賦

lü-shih	律詩
luan	亂
"Lung shih"	瀧使
Ma Chih-yüan (c. 1210–1280)	馬致遠
Mao Heng (second century A.D.)	毛亨
Mei Sheng (?–140 B.C.)	枚乘
Nan Hsiung-nu	南匈奴
Ou-yang Hsün (557–641)	歐陽詢
p'ai-lu	排律
Pan Ku (32–92)	班固
"Pei cheng"	北征
"Pei-fen shih"	悲憤詩
P'ei Ti (b. 716)	裴迪
pi	比
"P'i-p'a hsing"	琵琶行
pieh-hsiang	別相
pien-wen	變文
p'ien-wen (p'ien-t'i wen)	駢文
Po Chü-yi (772–846)	白居易
Po Ya	伯牙
"San li"	三吏
"San pieh"	三別
sao	騷
sao fu	騷賦

"Shang-lin *fu*" 上林賦

Shen Ch'üan-ch'i (c. 650–713) 沈佺期

shih 詩

shih 事

shih chih ch'eng hsing 詩之成形

shih chih suo yung 詩之所用

Shih ching 詩經

Shih Ch'ung (249–300) 石崇

"Shih-hao *li*" 石壕吏

shih-lei fu 事類賦

Shih P'in 詩品

Shih ta hsü 詩大序

"*shih yen chih*" 詩言志

shui 說

shui ch'u 說去

Ssu-ma Hsiang-ju (179–117 B.C.) 司馬相如

sung 頌

Sung Ch'in-tsung (r. 1126) 宋欽宗

Sung Hui-tsung (r. 1101–1126) 宋徽宗

Sung Kao-tsung (r. 1127–1161) 宋高宗

"*Ta ch'ih-mei tai-shu chi chia-jen*" 答魑魅代書寄家人

ta fu 大賦

T'ang Hsüan-tsung (Ming-huang, 684–762, r. 713–755) 唐玄宗（明皇）

T'ao Ch'ien (365–427)	陶潛
"T'ao-hua yüan shih"	桃花源詩
"T'ao yüan hsing"	桃源行
ti-li	地里
"T'ien wen"	天問
"ts'ai ts'ai chuan erh"	采采卷耳
Ts'ai Yen (Wen-chi, late second–early third century)	蔡琰 （文姬）
Ts'ai Yung (133–192)	蔡邕
Ts'ao Chih (192–232)	曹植
Ts'ao Ts'ao (155–220)	曹操
"Tseng Pai-ma Wang Piao"	贈白馬王彪
tu	獨
Tu Fu (712–770)	杜甫
tung	動
Tung Cho (d. 192)	董卓
Tung Ssu (late second–early third century)	董祀
"Tung Ssu chi chuan"	董祀妻傳
tza-chü	雜劇
tzu	自
"Tzu ching fu Feng hsien hsien yung-huai wu-pai tzu"	自京赴奉先縣詠懷五百字
"Tzu-hsü fu"	子虛賦
wai-chi	外集
"Wan lan"	芄蘭

wang	王
Wang An-shih (1021–1086)	王安石
Wang Chao-chün (Ming-chün, first century B.C.)	王昭君（明君）
"Wang ch'üan chi"	輞川集
wang hou	王后
"Wang Ming-chün *tz'u*"	王明君辭
Wang Ts'an (177–217)	王粲
Wei Chuang (c. 834–910)	韋莊
Wei Hung (first century A.D.)	衛宏
Wen Hsüan	文選
"Wen wang *cheng tsai*"	文王丞哉
"Wen wang *yu sheng*"	文王有聲
wo	我
wu	吾
ya	雅
Yang Hsiung (43 B.C.–A.D. 18)	揚雄
Yang Kuei-fei (718–756)	楊貴妃
yen	言
yen chih	言志
yen-ch'ing fu	言情賦
yen-kuei	魘鬼
yen-wai	言外
"Yi-wen chih"	藝文志
"Yi-wen lei-chü"	藝文類聚
yu	有
"Yu hu"	有狐

"Yung-huai ku-chi wu shou"	詠懷古跡五首
"Yung-huai shih"	詠懷詩
"Yung-huai wu-pai tzu"	詠懷五百字
"Yung shih shih"	詠史詩
yü	于
Yü Hsin (513–581)	庾信
"Yü Yüan chiu shu"	與元九書
yüan	願
yüeh-fu (*yüeh-fu shih*)	樂府 （樂府詩）

Selected Bibliography

Works in Chinese and Japanese

Chang Wei-ch'i. *"T'ao-hua yüan chi shih yi,"* *Kuo-hsüeh yüeh-pao hui-k'an* 1 (1924): 201–20.

張為騏. 桃花源記釋疑. 國學月報彙刊.

Chao Tien-ch'eng, ed. *Wang Yu-ch'eng chi chien-chu.* 2 vols. Peking: Chung-hua, 1961.

趙殿成. 王右丞集箋注.

Ch'en Yin-k'o. *"Ch'ang-hen ko chien-cheng"* ("Yüan Po *shih chien-cheng kao chih yi"*). *Ch'ing-hua hsüeh-pao* 14, no. 1 (October 1947): 1–34.

陳寅恪. 長恨歌箋證（元白詩箋證稿之一）.

――――. *Ch'en Yin-k'o hsien-sheng wen-shih lun-chi.* 2 vols. Hong Kong:

Wen Wen Publications, 1973.

陳寅恪先生文史論集．

——— . *Ch'in-fu yin chiao-chien.* Taipei: Hua-cheng, 1974.

秦婦吟校箋．

——— . "*T'ao-hua yüan chi p'ang cheng.*" In *Ch'en Yin-k'o hsien-sheng wen-shih lun-chi,* 1:183–93.

桃花源記旁證．

——— . "*Tu Ai Chiang-nan fu.*" In *Ch'en Yin-k'o hsien-sheng wen-shih lun-chi,* 2:339–45.

讀哀江南賦．

——— . "Yü Hsin *Ai chiang-nan fu yü* Tu Fu *Yung-huai ku-chi shih.*" In *Ch'en Yin-k'o hsien-sheng wen-shih lun-chi,* 1:201–03.

庾信哀江南賦與杜甫詠懷古跡詩．

Ch'en Yüan-lung (1652–1736), ed. *Yü-ting li-tai fu-hui.* Preface 1706. Reprinted, with an introduction by Yoshikawa Kōjirō. Tokyo: Chubun, 1974.

陳元龍．御定歷代賦彙

Ch'eng T'ing-tso. "*Sao fu lun.*" In *Wan shu ting yi.* Taipei: Li-hang, 1970.

程廷祚．騷賦論．晚書訂疑

Chi Yu-kung, ed. *T'ang shih chi shih.* Peking: Chung-hua, 1975.

計有功．唐詩記事

Chiang Tsung-p'ing. *Wei Tuan-yi shih chiao-chu.* Taipei: Chung-hua, 1968.

江聰平．韋端己詩校注．

Ch'ien Mu. *Chung-kuo wen-hsüeh Chiang-yen chi.* Kowloon: Jen-sheng, 1963.

錢穆．中國文學講演集

Chin Chü-hsiang. *Han tai tz'u fu chih fa-ta*. Shanghai: Commercial Press, 1931.

金秬香．漢代辭賦之發達

Ch'iu Hsieh-yu. *Chung-kuo li-tai ku-shih shih*. Taipei: San-min, 1969.

邱燮友．中國歷代故事詩

Chou Fa-kao. *Chung-kuo ku-tai yü-fa*. 4 vols. Taipei: Academia Sinica, 1959 and 1961.

周法高．中國古代語法

Chu Hsi (1130–1200), ed. *Shih chi chuan*. Reprint. Shanghai: Chung-hua, 1958.

朱熹．詩集傳

Chu Tzu-ch'ing. *Shih yen chih pien*. Taipei: K'ai-ming, 1964.

朱自清．詩言志辨．

Chu Yi-tsun (1629–1709), ed., and Ku Ssu-li (1669–1722), annot. *Ch'ang-li hsien-sheng shih chi chu*. Reprint. Taipei: Hsüeh-sheng, 1967.

朱彝尊．顧嗣立．昌黎先生詩集注

Ch'ü Wan-li. *Shih ching shih yi*. Facsimile edition. Taipei: K'ai-ming, 1964.

屈萬里．詩經釋義．

Chung Jung (fl. 502–519). *Shih p'in chu*, edited by Ch'en Yen-chieh. Taipei: K'ai-ming, 1958.

鍾榮（陳延傑）．詩品注．

Endō Toshio. *Chōhonka Kenkyū*. Tokyo: Kensetsusha, 1934.

遠藤敏雄．長恨歌研究．

Fan Yeh (398–445), ed. *Hou Han Shu*. Peking: Chung-hua, 1965.

范曄．後漢書

Fang Hsüan-ling, ed. *Chin Shu*. Peking: Chung-hua, 1974.

房玄齡．晉書

Feng Chih. *Tu Fu shih hsüan*. Hong Kong: Ta-kuang, 1961.

馮至．杜甫詩選

Hsia Ch'eng-t'ao. *Wei Tuan-yi nien-p'u*. Taipei: Shih-chieh, 1959.

夏承燾．韋端己年譜

Hsiao Ti-fei. *Han Wei liu-ch'ao yüeh-fu wen-hsüeh shih*. 1944. Reprint. Taipei: Ch'ang-an, 1976.

蕭滌非．漢魏六朝樂府文學史

Hsieh Hung-hsüan. *P'ien-wen heng-lun*. Taipei: Kuang-wen, 1973.

謝鴻軒．駢文衡論

Hsin Wen-fang (fl. 1304). *T'ang ts'ai-tzu chuan*. In *Pi-chi hsü-pien*. Reprint. Taipei: Kuang-wen, 1969.

辛文房．唐才子傳．筆記續編．

Hsü Fu-kuan. "*Chung-kuo yi-shu ching-shen chu-t'i chih cheng hsien.*" In *Chung-kuo yi-shu ching-shen*. Tai-chung: Tunghai University Press, 1966, pp. 45–143.

徐復觀．中國藝術精神主體之呈現．

Hsü Pang-ta. "'*Sung-jen hua jen-wu ku-shih' ying chi 'Ying luan t'u,' k'ao*" ("A study of the identification of a narrative painting as 'welcoming the imperial carriages'"). *Wen wu* 8 (1972): 61–63.

徐邦達．"'宋人畫人物故事'應即'迎鑾圖'考．

Hsü Shen (c. 30–124). "*Shuo wen chieh tzu.*" In *Shuo wen chieh tzu ku lin*, edited by Ting Fu-pao. Taipei: Shang-wu, 1966.

許慎．說文解字

Hu Shih (1891–1962). *Pai hua wen-hsüeh shih*. Shanghai: Shang-wu, 1928.

胡適．白話文學史

Hu Ying-lin (1551–1607). *Shih sou*. Shanghai: Chung-hua, 1958.
胡應麟．詩藪

———. *Ssu pu cheng o*. In *Ku shu pien wei ssu chung*. Reprint. Taipei: Shih-chieh, 1965.
四部正譌．古書辨偽四種

Huang Chieh, ed. *Han Wei yüeh-fu feng chien*. Hong Kong: Commercial Press, 1961.
黃節．漢魏樂府風箋

Juan Yüan, ed. *Mao shih chu shu*. In *Shih-san ching chu shu*. 1815. Reprint. Taipei: T'ai-hua, 1977.
阮元．毛詩註疏．十三經註疏．

Ku Chao-ts'ang and Chou Ju-ch'ang, eds. *Po Chü-yi shih hsüan*. Peking: Tso-chia, 1962.
顧肇倉．周汝昌．白居易詩選．

Ku Hsüeh-hsieh, ed. *Po Chü-yi chi*. 4 vols. Peking: Chung-hua, 1979.
顧學頡．白居易集

Kubo Tenzui (1875–1935). *"Biwaku no gokyoku."* In *Shina gikyoku kenkyū*. Tokyo: Jinbun, 1928.
久保天隨．琵琶行の戲劇．支那戲劇研究

K'ung Ying-ta (574–648), ed. *Mao shih cheng yi*. In *Mao shih chu shu*. 3 vols. *Kuo-hsüeh chi-pen ts'ung shu*. Taipei: Shang-wu, 1968.
孔穎達．毛詩正義．毛詩注疏．

Kuo Mo-jo. *Pu tz'u t'ung tsuan*. 1933. Reprint. Tokyo: Meiyu, 1977.
郭沫若．卜辭通纂．

———, et al. *Hu-chia shih-pa p'ai t'ao-lun chi*. Peking: Chung-hua, 1959.
胡笳十八拍討論集．

Kuo Shao-yü. *Chung-kuo wen-hsüeh p'i-p'ing wen-hsüan*. Reprint. Tainan: P'ing-p'ing, 1975.

郭紹虞．中國文學批評文選．

Lei Chia-chi. "Ts'ao Chih 'Tseng Pai-ma Wang Piao' shih ping hsü chien-cheng." *New Asia Journal* 12 (1977): 337–404.

'雷家驥．曹植贈白馬王彪詩并序箋證

Liu Chih-chi (661–721). *Shih t'ung hsiao-fan chu*. Reprint. Taipei: Kuang-wen, 1963.

劉知幾．史通削繁注

Liu Hsü, ed. *Chiu T'ang shu*. Peking: Chung-hua, 1975.

劉昫．舊唐書

Lo Chen-yü. *Tun-huang ling-shih*. Shanghai: Tung-fang, 1924.

羅振玉．燉煌零拾．

Lo Ken-tse. *Yüeh-fu wen-hsüeh shih*. Peking: Wen-hua, 1931.

羅根澤．樂府文學史

Nakashima Chiaki. *Fu no seiritsu to tenkai*. Matsuyama: Kankosei, 1963.

中島千秋．賦の成立と展開．

Okamura Sadao. "Sai En no sakuhin no shugi." *Nihon Chugoku gakkai hō* 23 (1971): 20–35.

岡村真雄．蔡琰の作品の真偽．

Ou-yang Hsiu, ed. *Hsin T'ang shu*. Peking: Chung-hua, 1975.

歐陽修．新唐書

Ou-yang Hsün (557–641). *Yi-wen lei-chu*, edited by Wang Shao-ying. Peking: Chung-hua, 1965.

歐陽詢．（王紹楹）．藝文類聚

Pan Ku (32–92), ed. *Han Shu*. Peking: Chung-hua, 1961.

班固．漢書

Pei-ching ta-hsüeh, Chung-kuo yü yen wen-hsüeh hsi: ed. *T'ao Yüan-ming shih-wen hui-p'ing*. Peking: Chung-hua, 1961.

北京大學．中國語文學系．陶淵明詩文彙評

―――. *Wei Chin Nan-pei ch'ao wen-hsüeh shih ts'an-k'ao tzu-liao*. Peking: Chung-hua, 1962.

魏晉南北朝文學史參考資料．

P'eng Ting-ch'iu et al. *Ch'üan T'ang Shih*. 25 vols. Peking: Chung-hua, 1960.

彭定求．全唐詩．

Shang Ch'eng-tso. *Yin ch'i yi ts'un*. 2 vols. Nan-ching: Chung-kuo wen-hua yen-chiu suo, 1933.

商丞祚．殷契佚存．

Shen Te-ch'ien (1675–1769), ed. *Ku-shih yüan*. Reprint. Peking: Chung-hua, 1963.

沈德潛．古詩源

Sun Kuang-hsien, ed. *Pei-meng suo-yen*. In *Ya-yü t'ang ts'ang shu*. Taipei: n.p., 1966.

孫光憲．北夢瑣言．雅雨堂藏書

T'ao Ch'iu-ying. *Han fu chih shih ti yen-chiu*. Shanghai: Chung-hua, 1939.

陶秋英．漢賦之詩的研究

Ting Fu-pao, ed. *Ch'üan Han San-kuo Chin Nan-pei ch'ao shih*. Taipei: Yi-wen, 1968.

丁福保．全漢三國晉南北朝詩

―――. *Shuo wen chieh tzu ku lin*. 12 vols. Taipei: Shang-wu, 1966.

說文解字詁林．

―――. *T'ao Yüan-ming shih chien chu*. 1927. Reprint. Taipei: Yi-wen, 1964.

陶淵明詩箋注

T'o T'o et al. *Chin shih*. Peking: Chung-hua, 1975.

脫脫．晉史．

———. *Sung shih*. Peking: Chung-hua, 1977.

宋史．

Ts'ai Yung (133–192). *Ch'in Ts'ao*. *Ts'ung-shu chi-ch'ang* edition. Shanghai: Shang-wu, 1937.

蔡邕．琴操

Wang An-shih. *Wang An-shih shih-chi*. Reprint. Taipei: Kuang-wen, 1974.

王安石．王安石詩集

Wang Chung-min. *Tun-huang ku-chi hsü-lu*. Shanghai: Shang-wu, 1950.

王重民．燉煌古籍叙錄．

Wang Fu-chih (1619–1692), ed. *Li Chi chang-chu*. Taipei: Kuang-wen, 1967.

王夫之．禮記章句．

Wang Kuo-wei. *Jen-chien tz'u-hua*. In *Hai-ning Wang Ching-an hsien sheng yi-shu*, edited by Hsü Tiao-fu. Peking: n.p., 1927–28.

王國維．人間詞話．（徐調孚．海寧王靜安先生遺書）

———. *Kuo-hsüeh chi-k'an*. Shanghai: Tung-fang, 1924.

國學季刊．

Wang Kuo-ying. "*Han fu chung ti shan-shui ching-wu*." *Chung wai wen-hsüeh* 9, no. 5 (1980): 4–34.

王國瓔．漢賦中的山水景物．

Wang Yi (second century A.D.), ed. *Ch'u tz'u chang-chu*. Reprint. Taipei: Shih-chieh, 1965.

王逸．楚辭章句

Wu Ch'eng-ch'üan (fl. 1711) et al. *Ku-wen kuan-chih*. Hong Kong:

Hua-mei, 1951.

吳乘權. 古文觀止

Yen Yü (c. 1180–1235). *Ts'ang-lang shih hua chiao-shih*, edited by Kuo Shao-yü. Peking: Jen-min, 1962.

嚴羽. 滄浪詩話校釋

Yü Kuan-ying. *"Lun* Ts'ai Yen *Pei-fen shih."* In *Han Wei Chin Liu-ch'ao shih lun-tsung.* Shanghai: T'ang-ti, 1953.

余冠英. 論蔡琰悲憤詩·漢魏晉六朝詩論叢.

Works on Chinese Literature in Western Languages

Allen, Joseph Roe III. "Chih Yü's *Discussions of Different Types of Literature*: A Translation and Brief Comment." In *Two Studies in Chinese Literary Criticism (Parerga* 3). Seattle: Institute for Foreign Area Studies, 1976.

———. "Early Chinese Narrative Poetry: The Definition of a Tradition." Ph.D. diss., University of Washington, 1982.

Alley, Rewi. *The Eighteen Laments.* Peking: New World Press, 1963.

Birch, Cyril. "Some Concerns and Methods of Ming *Ch'uan-ch'i* Drama." In *Studies in Chinese Literary Genres*, edited by Cyril Birch, pp. 220–58.

———, ed. *Studies in Chinese Literary Genres.* Berkeley: University of California Press, 1974.

Bischoff, F. A. *Interpreting the Fu: A Study in Chinese Literary Rhetoric.* Münchener ostasiatische Studien, no. 13. Wiesbaden: Franz Steiner, 1976.

Brower, Robert H., and Miner, Earl. *Japanese Court Poetry.* Palo Alto: Stanford University Press, 1961.

Bynner, Witter, and Kiang Kang-hu. *The Jade Mountain: A Chinese Anthology Being Three Hundred Poems of the T'ang Dynasty.* New York: Knopf, 1929.

Cahill, Suzanne. "Shen Ch'üan-ch'i; Poems in Exile." M.A. thesis, University of California at Berkeley, 1978.

Ceadel, E. B. "The Two Prefaces of the *Kokinshu.*" *Asia Major*, n.s. 7, nos. 1–2 (1959): 40–51.

Chan, Mimi, and Grey, Piers. "Three Poems on Yang Kuei-fei." *Renditions* 14 (Autumn 1980): 79–84.

Chang, Kang-i Sun. "The Concept of Time in the *Shih Ching*." *Ch'ing-hua hsüeh-pao*, n.s. 12, no. 2 (1979): 73–85.

——. "Description of Landscape in Early Six Dynasties Poetry." In *The Vitality of the Lyric Voice*, edited by Lin Shuen-fu and Stephen Owen, pp. 105–29. Princeton: Princeton University Press, 1986.

——. *The Evolution of Chinese Tz'u Poetry from Late T'ang to Northern Sung*. Princeton: Princeton University Press, 1980.

——. *Six Dynasties Poetry*. Princeton: Princeton University Press, 1986.

Chao, Yuen Ren. *Language and Symbolic Systems*. London: Cambridge University Press, 1968, pp. 102–5.

——. *Mandarin Primer*. Cambridge: Harvard University Press, 1948.

Chen Shih-hsiang. "The Genesis of Poetic Time: The Greatness of Ch'ü Yüan, Studied with a New Critical Approach." *Ch'ing-hua hsüeh-pao*, n.s. 10, no. 1 (1973): 1–45.

——. "The *Shih Ching*: Its Generic Significance in Chinese Literary History and Poetics." *Bulletin of the Institute of History and Philology* (Academia Sinica) 39, no. 1 (1968): 371–413. Reprinted in *Studies in Chinese Literary Genres*, edited by Cyril Birch, pp. 8–41. Berkeley: University of California Press.

Cheng, François. *L'écriture poétique chinoise*. Paris: Editions de Seuile, 1977. Translated by Donald A. Riggs and Jerome P. Seaton as *Chinese Poetic Writing*. Bloomington: Indiana University Press, 1982.

Chou Fa-kao. "Reduplicatives in the Book of Odes." *Bulletin of the Institute of History and Philology* (Academia Sinica) 34, no. 2 (1963): 661–98.

Chou Shan. "Allusion and Periphrasis as Modes of Poetry in Tu Fu's 'Eight Laments.'" *Harvard Journal of Asiatic Studies* 45, no. 1 (1985): 77–128.

Chow Tze-tsung. "Ancient Chinese Views on Literature, the Tao, and Their Relationship." *CLEAR* 1, no. 1 (January 1979): 3–29.

——. "Ancient Chinese *Wu* Shamanism and Its Relationship to Sacrifices, History, Dance Music, and Poetry" ("*Chung-kuo ku-tai ti wu-yi yü chi-ssu, li-shih, yüeh-wu, chi shih ti kuan-hsi*"). *Ch'ing-hua hsüeh-pao*, n.s. 12, nos. 1–2 (December 1979): 1–59; n.s. 13, nos. 1–2 (December 1981): 1–25.

——. "The Early History of the Chinese Word *Shih* (Poetry)." In *Wen Lin: Studies in the Chinese Humanities*, edited by Chow Tze-tsung, pp. 151–210. Madison: University of Wisconsin Press, 1968.

Coleman, John D. "Lute Song." *Renditions* 10 (Autumn 1978): 155–58.

Cutter, Robert Joe. "The Incident at the Gate: Cao Zhi, the Succession, and Literary Fame." *T'oung Pao* 71 (1985): 228–62.

Davis, A. R. *T'ao Yüan-ming*. 2 vols. Cambridge: Cambridge University Press, 1983.

Demiéville, Paul, ed. *Anthologie de la poésie chinoise classique*. Paris: Gallimard, 1962.

Dewoskin, Kenneth. "On Narrative Revolutions." *CLEAR* 5, no. 1 (July 1985): 29–45.

Diény, Jean-Pierre. *Aux origines de la poésie classique en Chine (T'oung Pao Monographie VI)*. Leiden: Brill, 1968.

Dobson, W. A. C. H. *Late Archaic Chinese: A Grammatical Study*. Toronto: University of Toronto Press, 1959.

———. "Studies in the Grammar of Early Archaic Chinese." *T'oung Pao* 46, nos. 3–5 (1958): 339–68.

Dubs, Homer H. "Han Yü and the Buddha's Relic: An Episode in Medieval Chinese Religion." *Review of Religion* 11 (November 1946): 5–17.

———. *The History of the Former Han Dynasty*. 2 vols. Baltimore: Waverley Press, 1944.

Egan, Ronald C. *The Literary Works of Ou-yang Hsiu*. Cambridge: Cambridge University Press, 1984.

———. "Narrative in the *Tso Chuan*." *Harvard Journal of Asiatic Studies* 37 (1977): 323–52.

Eoyang, Eugene. "A Taste for Apricots: Approaches to Chinese Fiction." In *Chinese Narrative: Critical and Theoretical Essays*, edited by Andrew H. Plaks, pp. 65–67. Princeton: Princeton University Press, 1977.

———. "The Tone of the Poet and the Tone of the Translator." *Yearbook of Comparative and General Literature* 24 (1975): 75–83.

———. "The Wang Chao-chün Legend: Configurations of the Classic." *CLEAR* 4, no. 1 (1983): 3–22.

———. "Word of Mouth: Oral Storytelling in the Pien-wen." Ph.D. diss., Indiana University, 1971.

Fang, Achilles. "Some Reflections on the Difficulty of Translation." In *On Translation*, edited by Reuben Brower. Cambridge: Harvard University Press, 1959.

Fang, Robert F. *Gleanings from T'ao Yuan-ming*. Hong Kong: Commercial Press, 1980.

Fenellosa, Ernst. *The Chinese Written Character as a Medium for Poetry*, edited by Ezra Pound. Washington, D.C.: Square Dollar Series, 1951.

Fokkema, D. W. "Cultural Relativism and Comparative Literature." *Tamkang Review* 3, no. 2 (1972): 59–71.

Frankel, Hans H. "Cai Yen and the Poems Attributed to Her." *CLEAR* 5, no. 2 (1985): 133–56.

——— . "The Chinese Ballad 'Southeast Fly the Peacocks.' " *Harvard Journal of Asiatic Studies* 34 (1974): 249–71.

——— . "The Contemplation of the Past in T'ang Poetry." In *Perspectives on the T'ang*, edited by Denis Twitchett and Arthur Wright, pp. 345–64. New Haven: Yale University Press, 1973.

——— . "The Legacy of the Han, Wei, and Six Dynasties *Yüeh-fu* Tradition and Its Further Development in T'ang Poetry." In *The Vitality of the Lyric Voice: Shih Poetry from the Late Han to T'ang*, edited by Lin Shuen-fu and Stephen Owen, pp. 287–95. Princeton: Princeton University Press, 1986.

——— . "Fifteen Poems by Ts'ao Chih: An Attempt at a New Approach." *Journal of the American Oriental Society* 84 (1964): 1–14.

——— . *The Flowering Plum and the Palace Lady*. New Haven: Yale University Press, 1976.

——— . "The Formulaic Language in the Chinese Ballad 'Southeast Fly the Peacocks.' " *Bulletin of the Institute of History and Philology* (Academia Sinica) 39, no. 2 (1969): 219–44.

——— . "Some Characteristics of Oral Narrative Poetry in China." In *Etudes d'histoire et de littérature chinoises offertes à Professeur Jaroslav Průšek, Bibliothèque de l'Institute des Hautes Etudes Chinoises*. Paris: Presses universitaires de France, 1976, 24:97–106.

——— . "*Yüeh-fu* Poetry." In *Studies in Chinese Literary Genres*, edited by Cyril Birch, pp. 69–107. Berkeley: University of California Press, 1974.

Frodsham, J. D. *The Murmuring Stream: The Life and Works of the Chinese Nature Poet Hsieh Ling-yun (385–433), Duke of K'ang-lo*. 2 vols. Kuala Lumpur: University of Malaya Press, 1967.

——— , and Ch'eng Hsi. *An Anthology of Chinese Verse: Han Wei Chin and the Northern and Southern Dynasties*. Oxford: Oxford University Press, 1967.

Galik, Marian. "The Concept of Creative Personality in Traditional Chinese Criticism." *Oriens Extremus* 27, no. 2 (1980): 183–202.

Gardner, Daniel K. "Principle and Pedagogy: Chu Hsi and the Four Books." *Harvard Journal of Asiatic Studies* 44, no. 1 (1984): 57–81.

Giles, Lionel. "The Lament of the Lady of Ch'in." *T'oung Pao* 24 (1926): 316–25.

Graham, Angus. *Lieh-tzu: A New Translation*. London: John Murray, 1960.

Graham, William T., Jr. *"The Lament for the South": Yü Hsin's "Ai Chiang-nan Fu."* Cambridge: Cambridge University Press, 1980.

Hartman, Charles. *Han Yü and the T'ang Search for Unity*. Princeton: Princeton University Press, 1986.

Haskins, John F. "The Pazyryk Felt Screen and the Barbarian Captivity of Ts'ai Wen-chi." *Museum of Far Eastern Antiquities Bulletin* 35 (1963): 141–61.

Hawkes, David. *Ch'u Tz'u: The Songs of the South*. Oxford: Oxford University Press, 1959.

———. *A Little Primer of Tu Fu*. Oxford: Clarendon Press, 1967.

———. "The Quest of the Goddess." *Asia Major*, n.s. 13, nos. 1–2 (1967): 71–94. Reprinted in *Studies in Chinese Literary Genres*, edited by Cyril Birch, pp. 42–68. Berkeley: University of California Press.

Hightower, James Robert. "Allusion in the Poetry of T'ao Ch'ien." *Harvard Journal of Asiatic Studies* 31 (1971): 5–27. Reprinted in *Studies in Chinese Literary Genres*, edited by Cyril Birch, pp. 108–32. Berkeley: University of California Press.

———. "Chia Yi's 'Owl Fu.'" *Asia Major*, n.s. 7, nos. 1–2 (1959): 125–30.

———. *The Poetry of T'ao Ch'ien*. Oxford: Clarendon Press, 1970.

———. "Some Characteristics of Parallel Prose." In *Studia Serica Bernhard Karlgren Dedicata*, edited by Søren Egerod and Else Glahn, pp. 60–91. Copenhagen: Munksgaard, 1959. Reprinted in *Studies in Chinese Literature*, edited by J. L. Bishop, pp. 108–39. Harvard-Yenching Institute Series, no. 21, 1966.

———. "The *Wen Hsüan* and Genre Theory." *Harvard Journal of Asiatic Studies* 20 (1957): 512–33.

Holzman, Donald. "Confucius and Ancient Chinese Criticism." In *Chinese Approaches to Literature from Confucius to Liang Ch'i-ch'ao*, edited by Adele A. Rickett, pp. 21–41. Princeton: Princeton University Press, 1978.

———. *Poetry and Politics: The Life and Works of Juan Chi (A.D. 210–263)*. Cambridge: Cambridge University Press, 1976.

Hopkins, L. C. "The Shaman or Chinese *Wu*: His Inspired Dancing and Versatile Character." *Journal of the Royal Asiatic Society* (1945, pts. 1 and 2): 3–16.

Hung, William. *Tu Fu: China's Greatest Poet*. Cambridge: Harvard University Press, 1952.

Idema, W. L. "The Illusion of Fiction." *CLEAR* 5, no. 1 (July 1985): 47–51.

Kao Yu-kung. "The Aesthetics of Regulated Verse." In *The Vitality of the Lyric Voice: Shih Poetry from the Late Han to T'ang*, edited by Lin Shuen-fu and Stephen Owen, pp. 332–85. Princeton: Princeton University Press, 1986.

———. "Lyric Vision in Chinese Narrative Tradition: A Reading of *Hung-lou Meng* and *Ju-lin Wai-shih*." In *Chinese Narrative: Critical and Theoretical Essays*, edited by Andrew H. Plaks, pp. 228–33. Princeton: Princeton University Press, 1977.

———, and Mei Tsu-lin. "Meaning, Metaphor, and Allusion in T'ang Poetry." *Harvard Journal of Asiatic Studies* 38, no. 2 (December 1978): 281–356.

———. "Syntax, Diction, and Imagery in T'ang Poetry." *Harvard Journal of Asiatic Studies* 31 (1971): 49–136.

Karlgren, Bernhard. *The Book of Odes*. Stockholm: Museum of Far Eastern Antiquities, 1950.

———. *Grammata Serica Recensa. Bulletin of the Museum of Far Eastern Antiquities* 29 (1957). Reprinted as a single volume. Stockholm: Museum of Far Eastern Antiquities, 1972).

Kennedy, George A. "The Fate of Chinese Pictographs." In *Selected Works of George A. Kennedy*, edited by Li Tien-yi, pp. 238–41. New Haven: Yale University Press, 1964.

———. "Fenellosa, Pound, and the Chinese Character." In *Selected Works of George A. Kennedy*, pp. 443–62.

———. "The Monosyllabic Myth." In *Selected Works of George A. Kennedy*, pp. 104–18.

———. "A Note on Ode 220." In *Studia Serica Bernhard Karlgren Dedicata*, edited by Søren Egerod and Else Glahn, pp. 190–98. Copenhagen: Munksgaard, 1959.

Kent, George W. *Worlds of Dust and Jade: 47 Poems and Ballads of the Third Century Chinese Poet Ts'ao Chih*. New York: Philosophical Library, 1969, pp. 52–56.

Knechtges, David R. *The Han Rhapsody: A Study of the Fu of Yang Hsiung (53 B.C.–A.D. 18)*. Cambridge: Cambridge University Press, 1976.

———. *Wen xuan, or Selections of Refined Literature*. Vol. 1, *Rhapsodies on Metropolises and Capitals*. Princeton: Princeton University Press, 1982.

————, and Swanson, Jerry. "Seven Stimuli for the Prince: The *Ch'i-Fa* of Mei Ch'eng." *Monumenta Serica* 29 (1970–71): 99–116.

Konishi, Jin'ichi. "Association and Progression: Principles of Integration in Anthologies and Sequences of Japanese Court Poetry, A.D. 900–1250." *Harvard Journal of Asiatic Studies* 21 (1958): 67–127.

Ku Tim-hung. "A Semiotic Approach to Wang Wei's *Wang River Sequence*: An Exploration of the Principle of Equivalance and the Principle of Disjunction." *Tamkang Review* 14, nos. 1–4 (Autumn 1983–Summer 1984): 339–54.

Kwong Hing Foon. *Wang Zhaojun: Une héroïne chinoise de l'histoire à la legende*. Paris: College de France, Institute des Hautes Etudes Chinoises, 1986.

Lattimore, David. "Allusion in T'ang Poetry." In *Perspectives on the T'ang*, edited by Denis Twitchett and Arthur Wright, pp. 405–39. New Haven: Yale University Press, 1973.

————. "From the Capital to Feng-hsien: Five Hundred Words to Chant My Feelings." *Ironwood* vol. 17, also known as vol. 9, no. 1 (Spring 1981): 52–4.

————. "The Journey North." Manuscript.

————. "Verbal Repetition in *The Canon of Songs*." Manuscript.

Lee Yu-ch'eng. "Hsieh Ling-yun: The Poet as Exile." *Tamkang Review* 14, nos. 1–4 (Autumn 1983–Summer 1984): 141–54.

Legge, James. *The She King of the Book of Poetry*. Vol. 4 of *The Chinese Classics*. Rev. ed. Shanghai: Mer Seng Press, 1935.

————. *The Shoo King*. Vol. 3 of *The Chinese Classics*. Rev. ed. Shanghai: Mer Seng Press, 1935.

Levy, Dore J. "The Trojan and the Hegemon; or, The Culture Hero as Slave of Duty." *Comparative Literature Studies* 22, no. 1 (Spring 1985): 136–46.

Levy, Howard S. "The Career of Yang Kuei-fei." *T'oung Pao* 45 (1957): 101–18.

————. *Lament Everlasting: The Death of Yang Kuei-fei*. Tokyo: n.p., 1962.

————. "Lute Song." *Literature East and West* 11, no. 3 (September 1967): 223–35.

————. "The Selection of Yang Kuei-fei." *Oriens* 15 (1962): 411–22.

————. *Translations from Po Chü-yi's Collected Works*. 2 vols. New York: Paragon Reprint, 1971.

Lin Shuen-fu. "Ritual and Narrative Structure in *Ju-lin Wai-shih*." In *Chinese Narrative: Critical and Theoretical Essays*, edited by Andrew H. Plaks, pp. 245–49. Princeton: Princeton University Press, 1977.

————. *The Transformation of the Chinese Lyrical Tradition: Chiang K'uei and Southern Sung Tz'u Poetry.* Princeton: Princeton University Press, 1978.

————, and Owen, Stephen, eds. *The Vitality of the Lyric Voice: Shih Poetry from the Late Han to T'ang.* Princeton: Princeton University Press, 1986.

Lin Wen-yüeh. "*The Tale of Genji* and 'A Song of Unending Sorrow,' " *Tamkang Review* 6, no. 2, and 7, no. 1 (October 1975–April 1976): 281–85.

Liu, James J. Y. *Chinese Theories of Literature.* Chicago: University of Chicago Press, 1975.

————. *The Interlingual Critic.* Bloomington: Indiana University Press, 1982, pp. 16–21.

————. "Time, Space, and Self in Chinese Poetry." *CLEAR* 1, no. 2 (July 1979): 137–56.

Mair, Victor H. "The Narrative Revolution in Chinese Literature: Ontological Perspectives." *CLEAR* 5, no. 1 (July 1985): 1–27.

Margouliès, Georges. *Anthologie raisonée de la littérature chinoise.* Paris: Payot, 1948.

————. *Evolution de la prose artistique chinoise.* Munich: Encyclopädie-Verlag, 1929.

Mei Tsu-lin and Kao Yu-kung. "Tu Fu's 'Autumn Meditations': An Exercise in Linguistic Criticism." *Harvard Journal of Asiatic Studies* 28 (1968): 44–80.

Miao, Ronald C., ed. *Studies in Chinese Poetry and Poetics.* Vol. 1. San Francisco: Chinese Materials Center, 1978.

Miner, Earl. *Japanese Linked Poetry: An Account with Translations of Renga and Haikai Sequences.* Princeton: Princeton University Press, 1979.

————. "The Objective Fallacy and the Real Existence of Literature." *PTL: A Journal for Descriptive Poetics and Theory of Literature* 1 (January 1976): 11–31.

————. "On the Genesis and Development of Literary Systems." *Critical Inquiry* 5, pt. 1 (Winter 1978): 339–53; pt. 2 (Spring 1979): 553–68.

Nienhauser, William, Jr., ed. and comp. *The Indiana Companion to Traditional Chinese Literature.* Bloomington: Indiana University Press, 1986.

Owen, Stephen. *The Great Age of Chinese Poetry: The High T'ang.* New Haven: Yale University Press, 1981.

————. *The Poetry of the Early T'ang.* New Haven: Yale University Press, 1977.

——. *The Poetry of Meng Chiao and Han Yü*. New Haven: Yale University Press, 1975.

——. "Transparencies: Reading the T'ang Lyric." *Harvard Journal of Asiatic Studies* 39, no. 2 (1979): 231–51.

Pai Hua-wen. "What is *Pien-wen?*" Translated by Victor H. Mair. *Harvard Journal of Asiatic Studies* 44, no. 2 (1984): 493–514.

Plaks, Andrew H. *Archetype and Allegory in the Dream of the Red Chamber*. Princeton: Princeton University Press, 1976.

——. *Chinese Narrative: Critical and Theoretical Essays*. Princeton: Princeton University Press, 1977.

——. "Conceptual Models of Chinese Narrative Theory." *Journal of Chinese Philosophy* 4, no. 1 (June 1977): 25–47.

——. "Issues in Chinese Narrative Theory in the Perspective of the Western Tradition." *PTL: A Journal for Descriptive Poetics and Theory of Literature* 2 (1977): 339–66.

——. "Towards a Critical Theory of Chinese Narrative." In *Chinese Narrative*, edited by Andrew H. Plaks, pp. 309–52.

Pollack, David. *The Fracture of Meaning: Japan's Synthesis of China from the Eighth to the Eighteenth Century*. Princeton: Princeton University Press, 1986.

Průšek, Jaroslav. *Chinese History and Literature: A Collection of Essays*. Dordrecht, Holland: Reidel, 1970, pp. 17–34.

Pulleyblank, E. G. *The Background of the Rebellion of An Lu-shan*. London: Oxford University Press, 1955.

Rickett, Adele Austin, ed. *Chinese Approaches to Literature from Confucius to Liang Ch'i-ch'ao*. Princeton: Princeton University Press, 1978.

——. *Wang Kuo-wei's Jen-chien Tz'u-hua: A Study in Chinese Literary Criticism*. Hong Kong: Hong Kong University Press, 1977.

Robertson, Maureen. ". . . 'To Convey What is Precious': Ssu-k'ung T'u's Poetics and the *Erh-shih-ssu Shih P'in*." In *Transition and Permanence: Chinese History and Culture*, edited by D. C. Buxbaum and F. W. Mote, pp. 323–57. Hong Kong: Cathay Press, 1972.

Robinson, G. W. *Poems of Wang Wei*. Baltimore: Penguin, 1973.

Rorex, Robert A. "Eighteen Songs of a Nomad Flute: The Story of Ts'ai Wen-chi." Ph.D. diss., Princeton University, 1975.

——, and Wen Fong. *Eighteen Songs of a Nomad Flute: The Story of Lady Wen-chi*. New York: Metropolitan Museum of Art, 1974.

Schafer, Edward. "The Last Years of Ch'ang-an." *Oriens Extremus* 10, no. 2 (1963): 133–79.

Seidensticker, Edward G., trans. *The Tale of Genji*. 2 vols. New York: Knopf, 1976.

Stimson, Hugh M. *Fifty-five T'ang Poems*. New Haven: Far Eastern Publications, 1976.

——. "The Rimes of 'Northward Journey,' by Duh-Fuu, 712–770." *Journal of the American Oriental Society* 93 (1973): 129–35.

Tőkei, Ferenc. *Genre Theory in China in the Third through Sixth Centuries (Liu Hsieh's Theory on Poetic Genres)*. Budapest: Akadémiai Kiadó, 1971.

——. *A kínai elégia szuletése. K'iu Juan és kora*. Budapest: Akadémiai Kiadó, 1959. A revised edition appears in French under the title *Naissance de l'élégie chinoise. K'iu Yuan et son époque. Les Essais CXXV*. Paris: Gallimard, 1967.

Tomita, Kōjirō. "Wen-chi's Captivity in Mongolia and Her Return to China." *Museum of Fine Arts Bulletin* 26 (1928): 40–45.

Ts'ai, Meishi. "Peach Blossom Spring: A Mythic Arcadia." *Tamkang Review* 11, no. 1 (Fall 1980): 1–22.

Twitchett, Denis, ed. *The Cambridge History of China*. Vol. 3, *Sui and T'ang China, 589–906*. Cambridge: Cambridge University Press, 1979, pt. 1.

——, and Wright, Arthur, eds. *Perspectives on the T'ang*. New Haven: Yale University Press, 1973.

Waley, Arthur. *The Book of Songs*. London: Allen and Unwin, 1937.

——. *Chinese Poems*. London: Allen and Unwin, 1946.

——. *The Life and Times of Po Chü-yi*. London: Allen and Unwin, 1949.

——. *The Nine Songs: A Study of Shamanism in Ancient China*. London: Allen and Unwin, 1953.

Wang, C. H. *The Bell and the Drum: A Study of the Shih Ching as Formulaic Poetry*. Berkeley: University of California Press, 1974.

——. "The Nature of Narrative in T'ang Poetry." In *The Vitality of the Lyric Voice: Shih Poetry from the Late Han to T'ang*, edited by Lin Shuen-fu and Stephen Owen, pp. 217–52. Princeton: Princeton University Press, 1986.

——. "Sartorial Emblems and the Quest: A Comparative Study of the *Li Sao* and *The Faerie Queene*." *Tamkang Review* 3, nos. 1–2 (October 1971–April 1972): 309–28.

——. "Towards Defining a Chinese Heroism." *Journal of the American Oriental Society* 95, no. 1 (January–March 1975): 25–35.

Wang, John C. Y. "The Nature of Chinese Narrative: A Preliminary Statement of Methodology." *Tamkang Review* 6, no. 2, and 7, no. 1 (October 1975–April 1976): 229–45.

Wang Yi-t'ung. "The Lamentation of Ts'ai Yen (c. A.D. 200)." *Delta* (January–March 1960): 11–14.

Watson, Burton. *The Columbia Book of Chinese Poetry: From Early Times to the Thirteenth Century*. New York: Columbia University Press, 1984.

Wilhelm, Hellmut. "The Scholar's Frustration: Notes on a Type of *Fu*." In *Chinese Thought and Institutions*, edited by John K. Fairbank, pp. 310–19. Chicago: University of Chicago Press, 1957.

——. "Shih Ch'ung and the *Chin-ku-yüan*." *Monumenta Serica* 18 (1959): 314–27.

Wixted, John Timothy. "The *Kokinshu* Prefaces: Another Perspective." *Harvard Journal of Asiatic Studies* 43, no. 1 (1983): 215–38.

——. *The Song-Poetry of Wei Chuang (836–910 A.D.)*. Occasional Paper no. 12, Center for Asian Studies, Arizona State University, 1979.

Wong Kam-ming. "Point of View, Norms, and Structure." In *Chinese Narrative: Critical and Theoretical Essays*, edited by Andrew H. Plaks, pp. 203–26. Princeton: Princeton University Press, 1977.

Yang Lien-sheng. *Studies in Chinese Institutional History*. Cambridge: Harvard University Press, 1961.

Yeh Chia-ying and Walls, Jan. "Theory, Standards, and Practice of Criticizing Poetry in Chung Jung's *Shih-p'in*." In *Studies in Chinese Poetry and Poetics*, edited by Ronald C. Miao, 1:43–80. San Francisco: Chinese Materials Center, 1978.

Yip Wai-lim. *Ezra Pound's Cathay*. Princeton: Princeton University Press, 1969.

——. *Hiding the Universe: Poems by Wang Wei*. New York: Grossman, 1972.

Yu, Pauline. "Metaphor and Chinese Poetry." *CLEAR* 3, no. 2 (July 1981): 205–24.

——. "The Poetics of Discontinuity: East-West Correspondences in Lyric Poetry." *Publication of the Modern Language Association* 94, no. 2 (March 1979): 261–74.

——. *The Poetry of Wang Wei: New Translations and Commentary*. Bloomington: Indiana University Press, 1980.

——. *The Reading of Imagery in the Chinese Poetic Tradition*. Princeton: Princeton University Press, 1987.

Zhang Longxi. "The *Tao* and the *Logos*: Notes on Derrida's Critic of Logocentrism." *Critical Inquiry* 11 (March 1985): 385–98.

Other Western Resources

Bernstein, Michael. *The Tale of the Tribe: Ezra Pound and the Modern Verse Epic*. Princeton: Princeton University Press, 1980.

Booth, Wayne C. "Distance and Point of View." In *The Theory of the Novel*, edited by Philip Stevick, pp. 87–107. New York: Free Press, 1967.

Bremond, Claude. "La logique des possibles narratifs." *Communications* 8 (1966): 60–76.

————. *Logique du récit*. Paris: Seuil, 1973.

Cary, Joyce. *Art and Reality: Ways of the Creative Process*. Garden City, N.Y.: Doubleday, 1958.

Cassirer, Ernst. *Language and Myth*. Translated by Suzanne K. Langer. New York: Dover, 1946.

Child, Francis James, ed. *The English and Scottish Popular Ballads*. 5 vols. Boston: Little, 1886–98.

Dumézil, Georges. *Mythe et epopée I. L'idéologie des trois fonctions dans les epopées des peuples indo-européens*. 3d. ed. Paris: Gallimard, 1979.

————. *Mythe et epopée II. Types epiques indo-européens: un héros, un sorcier, un roi*. Paris: Gallimard, 1971.

————. *Mythes et epopées III. Histoires romaines*. Paris: Gallimard, 1973.

Entwhistle, William J. *European Balladry*. Oxford: Oxford University Press, 1939.

Forster, E. M. *Aspects of the Novel*. New York: Harcourt, 1950.

————. "Flat and Round Characters." In *The Theory of the Novel*, edited by Philip Stevick, pp. 223–30. New York: Free Press, 1967.

Fowler, Alastair. *Kinds of Literature: An Introduction to the Theory of Modes and Genres*. Cambridge: Harvard University Press, 1982.

Friedman, Norman. "Point of View in Fiction: The Development of a Critical Concept." *Publication of the Modern Language Association* 70 (December 1955): 1160–84.

Friedrich, Paul. *Language, Context, and the Imagination*. Palo Alto: Stanford University Press, 1979.

————. *The Language Parallax: Linguistic Relativism and Poetic Indeterminacy*. Austin: University of Texas Press, 1986.

Frye, Northrop. *Anatomy of Criticism: Four Essays*. Princeton: Princeton University Press, 1957.

————. "Fictional Modes." In *Approaches to the Novel*, edited by Robert Scholes, pp. 31–39. San Francisco: Chandler, 1961.

Genette, Gérard. *Figures III*. Paris: Editions de Seuil, 1972.

———. *Narrative Discourse: An Essay in Method*. Translated by Jane E. Lewin. Ithaca: Cornell University Press, 1980.

Gerould, Gordon Hall. *The Ballad of Tradition*. Oxford: Oxford University Press, 1932.

Goodman, Nelson. "Twisted Tales; or Study, Story, Symphony." *Critical Inquiry* 7, no. 1 (Autumn 1980): 103–19.

Harvey, W. J. "The Human Context." In *The Theory of the Novel*, edited by Philip Stevick, pp. 231–52. New York: Free Press, 1967.

Iser, Wolfgang. *The Implied Reader: Patterns of Communication from Bunyan to Beckett*. Baltimore: Johns Hopkins University Press, 1978.

James, Henry. "The Art of Fiction." In *Approaches to the Novel*, edited by Robert Scholes, pp. 289–312. San Francisco: Chandler, 1961.

———. *The Art of the Novel*, edited by R. P. Blackmur. New York: Scribner's Sons, 1934.

Kahler, Erich. *The Inward Turn of Narrative*. Princeton: Princeton University Press, 1973.

Kenner, Hugh. "The Poetics of Error." *Tamkang Review* 6, no. 2, and 7, no. 1 (October 1975–April 1976): 89–97.

———. *The Pound Era*. Berkeley: University of California Press, 1971.

Kermode, Frank. "Secrets and Narrative Sequence." *Critical Inquiry* 7, no. 1 (Autumn 1980): 83–101.

Kittay, Jeffrey, ed. *Towards a Theory of Description*. Yale French Studies, no. 61. New Haven: Yale University Press, 1981.

Lockwood, W. B. *Indo-European Philology. Historical and Comparative*. London: Hutchinson University Library, 1969.

Maritain, Jacques. *Creative Intuition in Art and Poetry*. New York: Pantheon Books, 1953.

Meillet, Antoine. *L'Introduction a l'étude comparative des langues indo-européennes*. 1903. Reprint. University of Alabama Press, 1964.

Motsch, Wolfgang. "Situational Context and Illusionary Force." In *Speech Act Theory and Pragmatics*, edited by John R. Searle, Fernec Kieffer, and Manfred Bierwisch, pp. 155–68. Dordrecht: Reidel, 1980.

Mudrick, Marvin. "Character and Event in Fiction." *Yale Review* 50.1 (Winter 1961): 202–18.

Pöschl, Viktor. *The Art of Vergil: Image and Symbol in the Aeneid*. Ann Arbor: University of Michigan Press, 1962.

Poulet, Georges. *Etudes sur le temps humain*. Paris: Plon, 1976–77.

Propp, Vladimir. *The Morphology of the Folk Tale*. 2d ed. Austin: University of Texas Press, 1968.

Rabkin, Eric. *Narrative Suspense*. Ann Arbor: University of Michigan Press, 1973.

Recanati, François. "Some Remarks on Explicit Perfomatives, Indirect Speech Acts, Locutionary Meaning, and Truth Value." In *Speech Act Theory and Pragmatics*, edited by John R. Searle, Fernec Kieffer, and Manfred Bierwisch, pp. 205–20. Dordrecht: Reidel, 1980.

Richards, I. A. *Practical Criticism: A Study of Literary Judgement*. New York: Harcourt, Brace, 1935.

Ricoeur, Paul. "Narrative Time." *Critical Inquiry* 7, no. 1 (Autumn 1980): 169–90.

Rimmon, Shlomith. "A Comprehensive Theory of Narrative: *Figures III* and the Structuralist Study of Fiction." *PTL: A Journal for Descriptive Poetics and Theory of Literature* 1 (1976): 33–62.

Rogers, William Elford. *The Three Genres and the Interpretation of Lyric*. Princeton: Princeton University Press, 1983.

Ross, James F. "On the Concepts of Reading." *Philosophical Forum* 6 (Fall 1972): 93–141.

Rubin, Louis D., Jr. *The Teller in the Tale*. Seattle: University of Washington Press, 1967.

Scholes, Robert, and Kellogg, Robert. *The Nature of Narrative*. New York: Oxford University Press, 1966.

Schorer, Mark. "Technique as Discovery." *Hudson Review* 1, no. 1 (Spring 1948): 67–87.

Searle, John R.; Kieffer, Fernec; and Bierwisch, Manfred, eds. *Speech Act Theory and Pragmatics*. Dordrecht: Reidel, 1980.

Smith, Barbara Herrnstein. *Poetic Closure; Or, a Study of How Poems End*. Chicago: University of Chicago Press, 1968.

Trilling, Lionel. "Manners, Morals, and the Novel." In *Approaches to the Novel*, edited by Robert Scholes, pp. 231–47. San Francisco: Chandler, 1961.

Todorov, Tzvetan. "Poétique." In *Qu'est-ce que le structuralisme?*, edited by Oswald Ducrot et al. Paris: Seuil, 1968.

Vendler, Zeno. "Telling the Facts." In *Speech Act Theory and Pragmatics*, edited by John R. Searle, Fernec Kieffer, and Manfred Bierwisch, pp. 273–90. Dordrecht: Reidel, 1980.

Weisman, Herman M. "An Investigation of Methods and Techniques in the Dramatization of Fiction." *Speech Monographs* 19 (1952): 48–59.

Index

Dore J. Levy teaches Chinese and comparative literature at Brown University in Providence, Rhode Island.